Heroes of North East India

Attention Authors

'We Convert Fighters into Writers.' That's the motto of Manas Publications since more than four decades. Our message to the world is that India can win the battle not only by the bullet but also by the pen. There is no dearth of intellectuals in our country, but their knowledge is confined to them only. No sincere effort has been made by any other publisher to channelise their knowledge in national interest. That is why the talent of a large number of intellectuals remains latent. An author transforms his knowledge into a manuscript, and it is our job to spread his/her knowledge by converting it into a beautiful book. For over four decades, Manas has been motivating the intellectuals by publishing their manuscripts and would like to publish your manuscript too. So if you or your colleagues have any manuscript ready for publication or are working on it, kindly contact us with detailed synopsis and list of contents. We will transform your work into a valuable publication. If you wish, we can also suggest you the suitable subjects for writing the books related to your area of expertise. Manas is known for its publishing quality and commitments. We take utmost care in production and give wide publicity to the book as well as its author through our national and international distribution network.

Heroes of North East India

Sumitra Mukherjee

Manas Publications
(We Convert Fighters into Writers)
New Delhi-110002 (INDIA)

MANAS PUBLICATIONS
(We Convert Fighters into Writers)
(Publishers, Library Suppliers, Importers & Exporters)
4402/5-A, Ansari Road (Opp. HDFC Bank)
Darya Ganj, New Delhi-110 002 (India)
Off. ✆ 23260783, 23265523, Fax: 011-23272766
E-mail: manaspublications@vsnl.com
manaspublications@yahoo.com
manaspublications@gmail.com

ISBN 978-81-7049-424-9
₹ 695/-

Designed at
Manas Publications

Printed in India at
RK Offset, Delhi
and published by Mrs Suman Lata for
Manas Publications, 4402/5-A, Ansari Road
(Opp. HDFC Bank), Darya Ganj,
New Delhi-110 002 (INDIA)

Contents

Dedicated to

Abhishek, the hero, who lives on in our lives

Acknowledgements

During my research for the book I have had a lot of support from various people and institutions, my thanks to all who supported and helped me with valuable inputs to complete this book.

I have to start from the place, my interest developed; it was the CIJW School or the Counter Insurgency School at Vairengte, Mizoram. The library there is a store house of knowledge and the books there are invaluable. Of course, I got the privilege because my husband was the Commandant of the school in 1997-1998. The village people also talked about some of the heroes as some of the material was oral.

The National Library during my first visit was an eye opener for me, there were journals from the British times stacked from the floor to the roof, I did not know from where to begin! The books available were massive; I could sit for days reading them.

The library at USI - United Service Institution - also has a fair amount of material and my husband being a member gave me the advantage of using the Library.

The Eastern Command library was another place where I found a lot of material. I am quite indebted to the then GOC-in-C Eastern Command, Gen. VK Singh, PVSM, AVSM, YSM, ADC, for allowing me to use the library.

My profuse thanks to Hari Kishan and Ruchika Kaushik, final year MFA students (Dept of Graphic Art, Faculty of Fine Arts, Jamia Millia Islamia) for all the sketches. Last but not the least many thanks to my husband Brig. Trigunesh Mukherjee, AVSM, and our two daughters Aditi and Puja for their encouragement and for having faith in me.

Introduction
A brief insight into the history of the Seven Sisters

While going through the history of India one hears of Shivaji, Rani Laxmibai or Bhagat Singh but rarely does one come across a brave from the North East. Nor do we get to read or know mythological figures from the North East like Ram or Yudhistir, maybe a few lines on Rani Gaidinliu but that is all. The plains people of the Indian sub-continent know very little about the North East. Generally, the vast majority of Indians we find are ignorant of the people, culture, and the land of the North East, tucked away as it is in a distant and relatively inaccessible and mountainous part of the country. The first reason for the ignorance possibly is inaccessibility; it has been cut away by the Inner Line Regulations of 1873. As a result, the North Eastern part of our country has lived in isolation. Very little recorded history can be found of this region as most of the region has oral traditions. India's North East is home to the 'Seven Sisters'. Aptly called the 'Seven Sisters' as they have common origin, racial history, anthropological and linguistic kinships.

The North East or the 'Seven Sisters' as they are popularly called is home to the states of Arunachal Pradesh, Assam, Meghalaya, Manipur, Mizoram, Nagaland and Tripura. The people now realise that in spite of their division into separate political units because of administrative and other considerations the states have geographical, political and economical affinity.

The beautiful land of the 'Seven Sisters' is well-known for its richness of culture and heritage. Assam, the land of blue hills and red rivers is the land of 'Usha', who was enamoured of 'Anirudha, the prince of Dwarka'. Meghalaya, abode of clouds was the dreamland of 'Pramilla'. Arunachal where the sun rises above the snow-capped mountains was the homeland of 'Rukmini' whose beauty enchanted Lord Krishna. Manipur, the dale of song and dances was the land of 'Chitrangada' and in Nagaland the eastern sentinel of our country; Arjuna's 'Ulupi' was born. Tripura is the land of the queen Tripura Sundari and the damsels of the blue mountains of Mizoram are as colourful as the river Dhaleshwari herself. (Taken from the speech of the then Chief Minister of Assam, Sarat Chandra Sinha in 1976). These lines aptly describe the beautiful North Eastern states or our very own the Seven Sisters.

The North East is a multifaceted gem culturally. It is an anthropologist's paradise as there is hardly any racial type or any form of social organisation that is not represented here. Over thousands of years, wave after wave of migrants have been attracted by the enchanting hills and valleys of the region. Its ancient history is full of myths and legends and points to possibilities of intercontinental migrations. There has been a racial mixture among the population of Assam. The Mongoloid people are more because of the large number of tribes of this racial stock. Traces of Negroids are to be found among the Nagas. The Khasis speak an Austric language which could have been taken from some Proto-Australoid race before they came to Assam. The Kaibartar a schedule caste of Assam are said to be of Dravidian origin. Any ancient Indian race or tribe that settled here came from across the frontiers, eastern or western regions.

We find in all the seven states an overwhelming tribal population since they practically remained isolated from the mainstream of Indian events. They are not very often referred to in the historical writings of India. Though we do find in the epic of Mahabharata the names of Pragyotishpur (Assam) and Manipur, for instance the Rakshas Princess Hidamba and her son Ghatotkach by the second Pandav brother Bhima. Princess Ulupi whom Arjuna married was from the Zeliang area now in Nagaland. The Aryans took several centuries to spread eastwards along the Ganga valley. They say the Aryans reached Bihar in about 700 BC, so possibly they also came to Assam. There is evidence in the Ramayana and the Mahabharata (written between 500 BC and 400 AD) that there were contacts between the Aryans and Mongoloids. The Ramayana mentions a kingdom Pragyjyotisha (the ancient name of Assam) founded by Amutarajas whose grandson Vishwamitra performed sacred rituals on the banks of the Kausika - modern Kosi today. Both the epics describe the Kiratas or the Mongoloid people of Assam as "handsome and capable warriors". We can say that when the basis of Hindu culture was being laid by the Aryans, Austrik and Dravidians in the rest of India, the Mongoloids made their presence felt in the North East region. Possibly the Mongoloids arrived in Assam during the time when the Aryans came to India around 1500 BC. They say the Mongoloids made large scale movements from their original homeland China in the first millennium BC. These people traversed through Thailand, Indo-China, Burma (today Myanmar) and the Himalayan tract from Ladakh to Tibet.

The Bodos or Boros are a group of Mongoloid people and their number is the largest in North East India. They have spread to Bengal, Bihar, Assam, Tripura, Sylhet and Mymensingh of Bangladesh. The Bodo language comes under the Tibeto-Burman sub-family of the Sino-Tibetan languages. The Bodo first settled in the Brahamaputra valley and then slowly spread out. According to the late Bishnu Prasad Rabha, an Assamese who was a Bodo, Brahamaputra is an Aryanised or Sanskritised version of a Bodo expression '*bhulung buthu*" meaning "a great river of bubbling water", Goddess Kamakhya was originally "Kamakhe or Kamalakhi" of a Mongoloid race.

The Mizos or Lushais are migrants from the Chin Hills and speak a Kuki-Chin tongue of the Tibeto-Burman sub-family of the Sino-Tibetan languages. The Chutiyas who were later Hinduised speak a Bodo tongue. They belong to the Subansiri and Sadiya area which lies close to Arunachal Pradesh. Under the Hindu Brahmanical influence they trace their origin of kings to mythical times. The Miris or Mishings also from the Mongoloid tribes can be seen in areas of Lakhimpur, Sibsagar and Darrang. Possibly these people were the Tibeto-Burman speaking group which came down to the sub Himalayan hills of the North Brahamaputra valley and were among the Akas, Abors or Adis, Mishmis of Arunachal. The Koches ruled in North Bengal and West Assam. Some people say they are of a Dravidian stock but they clearly have Mongoloid physical structures. Possibly they are a mixture of both. They speak the Assamese language and are Hindus by religion. One of the Koch king Naranarayana was a great Vaishnava and follower of Sri Sankaradeva (1449-15690 AD). Cooch Bihar was their original state of administration which lies in West Bengal.

The Morans or Mataks spoke a Bodo tongue but later adopted Assamese. These people are to be found in the areas of Sibsagar and Drang like the Chutiyas and the Mishings. Later they were defeated by the Ahoms who not only annexed them but also influenced them in many ways.

The Ahoms are the only Mongoloid race whose activities have been recorded in the chronicles called '*Buranjis*' meaning 'store house of unknown things.' After the Bodos they are the only people who made their presence felt in the area. They ruled for a good six hundred years. The Ahoms spoke Chinese-Siamese. They belong to the Shan or Tai or Thai race, they have exercised a powerful influence over the fortunes of the North East. The Siamese are now the most important branch of this family. They are called the Burmese Shangyai, or eldest branch of the Shans. According to historians there was once a great nation of theses people occupying a tract known to the historians of Manipur as the kingdom of Pong, which touched the Tipperah, Yunan and Siam. The Ahoms a branch of the great Tai race of SE Asia ruled Assam for six hundred years (1228-1826 AD). It is during this time they came in contact with the tribes of the plains and hills.

The Ahoms realised that the people of the region should be taken over in a friendly way, by a policy of conciliation right from the beginning of their rule. The Ahoms removed the fears and suspicion of the tribes. Hso-ka-pha (Sukapha) the founder of the Ahom kingdom, after his conquest invited all the local people, the inhabitants to his new capital to acquaint the new comers with Ahom environment. The locals realised that though the Ahoms had dislodged them from their land they had shown sympathy. The policy of friendship and goodwill became the central point of the relations of the Ahoms with the local inhabitants. The tribes of the plains such as the Borhais and the Kacharis who were conquered gradually were treated with great sympathy. Though these tribes lost their political identity they never suffered from any social disability under the Ahoms. They also married girls from the tribes. This assimilation was necessary as the Ahoms realised their numbers had to be increased by bringing in local people into their fold for administration and expansion of their areas. The Tais in the past centuries had assimilated their hill neighbours. The Ahoms followed the same pattern of assimilation for peace and harmony. We can say the Ahoms could take the best out of other cultures and social life to improve their own identity. They never disturbed the existing beliefs and customs of the tribal.

To understand the people from 'the Seven Sisters' one needs to know that myths play an important role in the life of the people, they tell us the story of the origin of God, the origin of the world and the origin of man. Myths form the base of all our social institutions, they help in carrying religion from generation to generation and it also transmits other cultural traditions. At times a myth is regarded as representing a world picture and an insight into life. The myths also tell us of our ancestors and of many magico-religious performances. One of the myths of the Tangsas is that if they want to get a good crop they have to sacrifice an animal to the gods like a monkey. There are myths which say that in the olden days the Ron- Rangs performed a ritual called '*Dawan*' for the welfare of the people. This was a big ceremony where there was a human sacrifice to propitiate the gods. It has been stopped now. In Assam the Ahom king Gaurinath Singha stopped it in the 18th century. The Tagins a group of the Adi tribe believe in the Doini-Pollo or the Sun-Moon God, who reigns supreme in the heavens. In the Aryan society we find the Chandravamsa and Suryavamsa kings. They left their impression on the North East. We have Lord Siva being worshipped amongst the people of Assam. Another name of Siva is Pashupati. Cow worship is one of the first social consciousnesses among all civilised people in India. The Assamese in their 'Bihu' festival have some sort of cow worship.

Religion is an all pervading supernatural phenomena in man's life. Religion is universal; it has exercised the most profound influence over man's thoughts and behaviour. Among tribal people religion becomes all important because it is interwoven in their social behaviour. The tribal religion is most often very simple. According to Durkheim religion consists of two basic things, beliefs and rituals. Beliefs are static while rituals are dynamic. The basic form of religion in the North East consists of beliefs in a hierarchy of supernatural beings with rituals performed for fulfilment. The people all over the world believe in some kind of existence which is less material than that of solid bodies. So the idea of soul develops in the mind of man. Some primitive religions believe that the soul of man can go astray, it can be influenced by others, it can be captured by enemies. This belief in non-material 'spirit' is animism. To the people of the North East God is an embodiment of 'All Pervasiveness and All Consciousness'. The common forces of the Universe, the Sun, the Moon, the River and the Mountain provide the basic elements in the North Eastern philosophy of religion.

Arunachal Pradesh

Jungles, Rivers, Snow and First Dawn

Arunachal, 'the land of the rising Sun' is our easternmost state. The first impression of the state is green and greener as one drives in. Mention about Arunachal can be found in the epics of Mahabharata and Ramayanaa; it is the land of characters like Princess Rukmini, Lord Parusharam and King Bhismaka. The first tribal groups travelled from Tibet in ancient times and in recent past the present HH Dalai Lama too, who had to leave Tibet for political reasons. But even today very little is known about the history of Arunachal Pradesh. The Assam chronicles or '*Buranjis*' do show records of local chiefs and the Monpa kingdoms of Monyul that prospered between 500 BC and 600 AD and ruled the northern parts of the state. The Assamese and the Ahoms had control over other parts till the British took control in 1858. It was in 1913-1914, Sir Henry McMahon, the then British Administrator, drew the 550-mile McMahon line, a border between British India and Tibet during the Simla Conference as Britain wanted to advance its line of control and have a buffer zone in its colonies in South Asia.

Earlier, Arunachal Pradesh was called NEFA or the North East Frontier Agency, in 1972 the area became a Union Territory, later Arunachal Pradesh became a state on 20th February 1987, it was the 24th state of India. The state has been divided into sixteen districts for administrative purposes and the capital is Itanagar. It has been named after the 'Ita' or brick fort built in 14th century. Area wise it is the largest state of the 'Seven Sisters'. Arunachal Pradesh has green forests, mountains, plateaus and deep river valleys. The mountains belong to the Himalayan range and run north-south. The mountains divide the state into five river valleys, Kameng, Subansiri, Siang, Lohit and Tirap. All the rivers are snow fed and rise from the Himalayas except Tirap which rises from Patkai Range. The Siang is called Tsangpo in Tibet, later it becomes the Brahamaputra after it is joined by the Dibang and Lohit. The climate is warm and moist at the foothills or the Shivaliks to gradually becoming cold as we gain height. At the higher heights the snow cover is heavy. Nature has been indeed kind, as we have a variety of trees right from the equatorial to the alpine, rivers, lakes and waterfalls all put together in one place.

The lofty mountains have prevented the people from inter-communicating with other tribes in different river valleys; this geographical isolation has led different groups to evolve their own dialects and customs. The different tribes have their own fairs and festivals to show their respect to God and nature. The celebrations are accompanied by dance and music. Some of the important festivals of the tribes are, Apatani's - Myokoh, Dree and Murung, Nishi's Yulo, Monpa's Losar and Adi's Mopin. The people of Arunachal believe in a God or Super natural entity. 'Donyi-Polo' or more literally 'Sun and Moon' worship is followed by many tribes like Apatanis, Mishmi, Adi and Hill Miris of Arunachal Pradesh. Believers of 'nature worshipping' believe that all of Arunachal have a common ancestor who is 'Abotani'. The religion has no written records, but traditionally has been passed down orally. The people believe in a number of deities but the principal one is 'Donyi-Polo' or the Sun and Moon worshippers. The 'Donyi-Polo' worshippers believe in the oneness of all living creatures, from the smallest living creature to the largest, all living creatures have a role to play in their life. About 40 percent of the people follow 'Donyi–Polo', and followers of the Buddhist faith comprise of another 40 percent, Christians comprise of about 18 percent and Hindus the rest.

Arunachal Pradesh without mentioning Tawang is incomplete. The Tawang Monastery was founded near the small town with the same name. The monastery was founded by Merak Lama Lodre Gyatso in 1680-1681, according to the wishes of the 5th Dalai Lama.

The monastery belongs to the Gelugpa School and has religious links with the Drepung Monastery in Lhasa. Tawang Monastery lies very close to the border with Tibet, it has the Twang-chu which flows from Tibet. The word 'Tawang' means 'Horse Chosen'. Legend says that one day while praying to seek 'Divine guidance' Merak Lama after finishing his prayers came out to find his horse missing, the horse was found standing quietly on a hilltop, it is here Merak Lama decided to build the monastery of Tawang. The monastery was built by the local people of the village and even today it is looked after by these people. The Tibetan name of the monastery is 'Galden Namgey Lahtse' which means 'Celestial Paradise in a clear Night'. When one sees it on a clear moonlit night, the monastery seems to be shining in the Hillside.

The Sixth Dalai Lama, the only Indian born Dalai Lama, so to say was born in a place called 'Ugyenling' in 1683, very close to Tawang monastery. The monastery today is only a shadow of what it was. Though the place is very peaceful, when I visited it last I felt calmness within myself, yet in grandeur it has lost out to Tawang. The monastery was deposed off in 1706 by Lazang Khan (the last king of Tibet) and his forces to destroy the memory of the Sixth Dalai Lama.

Arunachal Pradesh is considered to be 'Nature's Treasure Trove' and is home to over six hundred varieties of orchid. A large part of the state's revenue comes from tourism, with 'trekking' and 'white water' rafting to name a few activities. Visitors to the state have a wide variety to choose from, the religious minded have 'Parasuramkund' and the Tawang monastery to visit, those interested in history and archaeology have Malinithan and Itanagar to see, to the nature lovers, who love the water there are Ganga and Sela lakes, the mighty river Brahamaputra, and of course snow clad mountains for trekkers.

1

His Holiness the Sixth Dalai Lama

The life of His Holiness the Sixth Dalai Lama has always fascinated me, specially his poems and why he gave up his life of pomp and religious power to lead a life as a normal layman. My quest to find more led me to Urgelling, the birth place of HH the Sixth Dalai Lama. Tsangyang Gyamtso the Sixth Dalai Lama is one of the most popular historical figures among Tibetans and the most colourful of the long line of Dalai Lamas. His poetry is the most iconic in Tibetan literature. Michael Aris, the authority on Tibetan culture says, "It is difficult to think of a more elusive figure in Tibetan and Himalaya history".

Urgelling monastery traces its root to the 15th century, around 1489 it was established by Urgen Sangpo as a Buddhist spiritual centre. The monastery is home to Lamas following the Lamaistic Mahayana school of thought. The monastery became a sacred place for the Buddhist since 1683 – the year the sixth Dalai Lama was born to Lama Tashi Tenzin (father) of Urgelling and Tsewang Lhamo (mother) of Bekhar. When we visited Urgelling we found an aura of peace and calm, something not felt in other monasteries of this area. We met a middle-aged lady here, who took us around the monastery and told us of the history of the place. The Sixth Dalai Lama was born in Urgelling, called Ugyenling in Tibetan.

He was born a Monpa, a group which speaks a language close to Tibetan but consider themselves different from the Tibetan high plateau. The two storey childhood home of the Sixth Dalai Lama has been turned into a pilgrimage centre. Candles adorn the main altar and prayer flags hang from a tree outside. The ground floor of the house has nine white stupas which has the remains of the Sixth Dalai Lama's relatives. We also saw a small wooden box with a stone inside that had faint foot prints, the footprints are supposed to be that of the Sixth Dalai Lama's. The young child though they say left Urgelling at age three and never returned.

A lot of stories about the birth of Tsangyang Gyamtso have been found. They say his mother Tsewang had experienced a few miracles before the birth of the Sixth Dalai Lama. During the first month of pregnancy the mother while husking rice/paddy found the mortar had water in it. (We were fortunate to see the same husking mortar or so we were told, lying outside in the courtyard of the monastery). On another occasion, the mother felt thirsty and went to drink water at a nearby place and found there was milk instead of water in the stream. The stream later happened to be called 'Oma Tsikang 'or literally known as milky water. Tsewang later gave birth to a boy; who was called Sanje Tenzin. As a baby when he did not drink his mother's milk as he was not well, two divine people were called to help the child recover from the illness. These people said a purificatory rite was required and that his name should be changed to Ngawang Gyamtso. Soon the baby improved and the credit went to the Dalai Lama's guardian deity Dorje Dakpa. The grandparents dreamt that the child was constantly being guarded by angels to look after the child. They say the Sixth Dalai Lama was a reincarnation of Chenrezig, a deity embodying compassion. Chenrezig is the patron deity of Tibet, also known as 'Avalokiteshvara', the Buddha of Compassion, and the 'Seeing Eye Lord'.

The Fifth Dalai Lama became the spiritual leader and had a sovereign rule over Tibet. During his reign a lot of work had been done on construction of monasteries and that included the home of the Tibetan head of State, the grand Potala Palace. The death of the Fifth Dalai Lama was kept a secret by his Regent or Desi. The Regent announced that the Fifth Dalai Lama had gone into a long retreat, a period of ten-year meditation. The death was possibly kept a secret as the Regent wanted to complete the Potala Palace.

The Sixth Dalai Lama was identified by search committees sent out by the Desi/ Regent. It was in 1685, his agents reported a child was born to Rigdzin Tashi and mother Tsewang Lhamo, on March 1, 1683 under mysterious circumstances, as the Sixth Dalai Lama's parents were members of a tantric sect of Buddhism. The boy, they say, was a descendent of Jingme Lingpa, the founder of a rare Buddhist text in Bhutan. The child was taken with his family across the Himalayas to a remote town called Tsona, here they lived almost under house arrest for about twelve years. The Sixth Dalai Lama studied Buddhist texts alone, even his relatives were not allowed to meet him. All visitors were screened; very rarely did he meet people. In 1697, mother and child were taken to Nakartse to the home Yardok Khripon, former Desi and uncle of the Fifth Dalai Lama. The Desi felt that it was time to reveal the truth about the death of the Fifth Dalai Lama.

(Some of the oldest Tantric schools involved certain secret disciplines involving a consort or yogic partner of the opposite sex. These helped to harness and transform sexuality, and other passions, as an aid to follow the path of enlightenment. The yogis and lamas of the oldest of these schools - the Nyingmas or the Ancient ones were often married laymen. Later these practices were misused, the Tantric teachings had degenerated to achieve worldly pleasures. As a reaction to this the Gelukpa emphasised a much disciplined monastic life).

When the Sixth Dalai Lama was finally enthroned in 1697 at age fourteen, he was a shy boy who was not prepared for the spotlight. When Tsangyang Gyatso ascended the golden throne it was a grand spectacle where a lot of dignitaries, Chinese emperors, Mongol princes and monks from the three major monasteries attended the enthronement. It is no wonder he rejected all the trappings of such a great responsibility. What else could a fourteen-year-old do? Had he focussed on ruling the land taking on his vows, the Sixth Dalai Lama could have consolidated the gains his predecessors had made and helped make Tibet a strong state. Gray Tuttle, a professor of modern Tibetan Studies at Columbia University says, "Because of his lack of training, lack of being raised as a Dalai Lama, he went off and did these activities. But the Tibetan people loved him for that and they loved his writings". The fifteen-year-old young Dalai Lama had grown up to be a handsome, intelligent person, he loved archery and roaming about the countryside with his friends. He showed no interest in spiritual studies, but that did not mean he had given up his studies, he studied political administration under the Desi, Buddhist philosophy under Panchen Rinpoche, loved music and archery. The Sixth Dalai Lama was a practical person and did not let the wealth and pomp go to his head, he remained much grounded and had no personal servants. He had a secret as during the day he followed his duties as a Dalai Lama and at night he would don a disguise and go out to Shol town, the disreputable section of lower Lhasa and spend the night with young ladies who took his fancy. But before sun rose he would come back to his palace. When morning came he was back to his duties. His night visits would have gone unnoticed if an attendant had not noticed footsteps in the snow leading to the backdoor of the Potala. The attentive attendant followed the footsteps which led to a tavern of Shol town and the his secret came out.

The Desi Sangay wanted the Sixth Dalai Lama when he was about twenty years old to take his gelong vows, but the Sixth Dalai Lama would have nothing to do with this. Finally, the help of Panchen Rinpoche was sought and a message was sent to the Panchen Rinpoche. He got to know of this and pretended he wanted to take his vows while all the time he was determined he would not, he felt it was time for him to renounce his vows. In a hall, full of people who had gathered for the ceremony, he fell to his knees in front of Panchen Rinpoche and asked for forgiveness for renouncing his vows.

Such behaviour, it was obvious, would draw the attention of people, specially the Desi who was very angered by the way he had given up his vows. The Lamas' and noble men tried to make him change his mind about giving up his being the Dalai Lama, but he was adamant and said if forced he would commit suicide. When things had reached this level the people backed off. The Desi wanted to get assassinated a close friend of the Sixth Dalai Lama, a man named Drungkhor Tharyasnas, whom the Desi felt was a bad influence on the Sixth Dalai Lama, but fortunately for Drungkhor Tharyasnas who had playfully exchanged his dress with his servant, and later it was found the servant got killed instead of Drungkhor Tharyasnas. The Sixth Dalai Lama did not give up and had the whole thing verified, an oracle was asked and it was found that the Desi had a role to play in the killing. The men who killed were put to death for their treachery.

Tsangyang Gyatso came back to Potala Palace as a layman. People were disappointed but his Dalai Lama title remained with him as nowhere is it written that a Dalai Lama has to be a monk. So the Sixth Dalai Lama remained at Potala Palace and led a carefree life. After the Sixth Dalai Lama renounced the vows of a novice monk he enjoyed a life of socialising with people of his age, wining and being with women, a very normal thing for a young man! Tsangyang Gyatso liked walking around the town of Lhasa instead of using the palanquins used by royalty. Often he would entertain his visitors by serving them tea which he had made. He enjoyed visiting the parks of Lhasa and many a night was spent on the streets of Lhasa. He visited the drinking houses or '*chang*'/rice or barley brew taverns of Shol town at the end of Red Hill. It is here they say he met a young girl called Makye Ame with whom he fell in love but never met her again. A lot of love poems were written, which even today can be read. A visit by the Sixth Dalai Lama into a home was always welcome and if he did spend the night with the daughters it was considered auspicious. The house roof of such houses was painted yellow and very soon a large number of houses indeed did have yellow roofs. Often he took on the name of Norsang Wangpo at night while drinking wine and singing love songs.

Sometimes in his poems he refers himself as 'The Turquoise Bee'. Wandering minstrels sang his songs on the streets of Lhasa, young men sang them at the pubs/ taverns, yak herds were heard singing on mountain tops, they all were heard singing the sweet stories of love and longing for a friend.

One of His Holiness' poems

I sought my lover at twilight
Snow fell at daybreak
Residing at the Potala
I am Rigdzin Tsangyang Gyatso
But in the back alleys of Shol Town
I am a rake and stud.
Secret or not
No matter.
Footprints have been left in the snow.

Gushri Khan King of Tibet was happy being a king in name only; he left the power in the hands of the Desi / Regent. A nomad at heart Gushri spent the last years of his life with his herd. In 1697 Gushri's grandson Lazaar Khan became the king and the leader of the Qoshot band of West Mongols in Tibet. The same year the Desi announced the death of the Fifth Dalai Lama, fifteen years after his actual death, and that he had found the Sixth Dalai Lama, who had been educated but under secrecy. The Sixth Dalai Lama had been enthroned and the Desi planned to be the Regent for the Sixth Dalai Lama. Lazaar felt insulted that the Desi had dared to keep his family ignorant of all this. Lazaar the new king of Tibet and the Desi soon became deadly enemies. The Sixth Dalai Lama's behaviour also irritated Lazaar Khan. The 14th Dalai Lama says, "The internal practice of the Fifth's Desi/ Regent was Nyingma, and the Sixth Dalai Lama was chosen by the Desi. The Desi gave the 6th Dalai Lama the Nyingma Dzochen teachings, which can involve sexual yoga". The 6th Dalai Lama's behaviour was also not what it should be. Lazaar Khan was a follower of Gelugpa and this was one of the reasons why the Desi and Lazaar Khan did not see eye to eye. Gelugpa means the 'school of the virtuous' is also known as the Yellow Hat Sect, which is the school of Buddhism founded by Tsongkhapa, a Tibetan religious leader. The first monastery is at Ganden.

Lazaar Khan killed the Desi in 1705 and in 1706 deposed the 6th Dalai Lama and sent troops to capture him from the Potala Palace and send him to exile in China. Lazaar Khan ordered the Sixth Dalai Lama to leave his Potala Palace and shift to a Mongol camp at Lhalu Garden near Lhasa. While he was under seize he composed a poem in haste to an unidentified woman in Shol town.

White crane!
Lend me your wings
I will not fly far
I will return near Litang

They say, two years later, the Seventh Dalai Lama Kelzang Gyatso was born in Litang.

The Tibetan people feared he would not come out alive. People from the surrounding three monasteries gathered in anger and brought out the Sixth Dalai Lama to safety and took him to the summer palace of the Drepung monastery where the Nechung oracle declared him a true reincarnation of the Fifth Dalai Lama. Not to give up easily Lazaar Khan had his guards surrounded the palace. Fearing a massacre the Sixth gave himself up to Qosot. His companions fought bravely but most were killed and he was taken to China. On 14th November 1706, at age twenty three the Sixth Dalai Lama vanished from Kokonor. Different stories are there regarding this, some say he was murdered, others say that through his tantric powers the Sixth Dalai Lama had a storm built up, with the help of this he vanished into the deserts of Mongolia where he lived for another thirty years meditating and leading a spiritual life. He led the life of a shepherd and when he died a temple was built by his followers. All this is still a rumour as his shrine has not been found as so far.

2

Tashi - The Singing Monk

Meeting Lama Tashi was a pleasure. It was in September of 2009 that we had gone to Arunachal Pradesh. From Gauhati we went to Tejpur and from there to Tenga by road. After lunch at Tenga we went to the Himalayan Cultural Institute. On the journey to Dahung, I kept wondering what lady luck had in store for me. As we got down from the vehicle, we were welcomed by a Lama and two girls. The Lama looked familiar but I could not remember him, wondering where I may have seen him! As we went in and sat down in his office and introduced ourselves and told him that we were looking for the 'Singing Lama' among a few other people. The Lama in front of us giggled an absolutely innocent laughter. The Hindi teacher at the institute said, "He is the same man", even then it did not register. After a while the history teacher said, "He is the Chant Master". I was stunned for I could not believe that I was with the world famous Grammy nominee. Such was my meeting with the Geshe Ngwang Tashi or Lama Tashi or The Singing Lama. It was destined to be as they say!

Geshe Ngwang Tashi Bapu ('Geshe' is equivalent to a doctorate in Buddhist Philosophy), was born into a family of farmers and yak grazers in far off Thembang (Arunachal Pradesh). (When we passed the palace on our way to Tawang it looked as if it was perched up on the mountains, it seemed to be a very steep climb, at least to me). That was the only house in that area. Tashi has three brothers and four sisters. As is the tradition in the monasteries (the rule was specially set up by Merak Lama) if a family had three sons then the middle son had to join the monasteries. His parents Krishok and Karma Tashi were farmers, Tashi's father had enrolled him in the local primary school at the age of six, and it is here at Pangona Government School Tashi studied till the eighth standard. The next three years Tashi studied at the Government school in Namshu. From there he went to the Gontse Gaden Rabgeyling monastery in Bomdila to complete his education. Since Buddhism is the dominant religion in the state it is but natural that bulk of the people are Buddhists and follow the Tibetan Buddhism. The Dalai Lama in 1983 had visited Arunachal Pradesh and it is at this time Tashi received his teachings and initiations from his Holiness the Dalai Lama. The simple life attracted Tashi to spiritualism and he decided to become a monk. His mother was not too happy at this happening in Bomdila; any mother would be to see her second son going away from home. She requested a cousin of Tashi's to stop him from joining the monastery as his elder brother was already in the monastery. But Tashi's brother being in the monastery helped in strengthening his resolve to join the monastery. It was on May 25th 1983, Ngwang Tashi Bapu at the age of 15 left home for the monastery in Karnataka.

About the original Drepung Loseling Monastery which is in Tibet. The monastery was known for the high standard of academic study and is sometimes also known as the Nalanda of Tibet, as Nalanda is an important centre of Buddhism in India. When the Chinese invaded Tibet in 1959, the 500-year old Drepung Loseling Monastery was one of the many holy places shut down by the Communist regime. Nearly 8, 000 Drepung Loseling monks were either executed or put behind bars. About a few hundred monks escaped to India, these monks worked hard to preserve Drepung Loseling Monastery's ancient heritage in the camps they lived in. Today the Monastery is located in South India on land given by the Karnataka government to the Tibetan community in exile by the then Prime Minister Pandit Nehru. The monastery has about 5000 celibate monks and about 2000 monks in Drepung Gomang (college). Every year many monks join the order, a large number are from families who came from Tibet.

Tashi was a brilliant student and his formal education started in 1983 at the young age of fifteen years. It is at the Drepung Loseling Monastery, he spent the next twenty years of his life. Tashi completed his studies with 'Philosophy in Debate System' which they say is a Socratic view of Tibetan Buddhism, as his major subject. Looking back Tashi says he loved the monastic life. With a smile on his face he recalls, "I loved the monastic way of life. During my entire childhood I was lost in monastic studies. Life was not easy, I had to get up at 5.30 am in the morning and study the whole day and go to bed at around 2 am in the morning. We did not have good food or the basic hostel facilities, but it has made me what I am today". From the day Tashi joined the monastery he was in love with chanting. In the first few days of his stay at Drepung Loseling a westerner had requested for a prayer service where the Head Abbot faces the altar and the Chant Master faces the crowd. To Tashi the chanting seemed familiar and often he was found imitating people. It was after two years the Head Chant Master noticed him, it was near the bathing area the Head Chant Master asked him to join his group of chanters. Lama Tashi was a little hesitant at first as he did not know if after his studies he could give time to chanting. Tashi in the beginning of his studies had to learn by heart sixty pages in a year which was difficuLt Later the Rinpoche asked him to join the group and the rest of course is history. Lama Tashi impressed his teachers and spiritual leaders so much that in 1991 he was chosen as one of the monks to travel the world on the 'Sacred Music and Dance' tour of 1991-1992. For almost a year he travelled all over the USA, Canada and Mexico performing on the tour. Later in 1996, we saw him performing as part of the Drepung Loseling Institute and Richard Gere Foundation. Tashi was fortunate to perform in front of the Dalai Lama in 1999, the Multiphonic Chant at Curitiba, Brazil.

Tashi's multiphonic chanting or the 'one voice chanting' or the commonly known 'one voice chant' arises from the throat of a person who has selfless wisdom. Multiphonic chanting is defined as multiple tones coming out from a single larynx. The frequencies developed by the human vocal chord are harnessed in the throat while singing. The result of the tuning allows the singer to create more than one pitch at the same time. According to Tashi, "Multiphonic chanting is in vogue in Mongolia, though it is prevalent here too. It is characterised by a deep, vibrating voice, which is produced continuously for 8-9 minutes at a stretch". It is believed by the Tibetan monks that in the creation of the '

One Voice Chord', the monks do not sing/make the sound; rather they become the instrument through which the sacred sound comes out. This is the basic principle found in the Tibetan Buddhist teaching of sacred sound. According to Tashi, "I mastered the multiphonic chant and was appointed as the 'Umzey' or the Head Chant Master of the Drepung Loseling Monastery in 1999. I served in that capacity for five years before coming back to Arunachal Pradesh in 2004". It was at Drepung Loseling Monastery Tashi mastered the Monastic Sacred Dance along with 'Deep Voice Chanting' too. The next year in 2000 he went to the USA and was the Head Chant Master of the Monlam Chenmo or the Great Prayer festival which His Holiness the Dalai Lama presided at the National Mall, Washington, before an audience of 50,000. In 2002 Tashi was the Choyang Umzey at the Great Prayer Festival at Bodh Gaya where the audience was over 250,000 people. This Tashi says was one of his most memorable experiences. The other memorable experience was in Central Park in New York where he had an audience of over 6,000 people. According to Tashi facing such audience gives you a great high; you almost feel you are flying around; the super natural powers have taken over. It is difficult to believe that a young monk at the 22 years of age from the remote village of Thembang (Arunachal Pradesh) left India to far off USA and achieved such success.

Lama Tashi had an interesting story to tell us about his chanting; way back in 1988 two groups of medical experts in the USA examined his throat to unravel the mystery of the vocal chord. They could not believe that one human being could produce a number of sounds at one time; it seemed as if a number of people were singing together. They even put a camera through his nose to find out the mystery. Tashi remembers that he felt very sleepy at the time when the tests were conducted!

When there was a talk on traditionalism and modernity Tashi feels, "If you live the Western way of life, you will become spoilt, you will become bad". At times Tashi feels maybe the monasteries should cater to the modern times. He says, "I seriously feel the monasteries and the outside world have a lot to offer to each other. The monasteries have their own world and the western world has its own rules of conduct. Monasteries should learn from outsiders and outsiders should also learn from Monasteries". Tashi has spent one third of his life in the monasteries and coming in contact with the outside world must have been a big change for Tashi, however he says, "he has not changed and has stuck to the vows he took when he joined the monastery, which are - 1. Shall not kill, 2. Shall not lie 3. Shall not steal, and 4. Shall remain a celibate. Tashi feels "the basic principles of life are disintegrating" in society.

Tashi and Grammy Nomination in 2006 - Lama Tashi missing the Grammy upset more his followers than Tashi himself. In an interview he says that the fact that he has reached that level in the Grammy was a big enough honour for him. Tashi was nominated for his album 'Tibetan Master Chants' produced by Jonathan Goldman an American musician who is into meditation and spiritual music. Thousands of monks from Arunachal Pradesh and Ladakh (Jammu and Kashmir) kept an all night vigil praying for Tashi's success which eluded him. Tashi lost out to Ali Farka and Toumani from Mali (West Africa). Tashi's album 'Tibetan Master Chants' is world famous today.

Can you guess when a Grammy winner and a Grammy nominee meet what do they do? They 'rattle and hum 'as they say! Both Pandit Vishwa Mohan Bhatt and Lama Tashi met on stage at Gauhati for a project called 'Rattle and Hum' organised by the North East Zonal Cultural Centre. Both Bhatt and Tashi with their 'veena and chanting' took the audience to a spell binding level that they had not thought of. What a fantastic performance it must have been, once in a lifetime chance for people hearing them.

Amongst the many incidents Lama Tashi talked about during our meet, the journey to the Drepung Loseling Monastery in Karnataka (South India) was an interesting one. It is from Bomdilla Tashi Rinpoche was to take him and two other boys to Karnataka. (Tashi is a disciple of Tsona Gontse Rinpoche. The Rinpoche was born in Kameng, Arunachal Pradesh and then went to Tibet for higher studies). The Deputy Commissioner of Bomdilla gave the Rinpoche a jeep to take him to Tejpur (Assam). The boys from Bomdilla had to travel in a truck of the agricultural department. The truck driver dropped the boys at Ballipara (today it is also famous for The Assam Valley school) in Assam to be picked up by the Rinpoche. Night had fallen and the boys were patiently waiting for the Rinpoche very tired and hungry, suddenly they found the Rinpoche driving past them, he had missed seeing the boys! The boys couldn't believe their bad luck. They somehow managed to remember the direction the Rinpoche's jeep had taken and found a place to spend the night. Next morning they took a bus ride to

Tezpur. On their arrival at Tezpur, they started looking for the Rinpoche but lady luck did not favour them, so they finally gave up their search at 5 pm The Rinpoche and Tashi's elder brother had reached Rangapara at about 7 pm By this time since Tashi and his friends could not find Rinpoche's group, they decided to go back to Bomdilla, what else could the boys do? One of Tashi's friends who had never seen a train (which is not very uncommon for hill people) wished that before they went back they visit a station to have a look at a train. After the train visit the boys went back to 'Sherpa Hotel' to their room. When they reached their room they found a lady waiting for them, who asked, "Are you the boys who are supposed to go with the Rinpoche"? She took the boys with her to Tezpur and the next day Tashi and his friends travelled with the Rinpoche by bus to Gauhati.

To make matters worse during the bus journey someone threw itching powder at the Rinpoche and this must have been very painful for the poor Rinpoche. The group stayed at Rajdoot Hotel in the night and the next day they left by train for Delhi. In Delhi the three new boys stayed at Ladakh Budh Vihar while the Rinpoche stayed with a Member of Parliament, PK Thungen. On 1st June 1983, the boys got a message that they should reach the railway station by eleven in the morning and that the Rinpoche was coming with the tickets. The young boys had to be careful with their money so they decided to pay the taxi by the meter. Later they realised the idea was not so good. As we all know the auto and taxi drivers of Delhi are well-known for duping passengers and these young boys were easy prey! As usual he took them around a long route, they drove all over the place and as a result the boys reached the station very late, so late that as they were running on the overbridge they saw the train leaving the platform. Totally disheartened they went back to Budh Vihar, this time they took an auto rickshaw instead of a taxi and it took them only twenty minutes instead of ninety. Later the boys went to the MP's house and were told to take the tickets back to the station and fend for themselves. The poor boys were tired but they had to get the tickets exchanged for the next day's train. As Tashi and the boys were standing on the station they heard a train whistle and when they turned around they saw a man being run over by the train. Perhaps this was the first time Tashi saw death and this upset him a lot as for a long time he was pale and felt queasy. The boys could manage to take the train next day, but that too with great difficulty. Tashi's elder brother was wiser, and knew how to get things done, what he did was pay a coolie Rs 20 per person to help them getting their seats. They had lower berths and the upper berths were occupied by a group of college girls who kept awake in the whole night talking, the chatter was a great disturbance and Tashi and his friends couldn't sleep much, never had they heard so much of chatter! All the while the friends kept thinking how people could talk so much! Finally, they arrived at Pune from where they had to change trains for Hubli. On the Hubli train the boys slept like logs as they had had a restless night and when Hubli came other passengers had to wake them up. Tashi's brother was the first one to get up and he had to drag the three sleeping boys with their luggage out of a speeding train. Getting down at Hubli the boys went to a hotel and freshened up and ate at a restaurant at the Tibetan camp. The boys were now ready to meet the Rinpoche. Finally, Tashi had reached the Drepung Loseling Monastery in Karnataka and what an adventure it had been.

Today Lama Tashi is the Principal of CIHCS (Central Institute of Himalayan Culture Studies), he came back to Arunachal Pradesh in 2004 to start a study centre of Tibetan Culture. He is busy today to make it a top class University. I am sure his centre will be a top class place as we all know, "Nothing succeeds like success".

3

Talom Rubko and Donyi Polo

Talom Rubko and Donyi Polo are inter-related. Golgi Bote Talom Rubko was a man who had faith in the old religion and tried to save it. Donyi Polo religion, which is animistic in nature, is under threat from Christianity and Hinduism as there are many converts to the new faiths. Arunachal Pradesh is one of the states where people still follow the old animistic religion. A movement was started by Talom Rubko in 1990-2000 to protect the Donyi Polo religion. We all believe that whenever society has too many wrong doings there comes a 'messiah' to save the people, Golgi Bote Talom Rubko – a community worker, was one of them. Here was a man who worked only for the good of the Arunachal society, it is no wonder that people love and respect him so much even after his death.

The people of Arunachal Pradesh, India's easternmost state have believed that Donyi Polo or the Sun and Moon are the greatest form of the Gods 'Bo Bomong' whom we cannot see. Worshipping both comes from the belief that life on earth is possible because of these two. The warmth of the Sun brings to life the flora and the fauna. The tribal people believe that the Sun and Moon are the two eyes of God and nothing can be hidden from them. Donyi Poloism was followed by most tribes in the yesteryears; today the faith has been diminishing with Christianity and Hinduism raising their heads. Most of the tribes like the Adis, Apatanis, Hill Miris and Nishis say their origin came from a common ancestor – Abo Tani. Donyi Poloism is a nature worshipping religion and believes every man and woman has a major role to play in this world. Some of the deities of Donyi Polo are Kine Nane, Doying Bote, Gumin Soyin, Dadi Bote and Pedong Nane. These deities are supposed to be protectors of Harvests, Home, Life and Natural Resources. One of the basic teachings of Donyi Polo religion is that everything has evolved out of nothing. The 'nothing' after a passage of time led to the creation of '*Jimi*', the origin of all living and non-living creatures in this world. All Donyi Polo followers believe their ancestors have come from '*Jimi*'. The soul of a man '*Ayik* or *Ayit*' grows in a man's body; man is blessed when he learns to live in harmony with nature and other creation of God. Donyi Polo followers believe that the soul does not take reincarnation. It is in this life we reap the harvest of our good deeds, sins cannot be washed away by confessions or holy dips. One can counter our ill-deeds with good deeds only.

The Sun, Moon and ancestral deities are worshipped. Sometimes the '*shaman*' or Miri tries to cure people, but he too at times seems to be confused with so many deities in today's world. Tamo Mindo a '*shaman*' has two deities in his home, that of the Donyi Polo God 'Yapom'- God of the mountains and the Hindu God 'Shiva' associated with destruction. Tamo Mindo feels that Donyi Polo and Hinduism have similarities in their basic faith and practices. Both the Gods are worshipped with equal devotion in his home. Tamo Mindo is one of so many trying to protect the old animistic Donyi Polo religion and also keeping with the changing times. The teachings of Donyi Polo which is peace, purity, kindness, truthfulness, equality and impartiality and the Adis would like to follow these values. They would like to shine like the Sun and Moon. People who follow Donyi Polo as a religion cannot be cheats or tricksters. To the Adis Donyi Polo is the truth, the light that enlightens us, it makes the world bright and beautiful. The Adis believe that due to greed there is violence and finally violence has to end and when it does end the Adis say ' Donyi Polo E Lendukn'/ meaning truth prevails upon ultimately. When in trouble, a Donyi Polo believer calls out to Donyi Polo or says 'Donyi-e' 'Oh! The Sun'. Honesty, integrity, compassion and peacefulness are components of truth, is what all Adis believe in. Donyi Polo helps a person to have a strong character.

Golgi Bote Talom Rubko was very concerned about the changes coming into his society that Christianity and Hinduism was bringing in. Talom Rubko warned all followers of Abo Tani that the western culture would ruin their own religion, their very roots. What upset him was that outsiders were taking advantage of the simple people of Arunachal.

Talom Rubko was born to Rukpaying Rubko and Odam Rubko on 1st December 1937 at a village of Pasighat. Talom Rubko went to Government High School, Pasighat and graduated from St Edmonds College, Shillong (Meghalaya). For some time he worked in government offices but could not hold on to these jobs as his heart was somewhere else.

Talom Rubko worked in Adi areas; he ensured that the Adis celebrated all festivals together. He formed a 'Adi Cultural and Literary Society' which was based at Pasighat. He started the 'Donyi Polo Spiritual Society' of Arunachal which today is no more functioning. Later he became the Assistant Secretary of 'Donyi Polo Vidya Bhavan' whose chairman was Gegong Apang, the then CM of Arunachal. He has attended a number of conferences on 'International Association for Religious Freedom' and had travelled to Delhi, Mumbai and Hamburg. One of the oldest religious faiths got a world platform to be appreciated. Talom Rubko carried the message of the Donyi Polo faith to the world which for generations has come down orally. He felt we must love and respect what we have inherited from our ancestors and not forget our past.

Talom Rubko was against conversion and once when he met a missionary after hearing the man out, spoke, "Give our people the knowledge of Science and Mathematics (for enlightenment and progress) but please avoid evangelisation and conversion activities as conversion tears the individual from his/her family, tears the family from the rest of the community. Acts of conversion, therefore, create social unrest and clashes. Hence, conversion is violence of the deepest and gravest kind". The evangelist being a learned man understood the importance of the words spoken. The incidents of conversion made Golgi Bote Talom Rubko realise the importance of a written script about his religion Donyi Polo. He asked the literate people to come forward and help to write. Talom Rubko believed in 'practice what you preach' so he started writing prayers and songs which were published and are still used by the people of the Donyi Polo faith, specially the Adis. He wanted to educate the younger generation about their own culture and religion. Some of the books are – 'Short Background of Adi Festivals, Folk Songs of Siang Valley, Donyi Poloism –A Religion and Dance and Dance Dramas of Adis'.

Talom Rubko helped form the group called 'Donyi Polo Yelam Kebang', this was formalised on 31st December 1986 at Pasighat and inaugurated by the man himself. Finally, Talom Rubko's dreams of spreading the old religion seems to have come true. He spread the message of the old religion by moving from village to village by talking to the people and was perturbed by the growing trends of youngsters turning towards western culture. Some people helped in building prayer areas or Ganggings from where the divine message of Donyi Polo, the Supreme Being could be spread. Golgi Bote Talom Rubko was concerned about the Adis as they had taken to drinking and other bad habits, he told them they were all true children of Apatanis, Nishis, Galongs, Tagins, Adis, Hill Miris and Mishings and that they should not forget their own culture. Golgi Bote Talom Rubko was a concerned citizen and worked towards a cleaner environment for all. Talom Rubko left for his heavenly abode on 30th December 2001, a man who was loved by all in Arunachal Pradesh.

Long live Donyi Polo as a religion or 'Bomyerung Donyi Polo! Bomyerung Donyi Polo'.

Assam

Legacy of the Mighty Ahoms

When one visits Assam the first impression is miles and miles or shall we say kilometres of lush green foliage with Brahamaputra flowing through. The mighty river flows through almost the entire state from east to the west. The area is at times also called Brahamaputra valley or Assam valley. Amongst the 'Seven Sisters' Assam is the most centrally located if one had to travel from the north towards the North East. Assam to its north has Bhutan and Arunachal Pradesh, to its east is Manipur, Mizoram to its south, Tripura to its south west. Assam in the ancient past was known as *Pragjyotisha,* in the historical past it was known as Kamrupa and in the present days it is called Assam which came during the period of the Ahom rulers. Assam has been mentioned in the epics of Ramayana and Mahabharata. Kings like Narakasura, Bhagadatta and Bhasakvarman were known in our ancient past. Two strong ruling powers were the Ahoms in the east and Koches, in the west of Assam. The bulk of the population today are Assamese Hindus amongst whom the Indo-Mongoloid or the Kirata element is visible. There are sizeable amounts of local Muslim population too; Sikhs and Christians are also found in small numbers. Hindu mythology is also a part of the life of the Hindu; Vaishnavism has been a great influence on the Hindus. A majority of Hindus are followers of Vaishnavism or Lord Vishnu. Oral traditions are popular and are passed down from one generation to the other through singing, story telling and dramatic performances. Assam in the past was a centre of Saivism and Saktism, specially the 'Tantric' variety. Lord Shiva is a popular deity amongst the non-tribal population. The culture of Assam is mixed as there are different groups of people living together. There are a number of tribes in Assam, the Bodo, Kachari, Miri, Mishmi and Rabha. Though there are no prominent caste systems like the rest of India, some of the effects of caste system still do exist. Assam is basically an agricultural state where a large number of people are farmers, weaving is also an important occupation.

The tribal people have their own beliefs and myths, the most interesting ones are the ones on the myths of creation. The Bodo-Kachari myth on creation is that Lord Anan Gosai – Binan Gosai was first in a formless state after which he decided that the universe and other living things had to be created. After some time the Lord /Sibrai felt lonely so out of his own form created his partner Siburi. The first man was Mansinsin from whom came mankind. In the beginning there was only water and no land. God later asked for a lump of clay to be brought up from the bottom of the water and thus came into being life on the earth. Another view has this to say, a pair of birds were born out of a wish of God, who laid three eggs. From one egg came the trees and spirits; from the other two came Mansinsin and Diba-Dibi from whom mankind was born. The stories are all similar to Adam and Eve.

The Karbis have also some stories on myths of creation, called *'keplang'*. The *'keplang'* say that there was a mythical bird called '*wo plakpi*' who laid a number of eggs and from them were born the Assamese, Nagas, Kacharis and of course the Karbis, without doubt the Karbis came from the largest egg.

Eggs also are important in the Dimasa mythology. It is believed by them that the world earlier was very still, later a couple came called Bangla Raja and Arikhidima who united in conjugal bliss. After some time Arikhidima became pregnant and gave birth to seven eggs at the confluence of two rivers the Dilaobra and Sangriba. From the first six eggs six gods were born and the seventh egg gave birth to spirits and ghosts. The Dimasa believe their ancestors are the gods and it is the evil spirits which bring illness and pain. These are only a few stories about creations.

In terms of folklore Assam seems to be very rich, it is full of oral literature, the entire rural life finds expression in '*Bihunama*' and '*Baghosha*' which relate to marriage and religion of the Hindus and '*Zikirs*' and '*Jaris*' of the Muslim devotional songs. The Assamese oral narrations are through ballads and are popularly called '*Sadukatha*' or a merchant's tale or tales sung by wandering minstrels.

Written evidences are found in the '*Buranji*' or historical written records of the Ahoms who were a branch of the great Tai race of South East Asia. The first one was started by the first Ahom King Sukapha in 1228. Later many such records were kept in the offices of 'Likhar Barua' or the person responsible for writing the records. The word '*Buranji*' means 'a store that teaches the ignorant' (in the Ahom language bu is ignorant person, ran is teach and ji is store). These chronicles give us a good picture of life in those days and also the neighbouring kingdoms. The language used was simple and the entries were always brief. These *Buranji*s were written on the bark of the 'Sanchi' tree or 'aloe wood'. Today a large number of them have been published but some still remain with individual families. The British who were busy annexing territories fought against the Burmese but were not helped by the Ahoms, the kingdoms controlled by them later passed on to the British after the Treaty of Yandaboo. This also marked the end of the medieval period. The mighty Ahoms had ruled for almost six hundred years (AD 1228-1826). During this period the Ahoms came in contact with the tribes of the plains and Hills since they realised that the people of the region should be taken over in a friendly manner by a policy of conciliation. The locals realised that though the Ahoms had dislodged them from their land, they had shown sympathy. The policy of friendship and good feelings became the central point of the relations of the Ahoms with the local inhabitants.

Assam was annexed and came under the Bengal Presidency, gradually under the British the manufacture of tea became successful and in 1839 the 'Assam Company' was started. Initially workers from China were brought in but later by 1843 the Chinese went back. The tea garden workers were brought in from tribal India and today they have become an integral part of Assam.

In Assam a new kind of society grew up – the owners and managements were called the 'Planters' and the labourers brought in from tribal India now popularly called the 'Baganias'. The initial

'Planters' were from England, Scotland and Ireland, they built their small world in far off areas and at times their culture was called the 'Bunglow Culture', some of this culture still remains with our Indian 'Planters' too. The tea seeds initially were brought from China as the British felt Chinese tea was superior to Assam tea. Later a hybrid variety came up and tea from China stopped coming to India. Assam has today become one of the largest producers of tea in the world, second only to China.

Assam has seen its territory being broken away as the non-Assamese population were given land, the Naga Hills district became Nagaland, Meghalaya was formed to its South, Mizoram and Arunachal Pradesh too got its own identity. Assam has also seen ethnic violence in spurts as there are diverse cultures, different people from different religions speaking different languages disagree over issues is most commonly seen.

Assam the gateway to the 'Seven Sisters' is a major tourist attraction. Some of the tourist attractions are the 'Kamakhya Temple' of the Hindus, people visit to pray to Goddess Durga in her many forms. The state is rich in archaeological ruins especially the Sibsagar area which was the Ahom capital for many years till the British came. One of the largest river islands in the world 'Majuli' is found on the Brahamaputra River. They say Lord Krishna played here as a child, the island also has monasteries and can be reached by ferries. The state because of its rich natural resources has areas that have become tourist destinations like the Kaziranga National Park which is a world heritage site as the Indian 'one horned rhino' can be seen here, Manas National Park has tigers. Manas is also a 'world heritage site', it is a 'Project Tiger' reserve and a Bio Reserve too. The National Park has endangered species like the Golden Langur, Pygmy Hog and Assam Roof Turtle. Assam is also fortunate to have the largest petroleum reserves in the country. The beautiful state has rolling plains, the finest tea gardens, shady forests and mountains all in one place.

4

Lokpriyo Gopinath Bordoloi

'Lokpriyo' is the right name for a man who loved and was adored by all. Gopinath Bordoloi was the first Chief Minister of Assam, in those days called prime minister. He has also been called the 'Architect of Modern Assam'. He is the one who saved Assam from merging with East Pakistan; today's Bangladesh, when the transfer of 'Power Act' was enacted by the British. He also saw the infiltration of Bangladeshis into Assam and initiated suitable steps to prevent the situation. Gopinath Bordoloi stands tall in the political annals of Assam.

The Bordolois belonged to the Brahmin Daivajna caste (astrologers) and originally came from Uttar Pradesh. Gopinath was a true follower of Gandhi and took to the path of non-violence as a political tool. He worked tirelessly for the land and people he loved. It is for this effort that the then Governor of Assam Jayram Das Doulatram conferred the title of 'Lokpriyo' on Gopinath Bordoloi. Gopinath, dreamed of an 'egalitarian society' where justice and fairplay were the order of the day. He believed that the different linguistic groups could live in harmony.

A tall and handsome man, Gopinath was born to Buddeshwar and Praneswari Bordoloi in 1890 at Raha. Buddeshwar was a doctor at Raha dispensary. Gopinath lost his mother when he was just 12-

year-old. He had five siblings and he was the third child. Shashikala, his eldest sister who had become a widow at an early age, brought up her other siblings. Since his boyhood, Gopinath showed interest in the scriptures and by age seven had read the *Mahabharata*. He was also interested in games, music and singing. Often he would sing about the places he had visited with his father. His father wanted him to do his graduation but unfortunately did not live to see it. Gopinath's family often faced hardship and Shashikala supported the family by weaving cloth, a common feature in the villages of Assam. Shashikala was a social worker and with her efforts she built a *namghar* or Prayer Hall at Silpukhuri for housewives to come and pray.

After passing his matriculation, Gopinath Bordoli joined Cotton College, Guwahati. From there he went to Scottish Church College and did graduation in 1911. To pursue his MA, he went to Calcutta and completed his Master's degree but could not complete his Law degree but later he did it in Assam. On his return from Calcutta, Gopinath joined Sonaram High School as Head Master. This was the first step towards improving education. Gopinath felt that only education is the viable alternative to help the people to improve themselves. Keeping this in mind, he set up a number of educational institutions. At heart, he knew that 'Swaraj' or freedom was incomplete till poverty and illiteracy were removed from the society.

Shashikala had started looking for a bride for Gopinath when he came back to Guwahati after completing his studies. At the same time, Gopinath came in contact with Tarun Ram Phookan who introduced him to politics. At times, Gopinath did wonder if he could balance marriage and politics together. Gopinath finally married Surabala, a young girl of thirteen and he being almost twenty-eight. When she came to her in-laws place Surabala had very little knowledge about cooking and household chores. Gopinath came to her rescue and helped her. He taught her to cook his favourite food - deer meat roasted and Rahu kaalia or salmon curry. Gopinath also taught his young wife how to embroider and sew clothes. There were a number of financial difficulties the family went through. During one such day, when funds were low there came a beggar asking for alms. Gopinath went out to see who it was, and told the beggar to wait. He came back inside and asked Surabala, if they had any food left. Surabala kept quiet and her silence conveyed the message to Gopinath that there was nothing left. So he went out and gave his share of food to the beggar. The younger son started crying as his father had nothing to eat. Gopinath then told the children it was 'Mahalaya' time and we used to offer prayers and food to our ancestors, so it was a good idea to share whatever you had.

Gopinath was a good musician and could play the Violin and Esraj well, a good singer too, he liked singing classical music, Rabindra Sangeet, Brahma Sangeet and Bihu songs. As a student at Calcutta, he had to his credit several theatrical performances and Bihu songs. Gopinath was a thorough gentleman and was ever willing to help others. Once he helped a Nepali milkman by carrying the bride's party to the groom's house in his own car, something unheard of even today. Gopinath was a strict disciplinarian and the rules were the same for his children and the outside world. His son Brig D Bordoloi fondly remembers the day; he did not return home at night and spent the night at his friend's house. At daylight, he ran home and to his horror found his mother standing at the door and in a tearful voice said father had asked him to leave the house as he had broken the discipline. The son wept his heart out and fell asleep on a chair. The next thing he knew was his father calling out his name, and wonder of wonders there was no anger in his father's voice. He just told his son 'unless you are disciplined you cannot be a good boy and attain your goals, now go inside your mother is waiting'.

Gopinath, a staunch Gandhian supporter, was a freedom fighter and strictly followed non-violence. He was greatly influenced by Mahatma Gandhi and his teachings. In 1921, Gopinath came in contact with Gandhi and there he changed dramatically - his love for fine clothes changed, he felt he could do without fashion. His mind and soul seemed to be transformed; the letters to Surabala, sometimes from prison, showed Gopinath's spiritual bent of mind.

When the first Congress Ministry was formed in 1938, Gopinath Bordoloi became the first Chief Minister of Assam and took education under his portfolio. When World War-II broke out the Congress High Command directed the Gopinath Ministry to resign in 1939, which it did. Gopinath joined the Satyagraha Movement and courted arrest. After the War, Congress again came to power and so did the Gopinath Ministry. Gopinath Bordoloi opposed the Cabinet's proposal to merge Assam with Bengal to form a Muslim majority area as demanded by Jinnah, no way would Assam be part of Pakistan were his feelings. Gandhi's advice to Assam regarding the grouping of Assam joining with East Pakistan was 'If Congress did not agree to have Assam with India, and then Assam should protest a kind of *Satyagraha* against the Congress for the good of Congress'.

He was instrumental in establishing Guwahati University, High Court of Assam, and Assam Medical College, Assam Veterinary College etc. Gopinath Bordoloi was also a gifted writer. He wrote several books like *Annaskaktiyog, Shreeramachandra, Hajrat Mohammad,* and *Budhhadeb* while in jail.

In his capacity as first Chief Minister of Assam, he worked tirelessly with Sardar Vallabhbhai Patel to maintain the sovereignty of Assam. He also helped organise the rehabilitation of millions of Hindu refugees who had fled East Pakistan due to widespread violence and intimidation in the aftermath of Partition. His work formed the basis for ensuring communal harmony, democracy and stability which effectively kept Assam secure and progressive right up to the 1971 war over East Pakistan's independence.

During his tenure as Chief Minister one of his greatest successes was the prohibition of opium in Assam. Gopinath had Assam's welfare in mind and so wanted the state to receive a share of the revenues coming in from mineral oil and tea. The Bordoloi government took steps to tax the wealthy land owners and became first amongst the contemporary Provincial Governments. Gopinath had always the hills people of Assam on his agenda, especially for the border tribes of Assam his policy was of non-aggression. The tribal people too knew he was their friend. Gopinath realised that the hills and plains men of Assam had to live in harmony as brothers otherwise Assam could not become a strong state.

The death of Mahatma Gandhi came as a jolt to Gopinath Bordoloi and Assam. Gopinath had a dream where Gandhi was saying to him, 'lots of things are to be done, and you come soon'. Strangely enough Gopinath Bordoloi passed away soon after that. The people suffered a rude jolt when he breathed his last on 6th June, 1950. The evening before, he had attended a theatrical performance and later had a massive heart attack. He was just sixty. The house he was born has been turned into a museum but has a run down look, all the artefacts are either crumbling or broken down. Let us hope and pray the museum comes back to its original glory. The 'Bharat Ratna' was conferred on Lokpriyo Gopinath Bordoloi posthumously in 1999.

5

Bhupen Hazarika — Assam's Pride

Bhupen Hazarika the 'bard' of the Brahmaputra as he was called was a brilliant singer, lyricist, film maker and a journalist, a creative man to the core. At heart Bhupen was a simple gentleman who loved his people; it is no wonder that when he left this world thousands came to pay homage to this man, who liked to call himself '*jajabor*/ wanderer'. To my mind when I think of Bhupen Hazarika the lyrics of "*O Ganga tum kyon behete ho*" flashes, the soulful music stays on in your mind for a very long time. Bhupen was a lyricist who wrote songs about humanity and universal brotherhood, his themes most often were on communal harmony, his lyrics are popular amongst the different religious communities of Assam. He is the man who brought Assamese folk music to the rest of India.

Bhupen was born in Sadiya, Assam in 1926 to Nilkanta and Shantipriya; theirs was a family of teachers. Nilkanta shifted out of Sadiya looking for better prospects to Bharalmukh, Dhubri and then to Tezpur in 1935. It is here in Tezpur Bhupen was discovered by Jyoti Prasad Agarwala and Bishnu Prasad Rabha when he was on stage singing a Borgeet which his mother had taught him. In 1936 Bhupen accompanied Jyoti Prasad and Bishnu Prasad to Calcutta where Bhupen recorded his first song at Arora Studio. Both these icons that is Jyoti Prasad and Bishnu Prasad started Bhupen on his musical journey. Jyoti Prasad also introduced Bhupen to the works of George Bernard Shaw and other literary figures. Both these two icons were also followers of Mahapurush Shankardeva, the 15th century poet saint who brought about a socio-cultural renaissance in Assam. Both Jyoti Prasad and Bishnu Prasad emphasised to Bhupen that Shankardeva brought about changes through music, drama and literature for social reforms. Later this fire to bring in social changes had ignited young Bhupen's mind, he acknowledges this in his autobiography, and "A fire had burnt in me since childhood to change society.... the fire is still burning. I was greatly influence by Shankardeva. The first lyric I ever wrote was for him. It expresses juvenile anguish at the hatred and violence in society and also the desire to guide it towards love and brotherhood". Jyoti Prasad helped Bhupen in his artistic and creative work and also taught him the beauty of words, Bishnu Prasad helped in shaping the revolutionary songs for the people. Jyoti Prasad had started a musical play called '*Joymati*' a heroine from Assam's Ahom history. During those days there was no soundtrack studio in Assam, so in 1936 a ten-year-old Bhupen went to Calcutta for recording at Arora Studio, the recording was so perfect that Senola Company decided to record a solo album of Bhupen – the cover had "Master Bhupen Hazarika (Amateur)" and he was dubbed as "The Youngest Artist of His Master's Voice of India".

Bhupen completed his school education from Gauhati in 1942 and his graduation in 1946 from Benaras University. Benaras Hindu University broadened his horizons as he realised a Marathi or a Gujarati student was similar to him, there was no difference from one to the other. Bhupen had African, Indonesian, and Japanese as fellow students; he also had a Muslim studying Sanskrit. It was total national integration and all living in harmony.

He got his PhD in Mass Communication from Columbia University and the Lisle Fellowship from Chicago, USA to study the use of educational project development through cinema. During his stay in USA, Bhupen had two good things coming into his life which would effect him a lot, they were, first, when he met the black singer Paul Robeson who was famous for the song 'Ol man River', Bhupen successfully used the song and turned it into a mega hit "*Bistirno parore O Ganga behti ho*" in Hindi, which most of us have heard and loved. Bhupen was greatly impressed by Paul

Robeson and had this to say, "Paul Robeson was a social singer with the power to change". Later he said like, "Jyoti Prasad and Bishnu Prasad Kokaideu (brother) he was responsible for moulding my philosophy of action. I also wanted to be a singer with the power to change society". The second good thing that happened was his meeting his wife Priyamvada Patel who was studying Political Science in the same area. Priyamvada came from a well-to-do family and the same lineage as Sardar Vallabh Bhai Patel, the noted freedom fighter. Priyamvada's father worked in Uganda but had to leave his job, so for a while they moved from UK to USA. After a whirlwind courtship they married in 1950 much against the wishes of Bhupen's parents. In 1952 their only child Tej was born. When the couple came back to Assam Bhupen took up a job with All India Radio but was fired for taking too many leaves. He had to make ends meet with odd jobs from singing assignments. Finally, he did get a teaching assignment in Gauhati University and for some time he could look after his wife and child. But this was shortlived as he was late in joining his duties and his pay was cut, Bhupen was coming back from a peace conference in Helsinki. This was the last straw and Bhupen as a protest resigned. Priyamvada could not take this poverty ridden stage as she came from a rich family; she went back to her parents. The separation was devastating for Bhupen, he felt humiliated, and his pride had taken a battering. One positive outcome of all this was his creative side exploded into his creating fantastic music. Priyamvada had got a job offer from Canada and both felt it was the best for them. According to him they separated as friends and occasionally met as friends. The son was brought up by the mother and at times Bhupen would feel guilty for not looking after his son Tej.

One person who perhaps knew Bhupen for the longest time was his sister Sudakshina Sarma also called Queen by some and she has had the privilege of singing his first compositions. She best describes Bhupen as a simple, soft hearted person ever willing to help others. She says the melody Bhupen had, had been inherited from the maternal side of the family though their father also used to sing '*bhajans*'. Sudakshina says her brother could compose music very quickly, "When Gandhiji passed away, he had to write a lyric within a night to be recorded the next night by All India Radio Calcutta...and he did just that". (Another incident which Kulkul Rahman remembers is quite interesting, Bhupen Hazarika as a person was very jovial and people loved his company, one day at their place Bhupen locked himself up in their guest room and everyone wondered why, it was because he was composing music for a song which he was to sing at Darrang College the same evening.) Sudakshina always spoke well of Priyamvada and found her very gracious. "*Bou* (daughter- in- law) was everything that an ideal Indian woman could be, full of love and concern for people around her. At times she had difficulty adjusting to local food habits but she never complained". One can understand the difference in eating styles of a Gujarati and an Assamese. One a total vegan, the other non-vegan. A Gujarati family in Tezpur when they heard that there was a girl with Gujarati roots in their midst they would often call Priyamvada and Sudakshina to their place, so every Sunday it was a much looked forward to outing for both. Priyamvada did try to hold on to the marriage but the final rift came when poverty and perhaps an old romantic interest surfaced, after this Priyamvada finally left Gauhati. Sudakshina remembers Priyamvada had called the ailing maestro, "Perhaps Dada was waiting for that call". Bhupen and Priyamvada's marriage lasted for about thirteen years, financial constraints may have been the most important factor for the marriage collapsing.

When Bhupen sings you can almost hear the voices of the lonely boatman on the Brahamaputra, the '*Palki*'/palanquin bearers, the women picking tea leaves or the happy beats of the '*bihu*'. Bhupen has worked tirelessly to bring about social changes through his music and has tried to bring Assamese culture to the forefront. His songs have a tribal beat and for this he has this to say, "As a child I grew up listening to tribal music, its rhythm saw me developing an inclination towards singing. Perhaps I inherited my singing skills from my mother, who sang lullabies to me. In fact, I used one of my lullabies in the picture *Rudali*". Bhupen sang his first song "*Biswa nijoy nojowan*" in Assamese for the film *Indramalati* in 1939 when he was only twelve years old, a tender age when most boys are playing football. He wrote lyrics for many Assamese, Hindi and Bengali films. He has also written many short stories and children songs.

Bhupen and rivers have a special bonding. He has said, "I have no fixed address. A flighty wandering life has been written on my forehead". Interestingly, the town of Sadiya was completely swept away by river Brahamaputra when it changed its course in 1950 after the great earthquake. It almost seems this river had conspired with heaven and swept away all that he felt was his roots. In his lyrics he calls river Brahamaputra as a living presence as it knows so many secrets and has seen so many civilizations. It brings in a message of harmony and unity. Bhupen loved the river and had spent many hours on its bank playing, swimming or just sitting on its bank enjoying the peace and tranquility. Bhupen's lilting voice was haunting at times and brought forward his love for humanity. The boatman's '*bhatiali*' song was later used in many of his lyrics; river Brahamaputra has been a great source of inspiration for Bhupen. Once while he was travelling in Assam, a man in Nogaon took hold of his hands and wept, "You promised so much in your songs. You made us hope, but life has been nothing like that". It has not been an easy life for Bhupen as he has had to live up to the expectations of the Assamese people. He is the man who has given Assam an identity and the people take pride in his work, but so much adulation comes with a tag – he has had to live up to the image of a hero.

On his return from America Bhupen had joined the Indian People's Theatre Association. Later he had gone to Mumbai to work in the Indian People's Theatre Movement with stalwarts like Salil Choudhury and Balraj Sahni. Hemant Kumar took him around to meet other great musicians. Later Bhupen wanted Lata Mangeshkar to sing for his first film as a director: 'Tunes from the Deserted Path', and she had obliged. The song was also one of Lata Mangeshkar's favourite songs. Bhupen had directed a colour documentary for the Arunachal Pradesh Government on tribal folk songs and dances called 'For Whom the Sun Shines' in 1974. Bhupen produced a 18-part documentary called 'Glimpses of the Misty East' on the progress of the North East India states from 1974 to 1997 for celebration of 50 years of Independence. Bhupen Hazarika is well-known in Bangladesh for his music, specially his song on the war for Bangladesh's freedom, "*Joi Joi Naba Jata Bangladesh*" (hail the new born Bangladesh), the song was very popular amongst the people of Bangladesh at that time. Once MF Hussain had called Bhupen from London, requesting him to compose music for Hussain's film *Gajagamini*. Hussain had said, "Bhupen, you paint when you sing. Your music paints, but my brush can't sing". This was genuine praise from one artist to another. To Bhupen music was life and always elevated his moods whenever he was down in the dumps.

Kalpana Lajmi and Bhupen Hazarika had an almost forty years long relationship, they first met in 1971 when Kalpana was just seventeen and Bhupen about forty-five. Kalpana is the niece of Guru Dutt, the director and daughter of Lalita Lajmi, the artist. After a few years of knowing each other Kalpana shifted in with Bhupen or Bhupso as she endearingly called him. At the age of eighty Bhupen did offer to marry her but she declined the offer as she said she did not need the 'wife' tag, the trust and respect they shared was more important to her. Kalpana Lajmi is best known for her woman-oriented films like *Rudali, Ek Pal* and *Daman* to name a few. Talking about Bhupen's family she says his former wife Priyam has called Bhupen on the phone and had talked to him, she has also visited them in Bombay. Bhupen has helped Kalpana in becoming a critically acclaimed director, film maker and at times gave music to her movies, *Rudali* (Lamenting Woman) was a hit and got a best music award at the Asia Pacific Film Festival. Kalpana has looked after Bhupen in good times and bad, she has constantly been by his side when he was ill neglecting her own career. She is also almost the sole beneficiary of Bhupen's property both moveable and immoveable. To Tej has gone what Bhupen inherited from his parents. In spite of the will saying that the funeral be performed by Kalpana Lajmi and a few other close friends finally it was his biological son Tej who performed the last rites according to Hindu traditions. Kalpana Lajmi rightfully says, "He was not just a singer but also a social reformer who brought the North East closer to the rest of India". Jhanu Barua said, "We have lost the Dronacharya of music. He was a creator whose quality compositions were easily identifiable and enjoyed by the common people". The maestro a poet, musician, lyricist, writer has received many awards. To name a few are the Padmashree Award in 1977, the 'Dada Sahib Phalke award' in 1992 and the Padmavibhushan (Posthomous) in 2012.

As the saying goes musicians may come and musicians may go but the music goes on for ever, so does Bhupen Hazarika live through his music and lyrics.

6

Kanaklata Barua

Assam since ancient times has given equal importance to both men and women in the social life arena. It is no wonder that when Mahatma Gandhi called his 'Do or Die' movement, the women of Assam came out of their homes in large numbers to fight for their motherland. Women folk in Assam led a series of attacks on the British; many had to lay down their lives. Amongst them was a young girl called Kanaklata Barua. She joined the movement when she was hardly sixteen or seventeen, sometimes one wonders what makes a young village girl, who had led a very sheltered life come out to fight for what she believes in.

Kanaklata Barua was born to Krishna Kanta and Karneswari Barua on 22nd December 1924 at Barrangbari, a small village under Sonitpur district of Assam. The family belonged to the Dolaksaria Barua lineage, (the Dolakeswari Barua were the guards accompanying the king when he went out on a sedan. These people or guards were also at times used as police constables) the grandfather Ghanakanta Barua was a hunter and was popularly called 'Ghana Chikari/hunter'. Kanaklata's father married twice, the first wife was Karneswari, Kanaklata's mother. Karneswari died young leaving behind three young children. It was the duty of

Kanaklata to look after her younger brother Rajanikanta and sister Dibyalata. The father later married again a girl called Jonaki and they too had three children, Mrigendra, Anada and Kalicharan. Kalicharan is alive and stays at the ancestral home.

Kanaklata was lovingly called 'Kanka' by the family, though at times her friends called her 'Koli' because of her dark complexion. Kanaklata was brought up by her father in the village environment, though she went to school for a few years and studied till class three, but had to give it up because of household chores. Kanaklata's mother died when she was five and her father died when she was thirteen. This young girl at such a young age was burdened with the task of bringing up her brothers and sisters, life must have been so difficult for Kanaklata despite the support from the joint family, and it was very common those days for grandparents and uncles to look after the rest of the family. Jonaki, Kanaklata's stepmother and grandmother tried their best to look after the orphans but life still seemed very difficult for Kanaklata as it sapped away all her energy, looking after the joint family was very taxing for Kanaklata who herself was a child.

Kanaklata was a quiet, reserved girl, somewhat different from girls of her age. Her interests were more into the political scenario to which she was introduced at a very young age. Slowly hatred for the British started creeping into young Kanaklata's mind and the words like 'Mahatma Gandhi, Congress and Independence' were familiar for Kanaklata. The words had started bothering her and soon she joined the Congress meetings, the songs of Jyoti Prasad Agarwala and the words of Bishnu Prasad Rabha really impressed her and now she was ready to fight. Kanaklata's grandfather Ghanakanta Barua did not like Kanaklata going out of the house as those days young girls roaming about on their own was not encouraged, the grandfather asked her not to muddle up her head with politics. Kanaklata, however, was convinced that this was what she wanted to do, so she took into confidence her stepmother Jonaki Barua and very reluctantly the mother gave her consent to join the group.

In one of the campaigns she met Pushpalata Das, another freedom fighter who advised all the participants to wear Gandhi caps, these caps and flags were made by the women's organisation 'Mahila Sangathan'. These women boycotted foreign cloth and started wearing home spun cloth. The 'Quit India' movement resolution was passed by the Congress Working Committee and everywhere people were protesting and as a result the Congress Party was banned by the British Government.

In Assam the 'Quit India' movement was comparatively peaceful, the Congress leaders of Tezpur area decided that they would go with the idea of participating in the 'Do or Die' movement. A secret meeting was held in the house of Brahamanda Barakakati, Amiya Kumar Das the Congress president fell ill and the responsibility of leadership fell on Jyoti Prasad Agarwal. Jyoti Prasad advised the Congressmen to fight back in a non-violent way. He told his group that they would go to the 'Thanas' of Tezpur and raise the national flag. He formed the '*Mrityu Bahini*' or Death Squad, Jyoti Prasad asked the volunteers to face death if the situation arose. The Congress volunteers went to Chaiduar and Dhekiajuli to get trained there for the final hoisting of the flag.

Kanaklata was very impressed by the plan of Jyoti Prasad and was ready to shoulder her responsibilities. She asked all members to go to the 'Thana' with flag in their hands. The appointed day was 20th September 1942. A brave girl indeed, who could think a seventeen or eighteen-year-old could shoulder so much of responsibilities. Kanaklata showed she was no less than Queen Joymati or Mula Gabhru, the words of Mahatma Gandhi 'Do or Die' kept haunting her.

In preparation for the final day on 18th September 1942, the Congress Party members met at the '*Kirtan Ghar*' or Religious prayer hall of Jeranial Satra (Satras are religious areas started by Sankardeva, the Vaishnavite saint) close to Kanaklata's village under the Presidentship of Maghiram Bora. Kanaklata was ready as a volunteer and had decided to join the 'death squad' to unfurl the national flag on 20th September 1942. Pushpalata Das another freedom fighter addressed the meeting; she encouraged the group to participate in the unfurling of the national flag. Young girls and women from the village sat below the shade of trees listening to the speeches. Pushpalata said India had been forced to participate in a war which was in Europe and the Indians were not consulted. The British were lowering the image of India, she even quoted the words of Gandhiji, "If you want help from us as friends, it's yours but we are not servants. We do not want to be involved in your war with money or manpower". Pushpalata, in her fiery speech, said that we Indians must not tolerate this injustice and this would be overcome by non-cooperation. The freedom fighters were put into two groups – the 'peace squad' and the 'death squad'. The 'peace squad' would maintain peace and harmony in the area, both in towns and villages. The 'death squad', on the other hand, had to fight for Independence and at times giving up their lives. Pushpalata's words sat heavily on Kanaklata's mind and after a lot of thinking she finally went on to register herself and join the 'death squad'. Pushpalata initially hesitated to register her as she was too young, but finally had to give in. Kanaklata now had the courage to go to her grandfather and tell him that she would not disgrace the family while hoisting the tricolour at the Gohpur police 'thana'. Many sleepless nights were spent thinking on what must be done. Finally, 20th September 1942 dawned, the day that was so important to all Assamese. Early in the morning Kanaklata finished her chores and had her meal with her brothers and sisters, she seemed somewhat sad as she told her siblings that she may not come back alive. After saying this she went to join the group of freedom fighters from the 'death squad' at Barangbari Chairali (where four roads meet). Kanaklata stood in the front of the female volunteers and soon they started walking towards the Gohpur police station which was about twelve kilometres away. The freedom fighters had the national flags in their hands and about four thousand people from Barangbari and the same number from Kalabari walked together. All along the way the group sang 'Vande Mataram' and shouted 'Freedom is our Birthright'.

Kanaklata led a big procession of people to the Gohpur police station to hoist the national flag. The British tried to stop the crowd but it was of no use, the crowd just came on and on like a big wave. Kanaklata requested the officer on duty to allow her to hoist the national flag but the request was refused, the British troops warned the group that if they came in they would fire. The British police force was led by RM Sunia, he did not allow the picketers to enter the compound of the police station. Kanaklata told the police that they could kill their bodies but not their souls. Hearing these words the group was all charged up and refused to turn back, death did not scare them, the very determined group refused to retreat. When the procession was going forward a sepoy named Mohan Kachari heard somebody shouting 'Fire, Fire', the man without thinking fired at Kanaklata and later at Mukanda Kakoti, both died instantly. Later, they say Mohan Kachari went mad and committed suicide by jumping into a well. Perhaps he could not live with the guilt of killing his own people.

Kanaklata's body was recovered and taken to her home where she was cremated. However, Mukunda Kakoti's body was taken by the British. The national flag was finally put up on Gohpur police station by Rampati Rajkhowa of village Kamdewal in the evening when the British were resting! On the same day, Dhekiajuli police station also had a similar situation when three teenagers, Tileswari, Numali amd Kahuli were gunned down by the British.

7

Lachit Barphukan – The Ahom Army Commander

Lachit Barphukan is a well-known personality of Assam, but outside his native place a large number of people have not heard of him. It is of late that he came into limelight. Lachit Barphukan like Chatrapati Shivaji is well-known for his military skills, a gold medal named after him has been installed at the National Defence Academy to be given to the best cadet officer for military skills. To pay respects to Lachit Barphukan a statue has been put up at National Defence Academy, Khadakvasla, Pune too.

Lachit Barphukan belonged to the Tai-Ahom group which has ruled over Assam for six hundred years before the British took over. The Ahoms started wet land cultivation here and so prospered in the bargain. The Ahom kings were called 'Swargdeos' meaning God of Heaven, the Ahoms believed the Kings were descendents of Lengdn or Indra. Lachit Barphukan belonged to the Lukhurakhun clan which was one of the oldest tribes of Assam and was linked to Sukhpha, the first Ahom King.

Lachit was the youngest son of Momai Tamuli Barbura. He was brought up like a noble man's son as his father was one of the Ahom generals, who fought against the Mughals during the reign of Jehangir and Shah Jehan. Momai Tamuli was born as

Sukuti and was a bondsman who was supposed to work for his nephew. One day, while Sukuti was working on making a 'bund' or barrier to store rainwater, the King Swargdeo Pratap Singh (1603-41) happened to pass by and noticed the meticulous way Sukuti was working. He, the King immediately released Sukuti from his bondage and appointed him Bar Tamuli or Superintendent of the Royal Guards. Being the dedicated worker that Sukuti was, he soon became the Barbura or the Commander of the army. During the Ahom-Mughal conflict he was responsible for the treaty with Allah Yar Khan (1639). Even the Mughals had to accept that with King Pratap Singh and Momai Tamuli as the head of the Army it was difficult to conquer Assam.

Momai Tamuli was a visionary and it was he who insisted that spinning and weaving should be done in all household. Even to this day we find in most Assamese village household, spinning is done at home. Momai Tamuli organised the Assamese hierarchy for administrative control and he also graded the functions of Assamese officers. Into such a background Lachit grew up, he learnt from his father the value of being honest and dedication to one's work. Lachit's early education was at home and in his father court room which was at their house. Young Lachit had the privilege of witnessing the official work and found his father delegating his duties and discussing business of the palace, Lachit was fortunate to learn the working of the state so early in life. Momai Tamuli had also got learned scholars to teach him about the '*shastras*' or religion and the history of the Ahoms. Military training was also not excluded from his learning.

As Lachit grew up he was made the scarf bearer of the Premier or the equivalent of a secretary, which they said was the first step towards a politician's life. Before he became the Supreme Commander of the army Lachit had served as Superintendent of the Royal Horses, being an excellent horseman he had managed to train the unruly horses of the king's stable. Later he became the Simulgaria Phukan or Commander of the levy generally stationed at Simulguri near the capital. Lachit also became the Dolakasharia Barua very soon. By today's standards it would mean Inspector General of Police. The king was very happy with Lachit and was seriously thinking of making him his Army General. One day, the king told him he was looking for a man who would capture Syed Firoz and Syed Sana from the Mughal side. The man had to be courageous, full of stamina and had depth of judgments. To this Lachit replied, "Could it be that there is no fit man in your domain, your majesty? What are enemies? After all they are mere mortals. Shall we not find men similar to them in our own country"? Hearing this, the king decided to appointment Lachit the leader of this army expedition. The king to make sure he had chosen the right man wanted to test Lachit again. One day while Lachit was in front of the king bowing down to pay his respects he found a man had come and snatched his turban away; this was a great insult as it meant that he had lost his prestige. Lachit ran after the man in anger with his sword, ready to strike, it is only then the king intervened saying that he had told the man to do so. It was to test his courage and quick thinking. After this, Lachit was made formally the army chief or Barphukan, and a golden sword was presented to him by the king.

The Ahom-Mughal conflict between 1614-1639: The Ahom and the Mughals had frequent clashes as is normal for two powerful rivals. The basic reason for the conflict was the natural resources like the forests and wildlife. The Mughals wanted the 'agar' wood (used for incense and perfume) for their king and this irritated the Ahoms, they captured the Mughal traders and plundered their boats also killing some of the traders. The conflicts continued for almost twenty-five years with victory and defeat on both sides. The monarch Swargdeo Pratap Singh guided them but the actual action was taken by Momali Tamuli Barbarua or Lachit's father. It was 1658, the Mughal king Shah Jehan fell ill and the Ahoms took advantage of this and they evicted the Mughals out of Gauhati and recaptured the lost Ahom territories. There were about seventeen invasions and out of these there was only one in which the invaders achieved some success. During this campaign Mir Jumla was the Mughal commander, who was the Viceroy of Dacca. The Mughal army came up to the river Brahamaputra and the Ahoms were badly defeated. The king Jayadhawaj Singha fled to the Hills and the Mughals won the battle momentarily. Soon the monsoon came and with it started problems of malaria and dysentery. Mir Jumla died during the retreat of the Mughal army. The Ahoms again were humiliated by Mir Jumla's treaty where two royal princesses were taken for the 'royal harem'. Some of the land had to be forfeited right from Manas to Gauhati, a sum of three lakhs had to be given as indemnity. The Ahom King Jayadhwaj died soon after the defeat and his nephew Chakradhwaj Singha became the king. It is here

Lachit Barphukan came into the limelight and took over the army; he was the one who changed the tide of war.

With Lachit Barphukan as the General of the Army all the preparations were done in 1667. It was in August 1667 the Ahom army sailed down the Brahamaputra river. Kaliabar was used to start the attack and the Mughal Governor Syed Firoz was taken by surprise and no reinforcements could be got from Dhaka. The Ahoms had a few easy victories and now they looked towards taking back Gauhati. Towards the south of Assam the Ahoms wanted to capture the fort of Itakhuli which was on the banks of the Brahamaputra, but by this time the Mughals had fortified themselves and the Ahoms suffered a setback. However the Swargdeo or King sent stern messages that the army had to go back and so they did. The spies from the Ahom camp pored water into the muzzles of the canons and the guns became ineffective. Finally, in November 1667 Itakhuli was captured back by the Ahoms and the Mughal General Syed Firoz Khan the Faujdar/Governor of Gauhati was also captured. The Ahom king Chakradhwaj Singha was now a happy man, he congratulated his generals and men saying, "I can now eat my morsel in peace. Long live the Ahoms".

This happiness was shortlived as the Mughals invasion of Assam started again in February 1669 and finished off in March 1671. When the loss of Gauhati reached the Mughal Emperor Aurangzeb he was fuming and immediately sent the Rajput Raja Ram Singh to establish control over Gauhati. The Ahoms came to know of this and started planning on how they would face the Mughal army. The king called for his 'mantris'/ ministers to find out the details and told them not to be caught napping. He also asked his General Lachit Barphukan about what he had found about the Mughals. Lachit said the Mughal army was led by Raja Ram Singh, son of Raja Jai Singh of Amber. Raja Ram Singh it was believed to have been sent by Aurangzeb for two reasons, one that Ram Singh was an able general, and second, Aurangzeb was not happy with Ram Singh as he felt Ram Singh had a role to play in the escape of Chattrapati Shivaji and Guru Tegh Bahadur while in Mughal custody. Lachit told the King Chakradhwaj Singh that Raja Ram Singh's deputy was Rashid Khan, the same man who was with Mir Jumla. Rashid Khan knew the Ahom language and the religion. Also both Ram Singh and Rashid Khan did not see eye to eye on most occasions and this Lachit wanted to make use of in times of need.

The Assamese King Chakradhwaj plan of action was to employ everyone to throw out the Mughals and get back their lost pride. Lachit Barphukan wanted to force the Mughals into a naval battle as he knew the Mughals lacked naval skills, so the Mughals had to be denied land access. For this he wanted defences put up on the Brahamaputra River around Gauhati. Next the king allotted duties to the Premier Atan Burgohain who was to look after fortifications around Gauhati on both the banks of the Brahamaputra River. Atan Burgohain got constructed ramparts on valleys so that two Hills could be connected; he also had anti-cavalry obstacles put up in front of the fortifications. On the river he put up walls at the landing sites and in the middle put up blockades so that naval advance could be stopped. He had put up artillery guns on the ramparts to cover all approaches. At regular intervals on the fortifications there were soliders guarding the plains and Hills. He also had commandos to support operations. The command and control was divided into two, the North and South banks. South bank of Brahamaputra was commanded by Lachit Barphukan and North bank by Atan Burgohain. Gauhati had adequate logistic support inside the fortification to last an extended war if that took place. In advance Lachit had repair material dumped close to the fortification for quick repairs. All soldiers had their clothes, arms and armour issued on time. On this Lachit Barphukan got his army ready to face the mighty Mughals.

Lachit's spies were working well in advance and all the movement of the Mughal army was getting reported to him. The news of Raja Ram Singh's departure from Dacca and his reaching Rangamati in February1669 was all reported back to Lachit. Lachit's army allowed the Mughals to come into the war zone of Gauhati, he made a few tactical withdrawals and left a few soldiers in the camps. The Mughals felt the Assamese were scared and had run away! The soldiers left behind were captured and taken to Raja Ram Singh who released them with a message for Lachit, "Tell your master to give me a fight for at least an hour". Hearing this Lachit was not too unhappy as this would give him an opportunity to gauze the number of men in the Mughal army. Delay in war was advantageous to the Ahoms as a few more blockades on the Brahamaputra had to be put up. Firoz Khan the ex-governor of Gauhati who was captured when the city was taken back by the Ahoms carried a message to Ram Singh from Lachit, "The city was never yours, and it was captured by the Ahoms from the Cooches". Battle of words continued through messengers. Raja Ram Singh tried to put pressure on the Ahoms by sending an arrow carrying a letter for King Chakradhwaj Singha. It stated Lachit had been paid one lakh rupees to evacuate Gauhati. The king understandably was upset over this and had a few doubts over Lachit's loyalty and integrity. But the Premier Atan Burgohain realised the trick and convinced the king that the message was only to fool him. Friction between Ram Singh and Rashid Khan had started and Rashid Khan had become very insolent and refused to accept Ram Singh as the leader. Ram Singh tried getting into the fort at Sarai through an underground passage but the Ahoms had filled the moat around the fort with water. Ram Singh fired cannons from temporary structures which broke the rampart walls but the Ahoms patched the wall quickly and started firing at the Mughal army and the Mughals had to beat a hasty retreat.

In June 1669, the Mughals attacked again, the Ahom commander Miri Sandikai Phukan fought bravely but Ahoms faced a few defeats and some war boats were captured by the Mughals. The king Chakradhwaj Singha sent orders to the Barphukan and Borgohain that the boats be retrieved immediately. But nature had other plans, the monsoons helped the Ahoms, the rain and floods separated the enemies camp, situations were similar to Mir Jumla's time. Raja Ram Singh seemed to be at his wits end trying to keep his men and horses safe. On the other hand, Lachit Barphukan was quite happy at the situation as it gave him more time to react and think of improvement. The Assamese army kept up the pressure with guerilla tactics, Raja Ram Singh called these 'thieves affairs', perhaps he had not heard of the saying, "Fight the guerilla like a guerilla". Raja Ram Singh fed up by the Ahom tactics, decided to withdraw his army during October 1669 and March 1670 as he was not going to fight like the Ahoms.

Lachit Barphukan felt he should also test Raja Ram Singh's skill on land warfare, so he sent Brahmin messengers to Raja Ram Singh saying, "Lions alone fight at night, while others fight during the day and night" The Ahom messengers said, "We cannot help but fight at night as we have thousands of Rakshas/ demons who are all man-eaters and night rovers". Raja Ram Singh at first did not believe this and said, "I believe the Assamese army is so powerful at night because they have Rakshas and cannibals in their camps, but I want proof of this to believe all this". When Lachit was told about this he praised the Brahmins for their quick thinking and decided to give the needed proof. Ahom soldiers who were dressed in black kept walking the ramparts the whole night, they had in one hand human legs or possibly human leg shaped sticks and burnt fish in the other. Raja Ram Singh saw this bizarre scene and could not help but think indeed the Ahoms had Rakshas in their camp! The Brahmins indeed had given the right news.

Raja Ram Singh tried all sorts of method to oust the Ahoms, right from trying to bribe the commanders with special gifts, a gem studded necklace was sent for Lachit Barphukan which of course he refused. Just when the battle was taking a critical turn King Chakradhwaj Singha died in April 1670, he was succeeded by his brother Udayaditya Singha, a capable monarch but he lacked experience in battle.

Battle of Alaboi, September 1670: The Ahom King Udayaditya Singh wanted his commanders to start an immediate attack by land to throw the Mughals out. At this time, the Mughals had collected an army at Alaboi Hills about 25 km away from Gauhati. There was an area of a vast plain in front of the Mughal camp; it had the Brahamaputra on the south and the Sesa River to the north. Lachit Barphukan an experienced soldier knew the Ahom army stood no chance with the mighty Mughals. Initially the Ahoms won as the Mughal king had been misinformed, the strength of the Ahom army was much more than it was thought to be. Quickly reinforcements were brought in and the Rajputs on the Mughal side attacked with vengeance, at the end of the day, ten thousand Ahom soldiers lay dead and the victorious Mughal army rode off to their camp with much fanfare.

Raja Ram Singh the victor pressed on for the evacuation of Gauhati, he even promised the sum of three lakhs as payment for the expenses of fortifying Gauhati. But the Ahoms were not to be swayed, so finally Raja Ram Singh agreed to fight the Ahoms on water which was perhaps their Waterloo! Raja Ram Singh was a desperate man as the Mughal Emperor Aurangzeb had threatened him with dire consequences, "If you can accomplish your mission you will be rewarded but if you fail, your head will be taken off and your children and relatives slain".

Lachit Barphukan fell seriously ill and was bed ridden; his absence from the battlefield affected his armed forces, the morale of his troops was down and this news reached the Mughal camp. Raja Ram Singh was a cornered man, he had Emperor Aurangzeb over his head and the news that Lachit Barphukan was seriously ill made Ram Singh take the plunge of fighting the Ahoms on water, a mistake he lived to regret.

Battle of Saraighat 1671: The final naval battle started in the last week of March 1671. The Brahamaputra is the narrowest between Kamakhya and Saraighat and there are Hills on both sides of the river with forests. Lachit realised that the river was an important means of communication and a moving army needed the river to move quickly. So the place had things in favour of the Ahoms. The Mughal armies were divided into four groups and were in the area of Ahom fortifications. The Ahom army was deployed on both sides of the Brahamaputra – the south bank had Lachit Barphukan as Commander and their headquarters were at Itakhuli. The north bank had Atan Burgohain as the Commander and their headquarters were at Lathia Hills; both were ably supported by junior commanders. The Mughal army had about 500 war boats while the Ahoms had about 3000 with almost 34,000 sailors. Raja Ram Singh was looking for an opening in the ramparts, on the sandbanks within Itakuli fort and the Kamakhya Hills. The Mughal army came with their guns booming and arrows flying and a breach was created, the Ahom army was taken by surprise and there was utter confusion in the Ahom camps. The Ahom soldiers missed their leader Lachit Barphukan in this difficult period. They retreated back and in the meantime the breach in the wall had been patched up as the material was readily available. All thanks to Lachit Barphukan's planning in advance. The Mughal army tried to attack the fort of Aswakranta both from land and water, the commander of Aswakranta asked for help as he found the going tough. Lachit immediately sent help but realised that for the Ahoms doomsday was not very far off without him. Lachit Barphukan ordered his men to put him on the flagship so that he could personally lead the Ahom army. The very presence of the man recharged the batteries of the Ahom soldiers. The Barphukan rushed ahead with six warships towards the enemy fleet. It is believed he said to the soldiers "If you want to flee, flee. The king has given me a task here and I will do it well. Let the Mughals take me away. You report to the King that his General fought well following his orders". This had an electrifying effect and the Ahom soldiers were all charged up. A fierce battle took place on the waters of the Brahamaputra and it was littered with corpses, boats and horses. The Mugahls could not stand the assault as they were attacked from land and water. There were heavy casualties on the Mughal side and the few who were alive beat a hasty retreat. By sun set the battle came to an end and it was a decisive victory for the Ahoms or the Assamese which was 'snatched from the jaws of defeat by Destiny's child, the one and only Lachit Barphukan'. Raja Ram Singh in his war impressions on Assam had this to say, "Glory to the King! Glory to the counselors! Glory to the commanders! Glory to the country! One single individual leads all the forces! Even Ram Singh, being personally on the spot, has not been able to find any loophole and an opportunity".

The victory in the Ahom camp was marred by the death of their leader Lachit Barphukan soon after the battle of Saraighat, his sick body could not take the strain; it was his indomitable spirit which kept it going. Lachit Barphukan at times has been compared to Lord Nelson who also died in the lap of victory. The battle of Saraighat was the largest naval battle ever fought in the 17th century. The hero's last remains lies in rest at the Lachit Maidan built in 1672 by Swargdeo Upaditya Singha at Hoolugapara close to Jorhat. Assam celebrates Lachit Divas on 24th November every year to keep the memories alive of this great man.

(Time Line of Kings)

1603-1641 Susenghphaa (Prataap Singha, Burhaa Rojaa, Buddhiswarganarayan, son of Sukhaamphaa)

1641-1644 Suramphaa (Jayaditya Singha, Bhogaa Rojaa, son of Susenghphaa)

1644-1648 Sutingphaa (Noriyaa Rojaa, son of Suramphaa)

1648-1663 Jayadwaj Singha (Bhoganiyaa Rojaa, son of Sutingphaa)

1663-1670 Supangmunga (Chakradwaj Singha)

1670-1672 Sunyatphaa (Udayaaditya Singha, brother of Supangmunga)

8

Maniram Dewan

(Assam's First Martyr of the War of Independence and a Tea planter)

Maniram Dewan Borbandar Baruah was born on 17th April, 1806 into a family of Marwari businessmen. His ancestors had travelled from Kanauj to settle down in Assam, looking for business, these men came and married local girls and took up local names to be part of the crowd. A Marwari they say can put up with any kind of hardships to become successful in life. There is an old saying that goes like this, "Where the bullock cart has not been able to go, the Marwaris have reached", nothing can stop a Marwari businessman. Maniram's forefathers had held high offices in the courts of Ahom Swargdeos. Maniram's ancestors were the first non-Ahoms to hold offices in the administration. Tradition of writing history by the Ahoms can be found in '*Buranjis*' or chronicles. Maniram Dewan also used to write history during the Ahom period.

Maniram, who had 'business' running in his blood, wanted to use traditional artefacts to start a business. He wanted to start a self-dependent economy under the Biritish East India Company. What they say Maniram had thought of for Assam can be still used in today's world. 'Entrepreneurial' courses in our academic system perhaps need to be given importance. Maniram had mastered the technique of iron smelting, gold procuring, boat making, brick kilns and salt manufacturing. He started black smithing around the Tiru Hills and made match locks, hoes and cutlery. He had also started weaving of *'Mugaand Paat'*, Assam silk. Name it and he had his hand in a number of businesses. Many in that area looked up to him as a demi-god.

Maniram grew up in an era which can be said to the bleakest period in Assamese history. The Burmese invasions brought in a reign of terror; Maniram was just about ten or twelve years old when the Burmese invaders struck terror by killing and burning. It was a reign of terror which most of us can't even think of, inhuman atrocities took place. Maniram's family with a few royalties shifted to Bengal between 1817- 1824. It is here they say Maniram met the British and was very impressed by them. He invited them to come and throw out the Burmese invaders and it is he who led the British towards Nowgaon in 1824. By virtue of his talent and intelligence Maniram became a loyalist of David Scott, the Agent under Governor General of India in North East India. Later he worked under Newfville. When Maniram took the British into Assam he thought that after the battle the foreigners would go back, but that was being naïve!

The British were also very impressed with Maniram and made him the *'Sheristadar'* or Land Agent. Later Maniram also became the *'Borbandar'* or the Prime Minister of the Ahom king Purandar Singha, who was a king only in name. Both the Ahom and the British were very happy with Maniram but this happiness was shortlived. The British hesitated to take over Upper Assam as the Burmese invasions had taken its toll, the land lay devastated and no revenues could be generated out of the place. The British were looking for an alternative to tea plantations as working in China did not seem feasible. So when they saw the wild jungles their thoughts of putting up a native king changed, on the pretext of the land taxes not being paid the area passed on to the British. Maniram did protest but it was pointless as the protests fell on deaf ears. Soon Maniram resigned from his post of Land Agent and with it went the powers that were given to him by the British administration. Maniram, of course, understood the implications of the British not wanting to go as the interest lay in the tea gardens.

In fact, it was Maniram Dewan, who introduced the indigenous tea plant to Robert Bruce in 1823. The tea plant grew wild in the Singhpo and Tikkar Hills of Assam region. The hill tribes of the area had used the leaves to boil or to chew them. The Singhpo and other tribes of Assam had been drinking the brew for ages. Some of the old medicinal textbooks in Sanskrit mentions leaves called *'Shampatra'* /dark leaves from which *'Shampani'* / dark liquid was made. This is the first mention of tea in India. The Dutch traveller JHVan Linschiten in 1598 noted that Indians ate the leaves as a vegetable and boiled the tree leaves to brew it as a drink. Probably, the tea leaves were discovered in the prehistoric Paleolithic age when the early tribesmen saw monkeys chewing the plant leaves and getting energized.

One day a British officer Capt Bedingfield who was posted at Sadiya had a Singhpo chief visit him and offered him a cup of Chinese tea brought from England. When the Singhpo chief saw the golden liquid in tea cups exclaimed *'phanapo'*. Maniram Dewan informed the British officer that 'Phanapo' was the tea made from the local tea bushes. Maniram explained that the brew helped in removing fatigue and had been used over centuries by the Singhpo tribes. Captain Bedingfield immediately reported this to the higher authority that is Lord William Bentinc, the Viceroy of India. This was followed by Lt Charlton and CA Bruce and formal initiative started to start tea plantations in Assam. The story of the tea industry has an interesting anecdote. The story goes like this, Bissagam the Singhpo chief wanted royalties from the tea gardens as the land was his. Once when his royalties were not paid the chief asked his men to chop off the tea plants cultivated by the British. Later it was found the tea bushes grew better after the cutting. Thus was started the technique of hedging, pruning of tea bushes. A method learnt by accident!

During this period various merchants were discussing the various types of tea found in the country at Kolkata, in one such gathering the seeds and plants were being discussed and it is here a young man exclaimed, "We have these seeds and plants in my part of the country". The young man was none other than Maniram Dewan. After the Ahom Kings, he was one of the most influential men of Assam. Bruce was commissioned by the British Government to open up new lands for tea gardens. The Bruce brothers claimed to start the first tea cultivation in Assam. In 1833 Lord William Bentinc appointed a Tea Committee to explore the possibilities of tea plantations and CA Bruce was appointed Superintendent of Tea Forests.

Not to be outdone Maniram Dewan who was a rich man also wanted to start his own tea gardens. He was determined to stake his share in the tea industry but before that he had to learn the techniques of tea cultivation and the manufacturing process. To learn all this Maniram joined the first tea company in India, The Assam Company in 1839. He joined as a Dewan or Land Agent and learnt the trade from the bottom of the ladder. It is from this period he came to be known as Maniram Dewan. After learning the trade he resigned from the Assam Company in 1845 and broke out on his own as a tea planter. The British Government tried its best to put spokes in the wheels and when Maniram applied for a land grant he was refused the concessions given to the Europeans. Maniram had to pay exorbitant prices for his two tea estates - Cinnamore in Jorhat and Selung in Sibsagar. Maniram Dewan's house has the factory even today and the plot is still called the Dewan plot. After his death his property was auctioned off to a George Williamson at a minimum price. But the property could not be kept as all the labourers and administrative staff did not want to work with George Williamson. So the property was again sold off and the money got was given to libraries.

Maniram Dewan's success in whatever he touched made him the envy of both the British administration and other planters. Maniram finally realised the policy of the British was one of subjugation. In his letter to Moffat Mills in 1853 he wrote, "The people have been reduced to abject poverty and hopeless state of misery from the loss of fame, honour, rank, caste and employment. The abolition of old customs and establishment in their stead of courts and unjust taxation, the introduction of opium in the state has ruined all". Maniram pleaded for a native ruler. The letter was thrown out as a 'curious' document from Maniram Dewan, and became a prime suspect for the discontentment that was growing throughout the country. By 1857, the country was in a mood to revolt and Assam too joined the group.

In 1856 Maniram Dewan went to Calcutta to request the British to enthrone Purandhar Singha's grandson Kandapeshwar Singha, when this request was turned down a very disappointed Maniram Dewan took to other means, he revolted against the British. The Sepoy Revolt of 1857 had an impact on the disillusioned Maniram Dewan who tried to take the revolt to Assam. He started getting people together and messages were sent through '*sanyasis*' or sages.

He kept sending coded messages to the Ahom King Kandarpeswar and Maniram urged him to join the revolt against the British with the help of Sepoys stationed at Dibrugarh and Golaghat. At the royal palace a plot was hatched and Indian soldiers of the British army like Subedar Nur Mohammad and Bhikun Sheikh were taken into confidence. The date of the uprising was to be the Durga Puja's time and Maniram Dewan was to come back to Assam and crown Kandarpeswar as the King. Unfortunately, the young prince was betrayed by his relatives and the British uncovered the plot very quickly. One such letter was sent to a wrong address and Maniram Dewan was arrested and later brought to Jorhat for trial. The trial was a farce as it was only a formality, it seemed that it had been decided that Maniram Dewan would be hanged. Capt Charles Holroyd was appointed Special Commissioner to preside over the 'Conspiracy Case'. Holroyd was both the jury and the judge and Maniram Dewan was not given the right to appeal in another court. The Ahom King Kandarpeswar Singha was first imprisoned in Alipur Jail, Calcutta and then shifted to Gauhati. Dutiram Barua, Bahadur Gaonbura and Sheikh Formud Ali were exiled to the Andamans, the infamous Kalapani area. Maniram Dewan was identified as the main culprit along with Peali Barua and was hanged on February 16, 1858. The hanging or so to say 'taming' of the lion – the spirited Maniram Dewan was a warning signal to all Assamese that the British would not tolerate any competition.

The writer Benudhar Sarma whose book on Maniram Dewan came out ninety two years after his death has described his hanging in detail. Sarma has described in detail the scaffolds and the gallows. Maniram Dewan has been described as a strong man who remained calm right till the end. They say he came out of his cell with his silver 'Hookah'/ Hubble in his hand with no scare on his face. He asked his sons not to take revenge; God would give punishment to them. When Maniram Dewan went up to the gallows he was heard saying, "He who has done this to me in spite of my innocence.... by false allegations will eat the head of his eldest child". Here was a man who never lost his mental balance whatever the circumstances were, he remained a calm man.

Maniram Dewan's death brought in a gloom for years. Ballads and '*Bihugeets*' have been written about him and he remains a legend.

9

Rupkonwar Jyoti Prasad Agarwala

Jyoti Prasad Agarwala, an Assamese cultural legend was a playwright, poet, songwriter and film maker. Jyoti Prasad was born into a family that was very cultured. Though born into a Marwari family of Rajasthan Jyoti Prasad was more an Assamese than a Marwari. He belonged to the Nabrangram Agarwala family which had come to Assam in 1811. They were a family of '*Saudagars*' or merchants of Tai village from Jaipur who had to leave their village due to rivalry from the locals. After a lot of struggle Nabarangram, Jyotiprasad's ancestors reached Assam, the land under the Ahom rule. Nabarangram worked hard and became the revenue collector of the Ahom land. The British deposed the Ahom king Purandhar Singha and the whole of Assam came under the British rule. Nabarangram imbibed the Assamese culture but retained his original Marwari title Agarwala. Nabarangram married twice, his first wife was Sadori from the Rajkhowa family whose son was Haribilas (grandfather of Jyoti Prasad). The second wife was Sun Pahi from the Saikia family. After the second marriage Nabarangram settled down in Assam permanently.

Haribilas, son of Nabarangram, settled down in Tezpur and built a house called 'Poki' which later became famous during our freedom struggle. Haribilas was spiritually inclined and published the works of Sankardeva and Mahadeva, the two Vaishnavite reformers of the 15th century. It was a big leap for Assamese literature. Now the works of Sankardeva and Mahadeva were available to the public. Into such a world Haribilas' children and grandchildren were brought up, that is Jyoti Prasad's father and uncle Chandraprasad, one of the 'leading lights' of Assamese literature. Jyotiprasad was greatly influenced by his father as far as music was concerned.

It is here Rupkonwar Jyoti Prasad Agarwala gave Assamese literature, drama and art a new life. The likes of Bishnu Kumar Rabha and Phani Sarma brought to life '*Ban*' Theatre in Tejpur. It is from here Jyoti Prasad discovered the talents of Bhupen Hazarika a living legend of our times. Today '*Poki*' is being looked after by the Assam Government as it is a heritage site for Assam.

Jyoti Prasad was born on 17th June 1903 in Tamulbari Tea Estate, Dibrugarh to Paramananda and Kironmoyee Agarwala. As a child Jyotiprasad was the family favourite and was somewhat restless by nature. Jyotiprasad showed no inclination towards sports or studies. He was happy to listen to music or sing with his mother Kironmoyee. Jyoti Prasad loved the natural surroundings around 'Poki'and loved the Assamese way of life. He was first sent to the Tejpur Town Hall School but had to shift to Dibrugarh to his uncle Chandra Kumar Agarwala's place. In Dibrugarh he went to George School and the Dibrugarh Government School. Jyoti Prasad was greatly influenced by his uncle Chandra Kumar, his philosophy, poetry and patriotism. As he grew older he came back to Tejpur and joined the Government High School. It was here in this school, while in Class 9 that he brought out a handwritten school magazine called '*Jonaki*' or 'Firefly'. By this time Jyotiprasad had started writing lyrics, poems and even plays. "Paramanand's talent, technique and love for music had very befittingly set an example for cultivation of art and music in the Agarwala household. As a result of Paramanand's dedication to music, the music world of Assam could rediscover the legacy in the midst of his successors as well", writes Jyoti Prasad in his 'Biography of Chandrakumar'. Chandrakumar, Jyoti Prasad's uncle maintained the cultural environment which was set by Haribilas.

The famous 'Sonit Konwari' or Princess of Sonitpur, a dance drama, which tells us the love story of Princess Usha and Anirudh,

Lord Krishna's grandson. Usha and Anirudh's love story an all time favourite is found in 'Haribangsha Puran'. Jyoti Prasad took the theme from here and adapted it for his play.

The story goes like this-

'Usha is the beautiful daughter of Ban, the king of Sonitpur. She was protected from all evil eyes and kept in 'Agnigarh', a fort which had fire all around it in the olden days. It is a fort on a hillock over looking the Brahamaputra. (When I saw it at night fully lit up it looked brilliant, almost surreal. A true princess's abode.) It was here Usha had a dream of a handsome young man, the man was none other than Anirudh, the grandson of Lord Krishna. Usha asked her friend Chitralekha to get the man to her. Chitralekha being a good artist drew a number of men from the heavens and Earth. Usha recognised the man from her dreams, it was Anirudh. So it was now Chitralekha's job to get Anirudh from Dwarka to Agnigarh. Usha and Anirudh had a 'Gandharva' style of wedding. Usha's father did not know of this meeting but the security men noticed Anirudh and duly informed the King. King Ban threw a challenge to Anirudh, who lost, and was put into prison. Lord Krishna came to rescue his grandson and the armies of Ban and Krishna clashed on the banks of the River Brahamaputra. To help Ban, Lord Shiva descended from the skies. They say there was a battle between the Lord Krishna and Lord Har or Shiva as they say between 'Har and Hari'. It was here Lord Brahma intervened and the battle came to a close. Ban realised Krishna was a reincarnation of God and now gave his daughter's hand in marriage to Anirudh very willingly. People still believe that the soil is red as so much blood was shed. Or it could also be that the soil is red due to the iron content in it!

Jyoti Prasad took this theme for his play 'Sonit Konwari', a regal love story. All the lyrics of the film were set to the folk music of Assam which started the trend of modern Assamese music, also folk music in films and plays. 'Sonit Konwari' was a mythological play and was retouched and revised a number of times before it was put up for publication. When he heard his father Paramanand singing an old folk song, the music kept haunting him and he could not sleep for a few days, the thought of utilising this music for his plays kept bothering him. So were born the lyrics of 'Sonit Konwari'.

It was in 1926, Jyoti Prasad had gone abroad to study at Edinburgh University. His mother, Kironmoyee, was definitely responsible for sending him abroad to study, as she wanted her son to get the best of education. As an artist his sole aim at that time was to blend Indian and Western music. His observing powers helped in learning the basic tonal differences of the two worlds of music. He also utilised the time to go to Berlin to meet Himanshu Roy. It is under him that Jyoti Prasad got his first training in film making. He is not only a trendsetter for Assam but for the entire North East India.

The period Jyoti Prasad was born was a period of difficult times for India. We were still under the shackles of the British Raj, and this inspired the feelings of nationalism and patriotism in young Jyoti Prasad. Gandhiji had started his non-cooperation movement and the year 1921 saw Jyoti Prasad join the movement after completion of his matriculation. He had joined the National College in Calcutta and due to the freedom movement the college was closed down and Jyoti Prasad had to come back home to Tezpur.

He started assisting his uncle Chandra Kumar in managing the '*Asamiya*' newspaper. The non-cooperation movement ignited the patriotic feelings of Jyotiprasad and he participated in all activities. He went to Chaiduar and Biswanath (areas around Tezpur) to organise the farmers as volunteers. Often he fell sick but this did not stop him from organising 'Volunteer Camps' which were banned by the British Government. It was on this account, Jyoti Prasad was arrested and put into Silchar prison. In prison Jyoti Prasad fell sick and the jail authorities decided to acquit him but on the condition that he would not participate in any anti-British activities. Jyoti Prasad refused and this surprised the then Governor of Assam Michael Kein and the Government wondered, "How can a person refuse getting out of jail" in spite of suffering from typhoid. Jyoti Prasad completed his full term and came out of jail only in 1933.

Pushpalata Das another freedom fighter remembered that in 1932 Jyoti Prasad organised camps for all the members of the '*Sevadal*' at Tezpur whose main aim was to hoist the national flag. Then came the 'Quit India' Movement, which to many was the final push or the last battle to be achieved. Jyotiprasad divided his group into '*Santi Bahino*' and '*Mrityu Bahini*'. Jyotiprasad had full faith in Gandhi, his mentor, and kept working for the cause of freeing India. The musical squads would arouse the masses with their songs, Jyoti Prasad at this time composed many patriot lyrics, and the songs were sometimes sung by Jyoti Prasad himself. The *Satyagrahis* or revolutionaries went underground to avoid the

British Government and decided not to give themselves in. When Mahatma Gandhi was released, he expressed his annoyance at those who did not give themselves up. It is at this time Jyoti Prasad surrendered to the Tezpur police.

Jyoti Prasad started a temporary film studio at Bholaguri Tea Estate and after a lot of difficulties made his first Assamese film '*Joymoti*'. The movie is based on historical facts:

'Joymoti was an Ahom princess, who sacrificed her life to save husband Gadapani from the clutches of Lor Raja, the tyrant king'. The historical legendary story by Birinchi Kumar Baruah inspired the renowned play writer Lakshmi Nath Bezbaruah. The historical aspect of the play showed Gadadhar Singha, at times also called Gadapani, prince of Tungkungiya dynasty. Before he became king, Gadadhar and his wife Joymoti had to flee but Joymoti was caught and tortured by Lor Raja, the tyrant or wicked king. Lor Raja wanted information about Gadadhar Singha. The 'Rani' did not reveal her husband's whereabouts and for that was tortured to death. Her husband came in disguise and asked her to reveal the secret but the Rani refused. She asked him to muster an army to defeat the wicked king Lor Raja.

Jyoti Prasad was both a film maker and a patriot; he utilised his film making skills to bring out the true spirit of the people of Assam. The film was released in 1935 by the film company Chitralekha Movietone. '*Joymoti*', to its credit is one of the earliest films which has a woman as hero or the most important character, something which was uncommon those days, and often even now. Jyotiprasad did not want a male to play the female character. He travelled all over the state looking for a heroine, and this was difficult as no girl from a good family was willing to venture out. Finally, he did become lucky as Adieu Handique was found. According to Adieu, Jyoti Prasad was the perfect artist as he explained and acted out the roles to his actors. Somewhere in 1933, little Adieu of Pani-dihinga village near Gauhati wanted to see a '*jahaz*' or a steamship, so her cousin took her to see one. When they boarded the ship little Adieu's excitement died down as she was very scared of the journey and kept crying, she wanted to go home. Adieu's cousin Dimba had tricked her into going as he had an ulterior motive, he would get a small part in the film if he could get a heroine for Jyoti Prasad. That is the reason he took her to Jyoti Prasad, looking at the crying girl Jyotiprasad scolded the cousin. Immediately, a telegram was sent to Adieu's father Nilambar Handique to come and only then the shooting of the film started. When the film crew saw the first pictures of Adieu they knew Jyoti Prasad had found his heroine, the beautiful young girl was just right to be Joymoti. When one looks at her pictures one understands why.

Adieu was taken to the Bholaguri tea estate which belonged to the Agarwala family. When Adieu cried the women of the family tried to console her, and kept telling her as soon as the shooting was over she would be sent home. While acting out the scene of the wicked king's men beating the Princess Joymoti, Adieu remembered the beating she got from the stick, her back hurt for days. The guards had perhaps been over enthusiastic. But this pain was nothing compared to what was coming next. When the family reached the village they were thrown out of the village, Adieu was excommunicated as she had defiled the village. Nilambar Handique, the father, tried to reason it out but to no avail, it was only after he paid a fine of 'one rupee and four annas' with a betel leaf and nut were they allowed in. In the days that followed her younger brother died and Adieu was blamed for this. No boy dared to marry her as she had called her co-actor 'my dear husband'. Sadder still was the fact that she had not seen her film. She said, "Where would I see the film? There were no cinema halls around". Recognition came to her in 1985 when the Assam Government celebrated the golden jubilee of Assamese cinema. Adieu fondly remembered, "They took me in a car to Gauhati and I was felicitated at a public function. Even Amitabh Bachchan was there". The Assam Government gave her an artist's pension in 1984. In 1991 the village youth set up a girl's middle school named after her, a big honour for someone, who had been thrown out of the village. In 2002 Adieu bid adieu to the world, the first lady of the Assamese Silver Screen was no more, a lonely life had come to an end.

Going back to period that 'Joymoti' was being made, Jyoti Prasad lost his mother Kironmoyee (1933) followed by his father Paramananda (1934). To add to Jyoti Prasad's misery the music director of his film let him down as the sound system failed, the whole film became soundless and precious time was lost. But never to give up easily Jyoti Prasad had to get all the recording done again. Finally, the film was released at Raunak Hall, Calcutta, on 10th March 1935. Laxminath Bezbaruah, on whose play the film was based, said, "I am extremely delighted to have seen my fancy character Dalimi being emerged as a real one. Shriman Jyoti Prasad has infused life into the character of Dalimi". The film was a great success and was the first movie of the whole of north eastern India. But at the box office it bombed miserably.

Jyoti Prasad to his credit is a pioneer for setting up a musical school in Tezpur. He started to establish a university in Assam and also prepared an architectural print of the University. In 1937, he also constructed '*Jonaki*' a cinema hall in Tezpur. Ill-health made him stay at the Tambulbari tea estate where he tried his best to look after the workers, but cancer overtook him and he died on 17th January 1951 at the age of forty-eight. To honour him his death anniversary is celebrated as '*Silpi Divas*' or 'Artist's Day'.

Jyoti Prasad made immense contribution to literature, plays, poetry, for adults as well as for children – a true artist.

10

Shah Miran–Azan Fakir

(The Muslim saint whom both Muslims and Hindus equally revere)

Azan Fakir, son of Muhinuddin Syed Miran Shah Baghdadi bin Auz Zahan was a Sufi saint originally from Baghdad and lived in the 17th century. Baghdad those days was a centre of learning in Islamic studies. Azan Pir or Hazrat Shah Miran learnt the Holy Quran, the Hadith and Islamic studies at Baghdad. After completing his studies Azan Fakir and other students had to go to different parts of the world propagating Islam, they had to carry the message of Allah. It is during this period of early 17th century these holy men came towards India. During those days the Mughal dynasty was flourishing and Mughal India may have attracted people from the Middle East. Alongwith soldiers and traders also came a group of men who had renounced the world for the love of the Almighty. A true Sufi loves God selflessly and spends his whole life in the worship of God; worldly affairs no longer attract him. A Sufi though is a part of the world, he is not corrupted by temptations and attachments. A true Sufi's only attachment is to Allah or the Almighty.

Hazrat Syed Shah Miran alias Hazrat Azan Pir, a Sufi preacher of Hanafi order, was accompanied by his brother Hazrat Nabi Pir. The two brothers travelled from Baghdad via Iran through the Khyber Pass, a rather difficult journey when everything was by road.

They travelled to Ajmer Sharif to the 'dargah' of Khawaja Garib Nawaz Moinuddin Chisti, later they went to the 'dargah' of Nizamuddin Auliya at Delhi. Both spent a few years here, Azan Pir later became a disciple of Nizamuddin Auliya. From Delhi the brothers went to Assam via Gaur in West Bengal. In Kamrup or old Assam, they first went to Hajo and later to Goregaon, the Ahom capital. At Hajo they spent a few years trying to learn the language and customs of the place. The two brothers finally settled down in Sibsagar. When the brothers reached Assam they realised they were not the only Muslims there.

Exactly, when the Islamic faith found its root in Assam is not known as very little written record has been found. The possibilities are that the Muslim invaders left behind people who settled down in Assam and intermingled with the locals. The earliest of these conquests was 1205 AD when Muhammad Bin Bakhtiyar came on an expedition to Tibet and reached Kamrup, but met with a disastrous end while trying to cross the mighty river Brahamaputra. There were many invasions by the Mughals and finally the Ahom King Gadadhar Singha defeated the Mughals in the battle of Itakhuli and Saraighat, the Ahom General Lachit Barphukan is still remembered for his valour and spirit for retrieving Gauhati. Dr Bhuyan says, "The nucleus of the present day Mohammedan population of Assam was formed during the period of Mohammedan conflicts. The main stock being strengthened, from time to time by fresh immigrant and conversion" (Annals of Delhi Badshahat). Sir Edward Gait also has the same view in his book *History of Assam*. He says, "The Assamese Muslims were Muslims in name only". Azan Pir had this to say about them, "You worship various gods.... There will be none to save you from the abyss". During that time the Muslims followed a path deviated from the normal Islamic faith, they joined in the '*Kirtan*' or community songs started by Sankaradeva to spread Vaishnavism. These Muslims also took 'Mahaprasad' which was uncooked food like gram, sugarcane, coconut and fruits; these were given out after the singing. To get back the strayed people of the Muslim faith, Azan Fakir started the custom of distributing '*Sinni*' which was made out of rice, these were given out after the singing of '*Zikir*' and 'Zari' (Muslim religious verses). Both the brothers kept trying to bring back the wayward people. After a few years Azan Pir had a few followers. He called these believers through the prayer or '*namaz*' call or as we know it as '*azan*'. The practice of '*azan*' was not there till Miran Shah or Azan Pir started the practice.

When Shah Miran came to Assam he saw something wonderful, it was the Vaishnavite musical performances and was very impressed by it. Sankaradeva's '*Borgeet*' were very popular all over Assam. Soon Azan Fakir started his own compositions and the tunes were all local. Azan Fakir was greatly influenced by Sankaradeva's Vaishnavite lyrics, '*Sarvo ghate ghate Alla*' is found very often in the songs. Azan Fakir was a brilliant singer and poet and he composed about a hundred and fifty *Zikir*s in Assamese. Though Islam does not promote music and dance for entertainment but it does allow music and dance for religious activities. To the Assamese, the music was familiar and the rhythm was the local Assamese, only the message carried was that of Allah, this was all according to the Quran. The spiritual and mystical philosophy of Sufism was brought out by the Assamese songs which are known as '*Zikir*s'. *Zikir* and Zari are Sufi music of Assam. The music and the tune are similar in nature but there is a difference, '*Zikir*' speaks of the teachings of Islam, while 'Zari' speaks of 'Karbala' incidents. Both '*Zikir* and Zari' took root in Assam around the 17th century. It is Azan Pir who made '*Zikir*' and 'Zari' so popular in Assam, even today '*Zikir*s' are regularly sung on special occasions like social and cultural gatherings. Groups of fifteen to twenty people sing together, and the group has a leader. Even today, some of the '*Zikir*s' can be heard on All India Radio. *Zikir*s tells us about the values of a pious and honest life, the religion Islam and extremely important was the inter-community relationship in Assam's society.

When Azan Fakir came to Assam he was a grey haired man and did not know the Assamese language. He adds, "*Bhikari ajane koiahu pordesh bina guru mukhe namor napai asu bhed*". Translated it means, "This beggar Azan is saying I have come to an alien land without the help of a teacher, I know not the mystery of the name". The Ahom kings did not bother about this Garia Fakir, who kept praying and singing. Soon the Muslim people of Darrangi (Darrang and Sonitpur of today) invited the two brothers to come and meet them. The two brothers came in two boats called '*Xukoli*' and '*Paroi*'. The people of Darrangi were very happy to have the two pirs/ saints with them barring one, he was Rupai Dadhra. The Ahom kings had appointed him as the armourer, he was an important official and very powerful. Seeing so much importance going to the two brothers he felt very envious. To show his power Rupai Dadhara threw a feast for the guests, he came on an elephant to invite the two brothers. Azan Pir did not like this and climbed on the roof top of his house to be at equal height with Rupai Dadhra and asked him to take the two brothers on his shoulders. This rebuff made Rupai very furious and it is from here Rupai Dadhra started disliking Azan Pir and his brother Nabi.

Rupai Dadhra started complaining to the Ahom king who initially ignored him and paid no attention to his words, but when the complaints became persistent the Ahom king gave him permission to do what he felt was correct. Rupai Dadhra put the two brothers in prison, but this was not enough so he brought in the charges of 'sedition' against Azan Pir, saying he was a Mughal spy and had kept hidden his soldiers in the forest. At the right time, Azan Pir would bring the soldiers out and occupy the capital. Hearing this, the Ahom king in a fit of rage ordered the blinding of Azan Pir. When Azan Pir heard of the royal orders or diktat he asked for a bowl to be brought to him, after praying to Allah he dropped his eyes into the bowl. The people around were stunned and the eyes were thrown into the river Dikhow. They say there was a deluge after this and the river flowed backwards after the eyes were thrown in. The whole area was flooded and the Dikhow River had water spilling out. People were so scared that no one dared to step out of their homes. Some of the *Zikir*s confirm the theory of gauging Azan Pir's eyes.

Rupai Dadhara's mother realised the mistake and took two bowls, one of silver and one of gold for Azan Pir. The saint turned her away saying, "Save your gold and silver, O Rupai's mother. Your son is sawing the big tree and you are pouring water". Within a few days of this, Rupai Dadhra was found murdered by people around him. Some mention of this incident has been found in archaic Assamese chronicles. The Ahom king sent his general the Hatibaruah to assess the situation. The Hatibaruah came back to say that the area around Azan Pir was safe, but the rest of the land was under water. The Hatibaruah understood the situation and tried wiping the tears away from Azan Pir's sightless eyes. The Saint blessed him for this saying, "May you always rise in office". When the Ahom king realised his mistake, to make atonement for his sins he conferred the title of *'Deewang'* meaning 'divine'. That is why they say the descendents of Azan Pir and other saints are called *'dewans'*. The king offered land to the saint near Xoraguri Sapori near Dikhowmukh and finally Azan Pir could settle down with his followers and lead a peaceful life. It is a wonder that in spite of so many problems here, Azan Pir decided to settle in Assam.

Azan Pir married an Ahom girl from a noble family; she was the daughter of Syed Usman Gani of Khandikar village in Rangpur.

The Muslims of Assam today have become part and parcel of the land even though they were left behind by invaders, the Mughal historian Shiabuddin Talish who came with Mir Jumla had this to say, "These Musalmans who had been taken prisoners in former times had chosen to marry there and their descendents are inclined to mingle with Assamese rather than towards associations with Muslims". The Muslim saints or pirs or fakirs were encouraged by the Ahom rulers to settle down in their areas and were given land to build mosques. Dr JP Wade records that, "The Swargdeos or Kings used to dispatch a pir or fakir called Newas to pray at Hajo after the Musalman fashion for prosperity". It is interesting to note that both Muslims and Hindus pray at the same place. There are many '*dargahs*' or tombs of holy men in and around Gauhati. One of them is the tomb of the famous saint Jalaluddin Tabrizi. Ibn Batuta, the famous traveller, in his book 'Tunbatnuzzar' mentions having met the saint at Kamrup.

The '*dargahs*' at Sibsagar:- They say four saints or pirs who visited this place in the early 17th century, Hazrat Khondkar, Hazrat Azan, Nabi and Chowal. Hazrat Khondkar had no sons of his own, but he got his adopted son married to Hazrat Azan's daughter. Azan Pir's descendents today are known as 'Syeds'. Azan Pir was survived by his three sons. Possibly, he died around 1690 and his body was interned at Dikhumukh on the banks of river Dikhu where the river meets the Brahamaputra. Both Hindus and Muslims come and pray at the '*dargah*', just as they celebrate '*Bihu*' together. An annual '*urs*' is held every year in his memory.

Two religious movements which have had a major impact on the life of the people of Assam are Azan Pir and Sankaradeva. They both are acknowledged spiritual gurus of Assam and have tried to produce a balanced society. Sankaradeva's '*namghar*' or prayer halls could be entered by all, irrespective of class, colour or creed as they say. It is believed that the main pillar, called 'Lai Khuta' of '*namghars*' are installed by Muslims with recitation from the Holy Quran.

Today we have a film based on the life of Azan Pir. Here was a man who came from Baghdad and could initially speak only Arabic, but later became completely immersed in Assamese culture. He not only learnt the language but also translated the Holy Quran in Assamese all for the love of the Almighty Allah.

11

Srimanta Sankaradeva

Srimanta Sankaradeva was born during an era when religion was going through an age of blind beliefs, superstitions and malpractices. It was the 15th century which saw a number of saints and 'pirs' and 'fakirs', like Ramananda (1360-1450), Chaitanya (1485 -1533), Tulsidas (1523-1623), and Sankaradeva in (1449-1568) from Assam. Sankaradeva the founder of Assamese Vaishnava (followers of the Hindu God Vishnu) movement is a well-known literary figure, a fine poet and writer of religious songs. Sankaradeva was a follower of Chaitanya Mahaprabhu, in spite of being younger than him. Most of us have not heard of Sankaradeva as his writings are not easily found in history books. Sankaradeva was a man who was visionary; he could foresee the degeneration of the society, the turmoil within the country that is why he dreamt of a religion which could take all into its fold.

Sankara as he was called by the family was born into a 'Kaistha' family, at a village called Bardowa/Batadrava in Aliphukri, which is close to Nagaon in Assam. Borduwa the village where Sankara was born was next to the river Brahmaputra but today the river has moved away in its meandering. They say Sankara was a strong boy and in his youth could swim across Brahamaputra. His ancestors belonged to the '*Bhuyan*' family, a family which had a good social standing. Sankara's father was the Shrimoni or Chief of the '*Bara Bhuyians*' as they were called; they were independent landlords of Assam. They say when Sankara was born their royal status had been taken by the Ahom kings. Now they were more like the 'Zamindars' or only owned the land. Alipukhri was raided by the Kachari kings and the '*Bara Bhuyan*' and his family had to flee to the jungle. Sankara lost his mother very early in life, not a very uncommon thing those days. His grandmother Khersuti brought him up and the early childhood was spent in playing around. It is only at the age of twelve he was reminded by his grandmother that his was a family of scholars and so he was sent to a Sanskrit 'toll' (school) run by a Sanskrit scholar Mahendra Kandali. Sankara found the initial school years difficult to concentrate on his books as he was unused to studying. Later on an incident happened which showed that he was no ordinary student. They say the tutor one day saw Sankara sleeping in class after his studies and to his horror saw a snake, possibly a cobra with its hood up trying to protect Sankara's face from the sun. When the cobra saw people around him it quietly slid away. Mahendra Kandli realised that this was no ordinary student, possibly one with divine powers, so from Sankara he became Sankaradeva. All the students were asked to call him Sankaradeva and he was excused from doing all the menial tasks like cleaning the school.

Though Sankara had religious leanings he had to go through some of the responsibilities in life, worldly things like being forced to become the Shrimoni Bhuyan by the elders. Later he also married Suryavati daughter of Harivagirri Kayastha. In spite of so many responsibilities, he continued with his studies. After a few years a daughter was born to them and they named her Haripriya, lovingly called Manu. Suryavati died shortly after Manu was born and Sankaradeva had to look after the baby. It is after the death of his wife, Suryavati that Sankaradeva turned towards spiritualism. Sankara waited for his daughter to grow up and at the age of nine or ten married her off to a young boy called Hari. It is only after this, did he think of going on a pilgrimage. Sankara left the house to his son-in-law and the administration of the Shrimoni to Jayanta and Madhav Dalai.

Sankara's retinue for the pilgrimage had about seven people; among them were his teacher Mahendra Kandali and his childhood friend Ramarama. Sankara visited a number of places on his journey of twelve years. He visited Puri, Mathura, Dwarka, Vrindavan, Gaya, Rameshwaram, Ayodhya and Sitakund, almost all the major places of Vaishnavism. All these places had a great influence on his mind and he wrote a number of lyrics for his '*Borgitas*' or hymns or songs. At Badrikashrama he composed his first '*borgeet*', '*man meri ram sharanhai*' or shall we say 'my heart lies at your feet Ram'. During his first pilgrimage he found the Bhakti movement in full swing. All the songs praised Lord Krishna and Rama. After twelve long years Sankaradeva came back completely immersed in Vaishnavism, he was deeply impressed by the neo-Vashnavite movement of north India and was now ready to fulfill the mission of his life.

On his return Sankara's relatives wanted him to marry again and raise a family, so at the age of forty seven or forty eight he married Kalindi daughter of Kalika Bhuyian. He had three sons and a daughter with his second wife. Sankara now refused to become the Shrimoni Bhuyan as he wanted to spend the rest of his life dedicated to Krishna. All this effect came after listening to Jagadisha who had explained the Bhagvad Purana; Sankara realised that this was the only way to worship Krishna. He was an intelligent man and to attract people he started writing the lyrics of the songs, verses to attract the people to his new religion. It is he who took on the task of reaching the public through his '*bhakti*', the new religion. After introducing the people to his religion through his songs he also started writing plays and organised 'dramatic representation through his paintings'. For the musical instruments Sankara had got made different drums like the 'mridanga' by the potters of the village, Kapilmukh and cobblers of Salmara, something unheard of in those days, a cobbler making things for the places of worship! He also got made cymbals to accompany the singing. Jagadisa when he visited Sankara in the temple, a '*Maha-Nata*' (play) was presented there; Sankara was ready with his music and presentation. It is only after Sankara understood the 'Bhagvad' completely did he start his religion. Sankara had a number of converts to his new religion, among them was a leper called Harirama who was later called Tulasirama. Sankaradeva's friend Ramarama and teacher Mahendra Kandali were his first converts.

Sankara now had to leave his Bhuyan territories for fear of the Kacharis as the Bhuyans were constantly being attacked, the group with Sankaradeva as the head moved from Singari, Rauta, Bhalukgunj and finally settled down in Gangman. It is here his sons were born. After a lot of movements they reached Dhuwat which today is Majuli, the island on the Brahamaputra (the largest riverine island in the world).

Sankara's greatest disciple was Madhavdeva who was a worshipper of '*Sakta*' or in other words a follower of Shiv and Shakti or Durga. Madhavdeva had actually come to have a battle of words with Sankaradeva as Madhavdeva's brother-in-law Gayapani had been initiated into 'bhati 'or Vaishnavite way of thinking. Gayapani, it seems, had refused to bring Madhavdeva goats for sacrifice, and it is for this, the anger on Sankaradeva. For a long time the tussle continued, Madhavdeva finally had to bow down and take Sankara as his 'Guru', his superior. Madhavdeva was a scholar, poet and an excellent singer; his joining Sankara's fold increased the value of the religious discussions and mass prayers.

Sankara's faith was open to all, irrespective of caste; all were equal in the eyes of God, Vishnu or Krishna. This of course led to a lot of ill feelings amongst the Brahmins as their importance was diminishing with the Brahmanical rites were done away with in Sankaradeva's new religion. The Brahmins complained to the Ahom King Shummung (1497- 1539) about Sankara interfering into their religious practices, this upset the Ahom king and he called for Sankara. After some discussions Sankara was let off, but the ill feelings continued. Sankara's son-in-law Hari was arrested and put to death, his friend Madhavdeva was put behind bars. Sankaradeva realised that it was time for him to leave the place as life had become unsafe.

It was during this period of 1534, Visvasimha the Koch king died and his son Naranarayan came to the throne and with his general was ready to attack the Ahoms, the Koch-Ahom hostility continued. After roaming around for a few years, Sankara finally settled in a place called Patbausi. It was from here Sankara went on a second pilgrimage to Puri via Gaya. They say he did not go to Vrindavan as his wife had asked Madhavdeva not to take him there as she feared Sankara might not come back. After a few months Sankara did come back home to settle down here. Sankara wrote a number of plays and poems while at Patbausi. The '*Kirtan Ghosa*' or the verses for the prayer had the last part written here and the 'Bhagvata' was written in Assamese. Sankara's life was the happiest here as his knowledge and wisdom had reached its peak; his new religion had become very popular. Later he had a large gathering of followers, who had converted to his religion. Again the Brahmins were up in arms against Sankara and the King Naranarayan sent his men to arrest Sankara, he escaped but his followers Gokulchand and Naranarayan Thakur were caught and put in prison, they were tortured but the Ahom soldiers could not get any information about the whereabouts of Sankara. Both the convicts were sold off to the landed Bhuyans but these Bhuyias released the two as they realised they were holy people. They were again arrested by two constables but this time the results were different. The two constables now converted to Sankara's faith. King Naranarayan being a learned man appreciated Sankara's knowledge and asked for forgiveness. Now the King and Sankara became friends at the first meeting and they remained friends till the end.

The Vaishnav movement in Assam was at its pinnacle now and Sankara's life was nearing its end, the final journey was close. King Naranarayan wanted to join Sankara's order, but Sankara hesitated to ordinate the king as he felt it was not the right thing to do. Sankara's passing away has left some doubts in our mind as they say he had a boil in his body; others say he meditated and willed his mind to leave the body. Whatever the reasons, it was in 1569AD. Sankara left this world at nearly the age of one hundred and twenty years. Thus ended the life of a 'Mahapurus', or a saint.

Sankaradeva has left a deep impression on the minds of the people of Assam. He was a handsome man and his physical appearance and intellect matched each other. He was a great administrator, social worker, poet, musician and painter. Sankara's religion was 'love humanity' and he helped the common man to rise above the selfish rich class. He had started putting up monasteries called *'Sattras'*, (possibly this was a Buddhist influence) in Assam, here celibate monks lived. Here the monks performed the *'Satrriya Nritya'* a dance form started by Sankaradeva as an accompaniment to the *Ankiya Naat* (one act plays). The stories of these plays were generally mythological in nature. The dance form until the early 19th century was performed in a highly ritualistic manner by male dancers alone. Today it has come out of the *'Satrras'* and is performed by both male and female dancers who maybe not a part of the *'Satrras'*. It now has been accepted as a classical dance form by the 'Sangeet Natak Academy' in 2000. In spite of so many years having passed, today it has still maintained its traditional form and has had no changes so far.

Sankaradeva was a monotheist and followed the principle of '*Eka saran nama dharma*' or there is only one God that is Vasudeva Krishna. The worship of other gods and goddesses was strictly prohibited. Sankaradeva had '*Namghars*' or prayer halls put up, a simple construction, where anyone could sit irrespective of class or creed. Sankara wanted all the class, caste barriers to go from society. This also applies to our society these days. Sankara's religion embraced the lowliest of the lowly; it taught people the concept of universal brotherhood.

12

Within the family-

Dr Umesh Chandra Mukherjee

(A Social Reformer)

Umesh Chandra Mukherjee was born in Piljanga, Khulna (now in Bangladesh) into a very orthodox Brahmin family. His ancestors had lived in Jessore before shifting to Piljanga, to the land belonging to '*debottar*' or dedicated to the God. Such land cannot be sold off but can be used by the family. The land around the mud house into which Umesh was born was a very fertile area. They had their own orchards of mango, banana, coconut, betelnut and jackfruits. In those days, people had their own ponds as well. The ponds were used as a water source and were full of fish too. A good way to keep the pond clean and also have your fish readily available! Being a patriarchal system of family, the male head of the family had to look after the welfare of the family. Often the male head of the family would move from house to house performing the '*pujas*' (religious ceremonies) of marriages, thread ceremonies or funeral rites. In return he would get rice, fruits, clothes or sometimes even money for the services rendered. The head of the family would bring home all the items received to support the family. Umesh's ancestors were not rich, but had enough to lead a comfortable life.

Umesh's parents Nanadakunar and Bama Sundari had nine children and Umesh was the fifth child. He lost both his parents at a very young age and was looked after by Sheetal Chandra who was a state singer or "Kalawat of Balihar Raj State'. It is from Balihar State School that Umesh passed his Class X or Matriculation. Young Umesh was determined that he would not become a priest. He wanted to break free from the traditional life. In pursuit of a better life Umesh left home to go to Calcutta to study science. It is later he joined Cambell Medical College with Dr Lavinton as the Principal.

Young Umesh realised that if he took up medical sciences there were chances that he would not have to go back to the family. Since he was determined to become a doctor nothing could stop him, there was no looking back for him. Umesh put his heart and soul into his studies and it is no wonder that he came out with flying colours and stood first in his batch. Soon after, he was offered a job as a doctor on a merchant navy ship in British Ship company. During those days going abroad was a taboo, crossing the oceans was a definite 'no, no'. So he had to give in to family pressure and started looking for a job in the inland waterways.

India at that time had just started using the Steam Engine for the railways. All the heavy loads were shifted by trains, it is only in the East or North East of India where there are large rivers or the land is connected with the sea and so large boats were used or are still used to move cargo. Tiny boats went across small rivers and large boats brought the cargo from ships to the interiors. Long journeys by these steamer boats at times took days to reach their destinations. Calcutta was the capital of British India and the hinterland of Bihar, Bengal, Orissa and Assam had raw material of jute, cotton, silk, wood and tea, which had to be sold. The British had then just learnt to enjoy tea from China and in exchange gave them opium from India. The British were now looking for places to grow tea in India and what better places to grow tea but in Assam, Meghalaya and Mizoram where the climate was warm and moist, the whole area was ideally suited to grow tea.

Coming back to Umesh, he started his career as a doctor in one of the steamships which travelled from Calcutta to the remote areas of Assam, through the rivers Ganga, Bhagirati, Jamuna, Padma and the Brahamaputra. The journeys through the dense forests were tedious and hazardous at times. The steamers carried cargo and people - coolies, tea planters, Marwari businessmen.

Most often people enjoyed the trip by singing, dancing and sightseeing the places. During one such trip, Dr Umesh faced an unpleasant situation when to his horror he found a poor coolie who was sleeping being kicked around by a drunken Englishman. Umesh protested and there were hot verbal exchanges which later turned out to be a brawl. Umesh was a strong man and since he exercised everyday he could manage to beat up the Englishman. Though he won the fight, it cost him his job on the ship. Since he was well liked by all, soon he was offered another job. But Umesh's trouble did not end here as the Englishman filed a case against him in the law courts, how could an Indian hit a British? It was a long drawn court case and finally Umesh won, but this victory drained him out financially.

One of his English friends offered him a job in a tea estate, Umesh took up the job as he had a young growing up family. This new job made Umesh happy as he could practice his medicine and also look after his family. His patients gave back the love and care he gave them in kind or working for him as the 'coolies and the gora sahibs' got the same treatment. Being an orthodox Brahmin, Umesh had all his life practiced yoga and prayed to Goddess Kali after bathing. One day when he was praying there was a knock on the door but Umesh did not get up from his prayers, soon the door opened and a young pregnant girl rushed in, she happened to be a tea estate worker. The girl screamed, "Doctor please save me, the goras are after me". Umesh without stopping his prayers indicated with his eyes to the girl to sit in one corner. After finishing his prayers he asked the girl why she was so shaken up and realised that two British officers were chasing her in a horse carriage. Umesh took his time and dressed up in his trousers and of course his hat! After this he went out to see the two drunken British officers waiting outside his house for the girl. The two British Officers were very annoyed to see Umesh and started abusing him in the choicest of English-Hindi-Bengali mix language. Umesh tried to reason out saying she was pregnant and married, he was her doctor and they should leave her alone. This infuriated the 'Gora Sahibs' and they wanted to whip him. Umesh by now had also become very furious and to stop further arguments and unpleasantness he just picked up the carriage and threw it into the nearby canal, all that was heard was a mighty crash and loud screaming as the horse bolted and the Englishmen were left kicking in the air. This was a story the whole family loved hearing time and again for generations! The poor hapless girl was taken home by Umesh. He continued his doctoring till he was summoned by the courts. He had English barristers fighting his case but they could not save Umesh as the case was lost in the lower courts. The case went to Higher Courts next but by this time Umesh had spent most of his savings on the case. Life was very difficult for Umesh as he had to look after a large family too. Providence came in the form of a kind lawyer Basambad Mitra. When Mitra heard the story he took it upon himself to fight for Umesh. The fee was very peculiar indeed as Umesh had to sing every time he came to Mitra's chamber. He was a well-known singer and often would be called to sing at many musical gatherings and functions. He also happened to be the first one to cut a music album in Assamese. Mitra finally won the case in Calcutta High court but it was a long drawn out case.

After Umesh won the case he moved to a new tea estate 'Oklajan' which was owned by an Indian, Bagchi. Here he worked as manager and doctor. It was at this tea estate he met a lawyer called Harish Bagchi who happened to be the same person who had worked for the English drunken men whose carriage had been thrown out. He was against Umesh. The atmosphere was uncomfortable and so Umesh decided to leave the place despite requests from people that he should mot leave.

It was in 1885 Umesh came to Dibrugarh and settled down here. Umesh's first wife Satyabati died leaving behind three young children and he found it difficult looking after the children, so he requested his old aunt, a child widow, to help him out. Later he married Hemnalini from West Bengal. Both Umesh and Hemnalini first lived in a place called Lichutala, Dibrugarh. From here the family shifted to a place close to Umesh's in-laws place. Umesh's brother-in-law worked in the Head Office of the Assam Railway Trading Company and so knew many Britishers, this helped in Umesh's practice.

Umesh was a large-hearted man and many benefited from him, relatives and friends would come and spend months looking for work or at times the young to study. His wife Hemnalini would cook food and look after the people in the house. The couple had a number of cows for milk, the kitchen garden was full of vegetables and the ponds had a lot of fish. The doctor himself did not have too much of money but he always looked after the poor free of cost. Sometimes the patients brought in bags of rice, lentils and even biscuits as a token of gratitude and love. Most drivers of public horse carriages were told to bring in people who were lost or were looking for a place to stay in Dibrugarh, something unheard of these days. Dinesh, his son, remembered that quite often he had to give up his bed to the strangers who came to the house.

Umesh's day started early with a swim in the river Brahamaputra with his children. This was followed by prayers and breakfast. The queue of patients was unending; sometimes his patients had no money so often Umesh gave them free medicines too. Later he started a charitable dispensary and a poor asylum for the people to stay at. Very soon Umesh found his Indian and English friends coming out to help him in his projects. The concerned man that he was, Umesh, found a lot of young boys whiling away their time in idle gossip, so he decided to start a club for these boys where they could play chess, carrom and sometimes cards too. Umesh also wrote plays and directed them too for these boys. The municipality of Dibrugarh was started by him and he became its first chairman. Umesh did as much as he could for the people around him; it was his idea to put rubber tyres on bullock cart wheels for smooth functioning. Umesh started a girls and boys school, and also a medical school. Since the British trusted him they came forward to help financially and with ideas for his projects.

Umesh's children went on to become responsible citizens. They became teachers, doctors, and sportspersons and so on. Many participated in the 'Freedom Struggle'. It was very unfortunate that Umesh did not live to see all this as he left for his heavenly abode in 1929. A scholarship in Dibrugarh Medical College has been set up by Dinesh, one of his sons in his memory. The "Umesh Mukherjee Memorial Scholarship" is given on the 3rd of November every year to the best academic student.

Umesh was an ordinary man who loved life and made friends from all walks of life be it a Christian, Hindu, Muslim, English, Assamese, Marwari or Bengali. He was ever willing to help; whenever a helping hand was required. A true hero, we miss such people in today's world.

13

Lakshminarayan Chatterjee

Lakshminarayan Chatterjee was born into a very traditional orthodox Brahmin family of singers, teachers and priests. The family had possibly moved from Chadannagar, a Dutch colony to Chinsura, a distance of about twenty odd kilometers. Lakshminarayan's father Kedarnath was completely disinterested in worldly matters and as a result did not earn adequate money. Kedarnath was a *Sakta* (worshipper of energy) and was widely known for his wisdom and knowledge. Kedarnath was a gifted singer and he would go around villages singing songs in praise of God, most often he came home with a little money that his admirers had given him. This would tide over the family for a short while. On one of these travels or visits he visited the Durbar of the Nawab of Dhaka. The women as was the norm were in '*purdah*', sitting behind bamboo curtains, enjoying the singing. Later one of the women called him and asked for his family background. On hearing about his family, she said they were from the same lineage. A very long time ago when Kedarnath's grandparents were bathing in the river Ganga a royal barge with the Nawab of Dhaka passed by, the Nawab was enjoying his 'hookah' (hubble-bubble) and looking around the place, his gaze fell upon a beautiful girl splashing in the water.

Soon the Nawab asked his guards to take a fast boat to pick up the girl, it happened so quickly that people had very little time to react. The whole family was devastated as they had fallen from grace! 'How could a Brahmin, go to a non –Brahmin household'? This was the thought in the minds of the people. The Nawab brought the girl home and got her married to his eldest son. The woman's son was now the Nawab into whose court Kedarnath had come to sing. The woman knew how poor Kedarnath's family was and so gave him a bundle of gold and silver coins, she asked him to build a brick house with the gift. The royalty (queen mother) came to visit Lakshminarayan when he was married.

Kedarnath had four sons and a daughter. Lakshminarayan was the third son and like his father was very hard working, in spite of poverty he continued his education. Before his matriculation or class ten examination his father died and within a week his eldest brother also died of plague. No one was ready to help in carrying the dead body to the cremation ground. Lakshminarayan had to go from house to house begging for help, as to take the body four people are required. Finally, a friend's mother helped as the friend was ill. All these incidents delayed the marriage by a year. The family fell from grace in the society as Lakshminarayan could not perform the last rites of his father on time. It took him forty years before he could perform the '*brisodasarga*' meaning bestowing cows yagna or sacrifice, to release the family from the 'fall' or disgrace of not performing the last rites of his father on time.

Laksminarayan had started a local school on the '*Guru Shiksha*' (a system where one teacher taught all the subjects) system also called a 'toll'. Here he taught Sanskrit, arithmetic and religious text. The school/ ashram was called 'Kedar ashram'. He tried to follow the age-old tradition of not accepting any payment as fees for his teachings, but possibly some contributions may have helped to run the institution. Life was not easy, but it was not an uncommon situation amongst the Brahmins of West Bengal.

At age nineteen, he was engaged to Sati Devi a rich landlord's daughter but the marriage had to be postponed by a year due to deaths in the family. When things had come back to normal Lakshminarayan's family requested him to marry Sati Devi, the same girl to whom he was engaged earlier. His only condition was that he would not accept a '*paisa*' or penny as dowry. His bride was to come with the least ornaments. Lakshminarayan decided that he would now give up his studies and take up a job. Fortunately, for Lakshminarayan an elderly gentleman from the village, Ashutosh Mukherjee came forward to help him with his studies. As usual this hard working man came out with flying colours in his first board examination and later won many scholarships from Calcutta University. To support his income he gave private tuitions to the children of rich families. His mentor helped him get a place to sleep; often he would have nothing to eat, this at times proved to be a boon as he could spend more time on his books was what he felt, he did not have to spend time on food! Which most of us find difficult to do. Lakshminarayan could concentrate on his work and focus onto whatever was required. It is said that once he had a carbuncle on his back and it required surgery, Lakshminarayan refused anesthesia and the doctors were at their wits end, thinking how best they could work. Lakshminarayan asked the doctor to give him half an hour to meditate and then start the surgery. Only after the surgery was over the doctors were told to inform him. After this he came out of his meditation. Lakshminarayan completed his education with MA in Sanskrit and Philosophy with gold medals in both the subjects. His wife was very proud of her husband and till the day she died no one could touch them as to them this was the most prestigious thing. After finishing his MA he went to Nabadwip (West Bengal) to study Hindu religion and philosophy under the guidance of priests and teachers. Later he was awarded the Vedanta-Shastri or one who can teach the Vedas. It was only after completing his education Lakshminarayan started looking for jobs.

Many opportunities came his way but the one job he chose was teaching Divinity in Sreerampore Baptist Missionary College. It is quite difficult to imagine a tall fair man in a dhoti, shaven head with the sacred thread of a Brahmin across his chest going for an interview in a Missionary Institution. But to the Christian interviewer he proved that he knew more about Jesus Christ and his philosophy than the rest of the Christians who had come for the interview. The Brahmins of Chinsurah protested by calling for a meeting, Lakshminarayan was questioned why he had to apply for such a job. Was he not disgracing the whole Brahmin community? Lakshminarayan listened to all of them with bowed head and after all had spoken he said: "I completely agree with you". There was stunned silence for a moment and then Lakshminarayan continued,

"In our society there are two types of Brahmins – the Acharyas and the Upadhyas. All Brahmins teach and preach. To meet the family's requirements the Upadhyas are allowed to accept remunerations for their work but the Upadhyas cannot take any fees or money. So what do they do? They need to look after their families and their students too. For this they depend on the society to look after their students and families. I request all of you to look after my students and family. If you all take care of this, then I will resign from my job". After listening to this talk from Lakshminarayan, there was pin drop silence and people in the meeting did not know where to look. Very soon the people left quietly.

So began Lakshminarayan's teaching career in Sreerampore (West Bengal). The job was a boon as he could now bring his wife to live with him. Later he brought his younger brother to live with him too. Very soon an offer to teach Sanskrit in Cotton College, Gauhati came his way and the offer was too good to resist. This brought about a change in his life, a life to live away from the joint family and village. Initially, he rented a house but soon built a house at Panbazar (Gauhati). Life had finally given him what he had always wanted, a house of his own with his wife and children. Lakshminarayan inspired many people around him and tried to educate as many as he could. Only the elder girls perhaps did not get a chance to go to school and they definitely missed that. He could recite the Gita and give discourses. He tried to spread Sanskrit through the 'tolls' all over Assam. His greatest advantage was that he could speak Assamese very fluently. Many a times Assamese students came to his house to study and stay with him. He helped them financially by paying their fees, later he started a 'poor fund' where others contributed and students could borrow and refund the money. Lakshminarayan's hard work was when he was asked to set question papers for the colleges, later he went on as examiner in different colleges and finally he became Principal of Murlichand College in Sylhet, it is from where that he retired in 1943-1944.

Lakshminarayan lived life according to his belief and philosophy. Once the Governor of Assam was visiting his college and everyone was supposed to be in formal suits. Lakshminarayan was the only one in his pristine white 'dhoti-kurta'. His colleagues had mocking glances and smirks on their faces almost saying 'how could you wear this'? But it so happened that the Governor's wife spent a fair amount of time talking to him. In the end the Governor's wife asked, "Chatterjee, I have never been inside an Indian home and I would love to know how it is"? Smiling Lakshminarayan said, "Why don't you come and have tea with us tomorrow". The very next day, she did visit with some other English women and was handsomely entertained with tea and biscuits. She went back happy after talking to Sati Devi through an interpreter; it was Miss Sudmerson, the daughter of the Principal of Cotton College, Gauhati. Miss Sudmerson and Sati Devi had become good friends, almost daily Miss Sudmerson would cycle down with her monkey. She would park the cycle and tie up the monkey outside the house and then go in. She enjoyed talking to Sati Devi and her children. A special bond had developed between Miss Sudmerson and the Chatterjee family, Miss Sudmerson had picked up Bengali. Now coming back to the tea party, the English guests did not know that this was the first cup of tea made in the Chatterjee household. The cups the English group used were later broken and buried in the ground as the British were untouchables and any object used by the British were not to be used by the so-called Brahmins. So Lakshminarayan's house was washed and wiped after the visitors left and the porcelain crockery was smashed and buried underground. It was not that Lakshminarayan was unhappy with his visitors but he drew the line between hospitality and custom.

Another incident which stands out is when Lakshminarayan had cycled down to Shillong which in those days was the capital of Assam. It was decided in college that they would have a cycle race. The discussion started with a lot of enthusiasm but finally only two people took part in the race, one a Muslim boy, the other was Lakshminarayan. They slept at the same place but when it came to food, Lakshminarayan had only fruits. The road was good but narrow and steep and vehicles plying up and down from Gauhati to Shillong left at the same time and crossed each other at Nongpo. The journey was long and tiresome but both were quite happy they could complete it.

Lakshminarayan had a happy married life but there were certain unfortunate incidents where he lost his children. Pinu the youngest son died of nephritis at age six. One daughter died of pneumonia, one committed suicide, yet another died at childbirth. His eldest son a botanist was murdered at the Botanical Gardens, Calcutta. Lakshminarayan took all this in his stride but his greatest tragedy came from another source. It was partition time when India was divided into two. There was great joy at India's independence and Assam wanted to become a separate state. The Britishers had built a rapport with the Bengalis as they needed people for their administration. The Assamese people resented this. Lakshminarayan became a victim of this agitation as his house was stoned at night. He came out and stood in front of them, a calm man in his pristine white 'dhoti and shawl'. Soon the angry mob quietly left in the darkness of night. He had to leave his house with his family in a matter of a few hours. His Assamese and Bengali friends took the family to the jetty on the river Brahamaputra and then in boats they went to Amingaon from where they took a train to Patna where their eldest daughter lived. Later on he went to Calcutta to live. Lakshminarayan's house in Gauhati was sold off and with that money he bought a house in Calcutta. Later his elder son who became the Superintendent of the Botanical Garden, asked his parents to shift in with him. The parents did shift but lived in a different floor as they did not want anyone to cook for them, especially not a non-Hindu! Though Lakshminarayan did not eat with others, he definitely came to see them every evening. Later he shifted to Meerut to live with his second son. He was fortunate enough to see a few great-grand children. He left for his heavenly abode in 1983 at the age of seventy-nine.

People from all walks of life, the young and old admired him for what he was, even if they did not agree with him always. He had his own human frailties, weakness and failings like all mortals.

(Information taken from Trilokesh Mukherjee)

Manipur

Of Drums, Dancers and Polo

"Manipur is the Jewel of India and Switzerland of the East" - said Pandit Jawaharlal Nehru. Manipur is a state in northeastern India, and its capital is the city of Imphal. Manipur is one of the smallest states of India, three fourths of the area is hilly and the rest is Valley. It is bounded by Nagaland to the north, Mizoram to the south and Assam to the west; it also borders the country of Myanmar to the east. Nature in Manipur is as beautiful as the people of the state. Its dance and music, rich cultural heritage, amazing martial arts performance, extremely rare orchid, flora and fauna and scenic beauties are beyond imagination. The place, the people and the climate allow the atmosphere to make Manipur an ideal holiday resort throughout the year but insurgency has taken its toll and the state has lost out on tourism. It is also the birth place of the game of Polo, a sport which earlier was played only by royalty. The history of Polo is as old as the history of Manipur. Polo locally is called '*Sagol Kangei*' and the historical Polo ground is 'Mapal Kangeibung' in Imphal, though originating in Manipur the game got its importance only after the British took it out first to Calcutta and then to the world. Legend says that the game was first started by King Kangba much before Christ was born. They say the first recorded match was between royal friends of 'King Nongda Lairen Pakhanagba' in 33 AD.

Manipur has Hills, green valleys, lakes and thick dense forests. Manipur literally means 'the land of the jewels'. There are a lot of stories about Manipur and various meanings have been given to the name 'Manipur'. Some say it means 'jewels'. They say Arjuna of Mahabharata was brought back to life from the nether world by a 'moni'/gem taken from here. Another version is that the whole area was under water and Lord Shiva was looking for a place for his Divine Dance and when he saw the place he drained out all the water, the Imphal river with its branches, Kongba, Iril, Nambul flows towards the south and enters an underground canal, there are three big holes in the mountain '*Chingnunghut*' form where the water drains out into the river Chindwin which joins the Irawadi in Myanmar. There are many underground passages for the water to pass through and this also supports the mythical story. They say many gods and goddesses joined in the dance with Shiva-Parvati. This dance is called '*Lai-haroba*'. They say that the gods brought with them jewels during this period. Another group says the land was called Mohendrapura but later came to be called Manipur by Babruvahana the son of Arjuna and Chitrangada (the daughter of the king Chitra Bahana). There are many stories about the origin of the name Manipur but the fact remains that it is so beautiful that people call it a 'jewel' of the northeastern states.

Manipur like the other 'Seven Sister states' has never been annexed by others, this may have helped the state having a special culture of its own. It was only in 1891 that Manipur came under British rule, the last of the north eastern states. During the Second World War, Manipur saw many fierce battles being fought between the Allied Forces and the Japanese. The Japanese were pushed back first before they could enter Imphal. Finally, in October 1949, Manipur became a part of India. It was in 1972, Manipur became a state of India.

Geographically, Manipur has two distinct physical features, rugged Hills and narrow valleys with flat plains. The Logtak Lake, one of the largest fresh water lakes of India, is an important feature of the central plain. The Logtak Lake today has hydro power project on schedule. History says that the lake was the property of the kings and when they used it the common man could not use it. Fishermen with permission from the king could use it to catch fish only when royalty was not around. Now of course rules have changed. There are a number of rivers which is used for inland navigation. River Imphal is one of the major rivers, the capital city Imphal has been named after the river, there are a number of small rivers and most of them are used for navigation.

The people of Manipur follow different religions and '*Sanamahism*' is the oldest religion here, it is the worship of the Sun god or *Sanamahi*. Ancient Manipuris worshipped a Supreme deity called 'Lainingthou Sorale' or 'following the footprints of ancestors' and animism. Later the people were influenced by Hinduism but retained some of the typical features worshipped by their ancestors. It was only in the 15th century people followed Vaishnavism during the reign of King Kyamba. Roughly about 47 percent of the population are Hindus, about 11 percent are *Sanmahis*, Christianity which was brought by the missionaries comprises about 34 percent of the religion and about 8 percent follow Islam. Most of the hill tribes today are Christians and the Meiteis follow Vaishnavism.

Theater in Manipur holds great importance as it is in other parts of the world. The culture spirit has not died in spite of all the problems the state faces. Theater has been a main part of the '*Laiharobi*' or festival of gods, this festival has been celebrated since ancient times, and stories of Lord Krishna's life are performed in temples which are still very popular. A classical dance form of the Manipuri style has emerged as '*Ras Leela*' which has as theme the love story of Lord Krishna and Radha. It was King Rajashree Bhagyachandra, who created the famous '*Ras Leela*' after his divine dream by the grace of Lord Krishna.

Manipur has people from the Hills and plains residing here, the plains man or the valley man call themselves 'Meities' and make up a large part of the population of Manipur. The meities are intelligent, hardworking and follow a strict form of Hinduism, Vaishnavism, it was made popular by Chaitainya Mahaprabhu who came from West Bengal. It is said that with the love of Vaishnavism, came another love, for fish. Like most Bengalis, Manipuris too love fish! Some of the festivals celebrated are *Laiharaobi*/ Festival of Gods, Cheraoba or the Manipuri New Year, Ningol Chakouba or Manipuri '*raksha bandhan*' where married girls of the family come home to a festivity of eating and gifts.

Manipur is a beautiful state almost picture perfect in its natural resources, Logtak lake is one of the largest fresh water lake in Manipur. We have the Rathband bazaar which is famous for being run by women and is also the largest in Asia. Manipur, literally the 'land of jewels' lives up to its name, Mother nature has been extra generous in giving her beauty. It stands out as the 'jewel in the crown' as they say of the 'Seven Sisters'.

14

Bir Tikendrajit

Raja Chandra Kirti's reign came to an end in 1886 and who would become the king became a problem. Chandra Kirti had six Queens who all bore him sons. The eldest or principal Queen's son Sura Chandra was nominated to be the successor. Sura Chandra was an easy going person who enjoyed all the privileges of a royalty but showed no inclination to shoulder his responsibilities for his subjects. Tikendrajit Singh was born on 29th December, 1856 to the fourth Queen – Chongtham Chanu Koueswari Devi of Chandra Kirti. When the third Rani's son Jhalakirti died, Tikendrajit became the king's Senapati or Commander of the Army. It is said that Tikendrajit married eleven times (Snahal Singh recorded on 14th September 1967) and at the age of twenty-four, he became a Vaishnava.

When Tikendrajit's father, King Chandra Kirti died Tikendrajit was in his mid twenties and one of the most popular prince. He was good looking and had the physical strength and martial art skills that behoves a prince. Tikendrajit was excellent at weight lifting and was good in playing polo. He dressed well and had the right social etiquette, even though Tikendrajit had never been to school he had a flair for languages and could speak fluent Bengali and Hindustani. He also had military training from his childhood and for his heroic nature, Tikendrajit was given the name *'Koireng'* (brave). It is said that when he was about twelve years he went with Col J Johnstone, (the then British Political Agent) in his Naga Hills campaign. Tikendrajit was fond of shooting tigers and at times was called 'Lion King' for his shooting prowess; the British Government also complimented him for shooting tigers and said he was as fierce as a tiger. All this impressed Grimwood and his wife, the then Resident of that area. Lady Grimwood in her book wrote about Tikendrajit, "He was manly and generous to a fault, a good friend and a bitter enemy. We liked him because he was so much more broad minded than the rest". Lady Grimwood liked watching him play polo and her husband enjoyed his company and expertise in duck shooting and hunting.

During this period there was unrest and sometimes jealousy in the royal family, even for petty matters like a girl (a local beauty called Maipaki). Later there seemed to be two camps Paka Sana and his two brothers against Tikendrajit. Things came to a head in 1890 when Zilla Singh and Paka Sana had violent exchanges. Paka Sana persuaded the King Sura Chandra to throw out Zilla Singh and withdraw his powers. Tikendrajit hatched a plot with Zilla Singh and Angou Sena which changed the history of Manipur. This at times has been called the 'Palace Revolt'. Tikendrajit put up Kula Chandra as the king and he himself became the Jubaraj/Prince. Sura Chandra and his three brothers rushed to Calcutta and appealed to the British government for help. The British government was waiting for such an opportunity and took this internal rift seriously. They interfered into the internal administration of Manipur. The then Viceroy of India Lord Landsowne and JW Quinton, Chief Commissioner of Assam decided that-1) Senapati Tikendrajit had to be removed, 2) Kula Chandra had to become the Maharaja, and 3) Quinton had to visit Manipur.

On 22nd March, 1891, Quinton went to Manipur and asked Kula Chandra to hand over Tikendrajit. He asked for a durbar the same day. The durbar met but the Senapati did not come as he, Tikendrajit, had information that he might be arrested. On the 24th of March, 1891 the British attacked the palace of Jubaraj Tikendrajit Singh killing many civilians who had gathered for *Raas-Leela.* The Manipuri army was successful in its offensive and Quinton's mission turned out to be misguided, the palace was ready for the British attack, and they say it had more than six thousand Manipuri troops ready. The information that Tikendrajit would be arrested in the Durbar Hall had leaked out and this infuriated the local people. As the British officers were leaving the Durbar Hall the angry Manipuri people attacked Quinton, the Chief Commissioner, Col Skene, Cossins, Lt Simpson and the bugler were beheaded by the public executioner just in front of the two dragons at the orders of the Jubaraj Tikendrajit Singh and General Thangal. It is interesting to note that the manner in which the British were killed was not the Manipuri way, as beheading was not normal. The Manipuri way of killing was by drowning. Beheading was introduced by the British Political Agent Col J Johnstone as he felt drowning was too gruesome. After this the Manipuri troops attacked all the outposts of the British army. There is a controversy between the Manipur Chronicles and Lady Grimwood's account whether Tikendrajit was present at all during the attack. This has left doubts in many minds whether Bir Tikendrajit was actually responsible for the killing of the British. Soon the British sent troops from three directions, Kohima, Kachar and Burma to control the Manipuris. Many sons of Manipur lost their lives in this fight like Yaiskul Lakpa, Chinglensana, Brajabasi Paona. On 27th April, 1891 the British hoisted their flag at Kangla and after this time Manipur came under the British control. The Manipuris had fought bravely under the leadership of Tikendrajit but under heavy odds could not keep up the struggle. The Manipuri people say they were the last to come under the British rule, it could be that Manipur was a remote area not easily accessible or the people did not give up easily their kingdom. Manipur became a princely state and Chura Chand Singh, a minor was put on the throne. After this Tikendrajit went underground but was finally arrested.

The trial of Tikendrajit started on 11th May, 1891, the special court was formed under Lt Col J Mitchell. The court found Kula Chandra, Tikendrajit and Thangal General guilty. On 10th June, 1891 Lt Col J Mitchell, Maj RK Ridgeway and Assistant Commissioner AW Davis pronounced their findings and sentence: "The court finds that you, Tikendrajit Singh, are guilty of the first and second counts of the charge, that is to say that you, on or about the 24th March, at Manipur waged war against the Queen Empress and abetted the murder of the Chief Commissioner of Assam, Quinton; Col Skene, 42nd Gurkha Rifles; Lt Simpson, 43rd Gurkha Rifles; and of Mr Cossins, Assistant Secretary of the Chief Commissioner of

Assam… the court directs that you, Tikendrajit Singh, alias Jubaraj, alias Senapati, be hanged by the neck until you are dead".

The people started asking even in England, "Did the Manipuri Prince obtain a fair trial"?, and were critical about the trial. Queen Victoria had shown concern and voiced her opinion, " It will never do to hang a Maharaja" she even sent a telegram to the Lord Cross saying, " Shut him up for life in a far off place, I think no prince was ever hanged". What troubled the Queen was the manner in which Tikendrajit was to be taken in at the Durbar Hall and almost accused the Chief Commissioner of deviousness and incompetence. Queen Victoria had met Lady Grimwood and found that she held Jubaraj in high regard. Queen Victoria after the meeting with Lady Grimwood sent a telegram to Lord Cross that since Jubaraj Tikendtrajit had not been convicted of the actual murder he should not be executed. All these effort were wasted as the Viceroy called back saying that the hanging of Tikendrajit had been successfully carried out. The irony was that the execution had been carried out in the name of the Empress Queen Victoria, the queen who had sought his reprieve. Bir Tikendrajit and Thangal General were publicly hanged on 13th August, 1891 at 5pm in the evening at Kangei-bung (Polo ground) in Imphal. After independence this ground is called Bir Tikendrajit Park.

The Manipuri Chronicle -1891 says "Soon after Koireng Jubaraj was hanged, while the bodies were still hanging on the gallows, a rider on horseback galloped into the palace bearing a reprieve from the Queen". But it was too late; a life had been lost, the most lasting loss of 1891.

The public execution agitated the Manipuris and people of Assam and it gave a boost to the freedom movement to put an end to the British Rule. Tikendrajit is one of the first freedom fighters of Manipur. The state of Manipur celebrates August 13th as 'Patriot's Day' to remember the role of Bir Tikendrajit as a patriot. The Manipur House in Delhi has been named after Bir Tikendrajit, the 'Lion King' as we would like to remember him.

The life story of martyrs Bir Tikendrajit and Thangal General, their trials and martyrdom are well-known to all Manipuris, of course for this one has to thank the meticulous records of the British. During the British rule in 1890, a period when the 'sun never set in the British Empire', some historians called it a time of peace and tranquility which was shattered in 1891 by a tiny state in the North

East – Manipur. The British suffered heavy losses and this was the first time a native force had defeated the mighty British, something unheard and unthinkable of those days. After the Mutiny of 1857 or the First War of Independence this was the first time the British were defeated at the hands of the Indians. This defeat was appreciated all over the country and covered by most newspapers. Ballads had been written and sung in Bengal. The idea of patriotism had come into the minds of all Indians.

The French Newspaper *Solien* thus wrote "We regard the catastrophe as indicating the spread of ideas of political emancipation in India. The day is perhaps not far off when a well organised party will spring up claiming India for Indians of which even England's domination in India will be seriously threatened". Proved to be so true.

15

Chitrangada and her son Babruvahana

Chitrangada

Great stories and plays have been written about Chitrangada, the Crown Princess of Manipur whose life impressed Rabindranath Tagore so much that she became his muse for a play –'Chitrangada'. Manipur, according to *Prachin Manipurer Itihas* by Mahendra Kumar Singh states that this place, with Lake Logtak in the centre, surrounded by hill-bounded plain land, was the kingdom of Chitra Bahana, a Gandharva king as per the epic *Mahabharata*. Shantidas Goswami has also written in Bengali a chronicle called 'Vijay Panchali' where he talks about Manipur and the first King of Manipur to Chandrabhanu whose daughter was Chitrangada who married Arjuna, the Pandav Prince Chitrangada's life was full of adventure, excitement and romance. Her father the King of Manipur who was son hungry like most people of India brought her up like a son. Chitrangada could fight in battles without any fear and knew all the different types of martial art. Chitrangada, the Manipur princess was brought up to be a good hunter as good as any man.

According to *Mahabharata*, the King's daughter Chitrangada (or Chitranggoda) was attracted to Arjuna from Hastinapur and once when Chitrangada dressed like a man was furiously hunting wild animals she happened to meet the Pandav Prince Arjun, who was wandering about the Hills in his eleventh year of exile (the exile was for disturbing Yudhistir and Draupadi in the night). It was love at first sight for Chitrangada. A heated argument took place between the two and Arjun told the young man he/she did not have the charm of a young woman/man and found her/him very unattractive, he did not know then that Chitrangada was a woman. It was till then a one sided love affair as Chitrangada had hopelessly fallen in love with Arjun and the word 'unattractive' hurt Chitrangada.

The spurned woman in Chitrangada provoked her to pray to Lord Madana (Kaama - Cupid - Eros) and persuaded him to transform her into a young woman of incomparable, 'irresistible' beauty; she asked only for a year to become a beauty to fulfill her desires and capture her man's heart that is Arjun. Lord Madana granted her the boon which made her very beautiful. The god had turned her into a beautiful, lissome young woman whose beauty everyone praised and talked about. Now that Chitrangada's wish was granted and she had turned into a beauty, her attention was now on Arjun to tempt him to fall in love with her. Arjun fell in love with her as he was bewitched by her (according to history Arjun had a weakness for beautiful women). They enjoyed a blissful romantic life and found great happiness in each other's company.

Later Arjun asked for Chitrangada's hand in marriage from the King. The King of Manipur had hesitated at first to give his daughter's hand in marriage as theirs was a matrilineal society and any child of Chitrangada would be heir to the throne. Arjun respected that and said he had no intentions of taking Chitrangada away as she must look after her people and her responsibilities.

One day Chitrangada's manly prowess as a hunter came into the forefront as Arjun chanced to see Chitrangada handle a group of robbers in the forest. Arjun saluted her in admiration and his love for her did not diminish, their marital life was not overshadowed by her martial status. Arjun no longer loved her for her beauty but as an individual.

After a year when Chitrangada went back to her original physical state, Chitrangada advised Arjun that she should be taken as his life partner in all senses and not be taken lightly. She was a man's equal and should not be viewed lightly. She must be accepted as she was irrespective of her not being as beautiful as she was earlier.

The point she drove home was that what matters most is the true values in life, not the superficial beauty and Chitrangada demanded a rightful place for herself in his life. She told Arjun that she was a princess and not a commoner. She was not someone either to be kept on a high pedestal and worshipped, or to be neglected and left to fade and languish in the background. He should allow her to be forever by his side in both happy and difficult times. According to legends Arjuna stayed for three years in Manipur.

Later a son was born to Chitrangada and Arjun and they named him Babruvahana. But before going on about Babruvahana, a mention about Uloopi - the Naga princess who helped in looking after Babruvahana, the snake princess they say nursed Babruvahana when he was a young child. Uloopi or Ulupi was one of the four wives of Arjun. While Arjun was in Manipur Uloopi was so infatuated with Arjun that she abducted him to her place. There she fed him with potions that made him her slave and Arjun very unwillingly agreed to marry Uloopi. A son was born to Arjun and Uloopi and was called Iravan or Iravat as some historians say. Later she returned Arjun to a lamenting Chitrangada.

The story of Chitrangada and Arjun has gone through a change in name, Arjun was renamed Urangangjuba and Chitrangada was called Laiyeklaikhotehanoo. Babruvahana was called Kupireng.

Babruvahana

Babruvahana was born to Chitrangada and Arjun when he was away on his exile. Arjun could not take Babruvahana away with him as according to the matrilineal society, any child born to Chitrangada, the Crown Princess, would inherit the throne. Babruvahana was adopted by his maternal grandfather and lived in the lap of luxury as is normal for an heir-apparent. After the death of the King of Manipur, Babruvahana inherited the throne as his successor and ruled for a long time.

There is a place called Shagol Bandh, which is not very far away from Kangla, in Imphal town. Manipuris believe that the son of Arjun and Chitrangada resisted the movement of an *asmavedha* horse of Arjun. Babruvahana caught hold of the horse and tied it to a tree at the place of Shagol Bandh, (in Sanskrit '*Shagol*' is horse and '*bandh*' is to tie). One day there was an encounter between Arjun and Babruvahana and Arjun was badly injured. Chitrangada had to disclose the truth, that Arjun was the father of Babruvahana.

Uloopi the Nag Kanya (princess of Nagaland) who was also married to Arjun arrived with a team of physicians. The physicians knew the art of *Sanjiwani buti* cure and they cured Arjun. The fight ended and the family was united. Some historians say that Babruvahana killed his father with an arrow. Later when he came to know who Arjun was he repented for his deed and wanted to kill himself. Uloopi again came to his help and gave Babruvahana a gem which brought back Arjun to life. After the family united Babruvahana went back to Hastinapur (the Pandav kingdom) with Arjun.

The family got established; the descendents of Babruvahana, Jobista also called Pakhangba became the first ruler of Manipur in AD 33 and ascended the throne.

16

Irabot Singh – The People's Man

Irabot Singh is remembered with respect and love even today though he died in 1951. Hijam Irabot Singh was born on 30th September1896 in a middle class family. Those were turbulent days as the British took control over Manipur. Irabot's family had to be shifted out of their ancestral home and both his parents, father Hijam Ibunohal Singh and mother Chongtham Ningol Thambalngambi died while he was very young. Dame fortune was on Irabot's side as his maternal aunt Songijam Ongbi Ibeton Devi who was related to the royal family by marriage took on the responsibility of looking after him. Irabot was admitted to school here, the Johnstone Higher Secondary School was his first school for him. Irabot studied here till Class 7. From a very young age Irabot Singh was very politically motivated. It was here he founded two student bodies, '*Bal Sangha*' and '*Scout and Chatra Sameloni*'. Once, it is said, he went on strike to protest against the misadministration of the teachers as one of Irabot's classmates had been badly beaten up by the teachers in front of other students. It is said that this was the first strike by students in Manipur.

He went to Dhaka to act as a companion-cum-assistant to his brother and also to complete his education. But life had other plans and he had to give up his education due to paucity of funds. In Dacca he met a number of Meiteis and this started his interaction with the Meiti culture. It was during this period Irabot came in contact with the 'Swadeshi' freedom movement workers. The thoughts of 'independence' had been sown and after he came back to Manipur he got together young people to and started the 'Swadeshi' movement, often secret meetings were held in the woods outside the town of Imphal. Since these meetings were hush-hush, no one knew of the meetings and so this did not affect his relationship with the king.

When Irabot came back to Imphal, he could not go back to his aunt's place because of ideological differences between his cousin and himself. It must have been a painful time for Irabot, the very feeling that you have nowhere to go is surely uncomfortable! It was Maibam Samden of Wankher who later gave him shelter. Irabot Singh's prominence in the Meitei society brought him to the notice of the King Churachandra Singh. The king realised that here was a man who believed in his principles and stood by it, this impressed the king a lot. The Raja decided to get his elder brother's daughter Princess Khomdonsana married to him. Irabot Singh as the royal son-in-law or 'Mamuk Ibungo' as they say in Manipuri, enjoyed some privileges. In 1930, he was appointed as a member of the Sadar Panchayat Court (today it is the post of a magistrate) and a lot of land was given to him. As a member of the Sadar Panchayat Court Irabot was given a salary of Rs. 25/- a month. Irabot Singh a man of sound principles never misused the powers he had got. He did not deviate from the path of supporting the poor, the downtrodden. The first argument with the king came when Irabot objected to people being excommunicated or as they say in Manipuri 'Ameng Aseng' because of differences with the king. The objection, since it came from the 'Mamuk Ibungo' was taken as a work of courage by the royal court and the king had to overlook the situation. The king had imposed a tax on the people for applying 'Chandan' or sandalwood paste on their forehead. Taxes had to be paid for fishing on the Logtak Lake and sometimes for threshing cotton. The poor had to undergo a lot of hardships. The king's rule had to be obeyed or he/she had to face punishment. Irabot Singh tried to advise the king to have more humane laws but it fell on deaf ears. When Irabot's efforts failed he resigned from the Panchayat, as he felt great injustice was being done to the poor. Irabot felt the farmers should own the land that they were tilling and the feudal system should be abolished. The most hated one was 'Pothang' or forced labour imposed on the common man for the comfort and safety of the villagers. Irabot Singh always found ways to call for meetings and the essence of the meetings was a serious attempt to also remove the differences between the poor and rich. Irabot had the support of writers and social workers.

Irabot Singh was keenly interested in literary works. He has the distinction of bringing out the first magazine in Manipuri, called 'Metei Chanu', and it was indeed unfortunate that due to paucity of funds it could not survive. Irabot Singh wanted to bring out original literary works as he found there was the need of Manipuri books in High Schools, later he brought another book called 'Saidem Seiring' which was prescribed as a text book for Class V. He also wrote a novel 'Mohini' which was first published in a journal by Dr Leiren. In 1933 he brought out a book titled 'Dahil Amasung Darkhast Iba', to bridge the gap between the public and the Manipur State Durbar. In 1937 and 1938 Irabot Singh became the general secretary of the Manipur Sahitya Parishad. In 1947 he brought out a journal 'Anouba Jug' or the 'Socialist Age'. Today we can call him the pioneer of Manipuri journalism. Some of Irabot Singh's poetry can be found in school textbooks.

Irabot Singh excelled in the performing arts too and had many dramatic performances to his credit. He had an active role in plays like 'Nar Singha' as he played the role of the leader, (some say Irabot was obsessed with the theme as it depicted the 'Manipuri protest against the Burmese'), 'Satee Khongnang' and 'Devala Devi' to name a few. It is here Irabot realised what a powerful medium the theatre could be for expressing an idea. He was a good painter and a sportsperson too. He was also one of the founder members of the Manipur Sports Association. Irabot Singh wanted people to learn the traditional Manipuri style of self-defence called the 'Sat-Jal'.

A social reformer at heart Irabot Singh started the 'Nikhil Hindu Manipuri Mahasabha' in 1939. This party brought into its fold a large number of Manipuris and the king Churachandra Singh was the Chief Patron. The first session was held at Imphal in 1934. It had sessions in Silchar in 1939 and Mandalay, 1937. The king was the President in the first three sessions and in the fourth session Irabot Singh became the President on 30th January1938. In his first Presidential speech he advocated the abolishment of the Manipuri State Durbar and wanted to start the 'Electoral System' in Manipur.

He openly told the people to vote against the State Administration after he quit the Sadar Panchayat March in 1939. Later he started his own party called the 'Manipur Proja Sameloni'. In January 1940 he was arrested and put behind bars for giving inflammatory speeches. Irabot was first put into Imphal jail but later shifted to Sylhet (now in Bangladesh) jail. It was during his stay in Sylhet jail he met many leaders from the Congress and Communist Parties. Irabot was greatly influenced by Leninism and Marxism. He was released from Sylhet jail in 1943 but was not permitted to enter Manipur. So from Sylhet, Irabot travelled to Cachar in Assam and took part in the 'peasant movement'. Irabot Singh attended the first Communist Party meeting in Bombay in 1934 as an observer. In 1944 he was again arrested for being a Communist. It was only in 1946 he was finally allowed to go to Manipur. There he started a new party called the 'Manipur Praja Mandal' the same year. He was thrown out of the Nikhil Manipuri Mahasabha as he was a member of the Communist Party. In the first Manipuri State Assembly, Irabot Singh contested from the Ulton constituency and won by a clear margin.

In 1948 there were talks of 'Purbachal Pradesh' or an Eastern State which would comprise of Manipur, Mizoram, Tripura and Assam's Cachar and Karbi Anglong Districts. Irabot Singh called for a meeting to protest against the proposal. To think that Manipur would be a district of the 'Purbachal Pradesh' and the Chief Minister's Secretariat would possibly be at Silchar seemed unthinkable to Irabot Singh. He met many leaders from these hilly areas and tried to make the people aware of the situation. The protest meet was held at Imphal on 21st September 1948. The police stopped a group of people at Pungdongbam near Imphal and this led to a tussle between the police and the people. To control the crowd the police 'lathi' (stick) charged and many people were hurt. Irabot Singh realised he would be held responsible for the fiasco so he went underground.

The first Communist Party of Manipur came into being on 23rd August 1948. But due to the incidents at Pungdongbam (meeting held by Irabot Singh) the group had to go underground, with its President Irabot Singh. The people's man, Irabot, still felt the poor people were being oppressed. The state government felt he was a hindrance to their working and so announced a reward of Rs. 1000/- for his arrest. The anti-communist drive continued with the help of the Manipur Rifles, Assam Rifles and Manipur Police. Irabot Singh never came out of hiding and he turned this into an opportunity, now he could start a Communist Party in Manipur.

While Irabot Singh was on the run he developed typhoid and succumbed to the illness on 26th September 1951. He died before he could celebrate his forty fifth birthday. Thus ended the life of a man who tried to uplift the poor, it is no wonder he is popularly called the 'Robinhood of the Poor'. Hijam Irabot Singh stands tall in Manipuri's history, it is unfortunate that he died young, here was a man totally devoted to the cause he believed in. The people still remember him on his birth anniversary as they do Bir Tikendrajit or Thangal General.

17

Irom Sharmila — The Iconic 'Iron Lady'

Irom Chanu Sharmila is one woman who fights for her people, the Manipuris for a better tomorrow. Born on 14th March 1972 at Kongkham Leikai, Imphal to Irom Nanda Singh (an employee of the veterinary hospital at Imphal) and Irom Ongbai Sakhi Devi (housewife). Sharmila was the ninth child; she has five brothers and three sisters. They say when Sharmila was born a storm swept the village as if to indicate that a legend was born. When she was about fifteen days old she had to be fed with boiled rice water as her mother could not nurse her. Sakhi Devi, Sharmila's mother was in despair, she wondered how the baby would survive. It was Sharmila's elder brother Singhajit who would take her to houses which had newborn babies to feed her. Anyone who came to the family grocery shop with a baby was requested to feed Sharmila too. Sharmila grew up being fed by many mothers. This may have made her socially concerned and committed.

In spite of having so many siblings Sharmila went to school regularly. Her first one was Khanglabung Child Centre, Khunai. Soibam Leikai (Nursery to Class V), from class VI to class X it was Ananda Singh Academy, finally from Ibotonsns Girls High Secondary School, Imphal she finished Class XII. She has not been to college. Sharmila is a shy soft spoken person, more an introvert. Her brother Singhajit says she was withdrawn and different from the rest in her youth. Sharmila grew up in turbulent times as the 70s saw Manipur struggling to keep her identity. All the violence around her made her unhappy; there was constant struggle between the security forces and the civilians. From her youth Sharmila has been a peace activist and had met people who were affected by the AFSPA (Armed Forces Special Powers Act), women who had been raped, children orphaned or men wrongly imprisoned. The AFSPA came into force in 1958. This act was imposed on Manipur and some other North Eastern States in 1980. The act allows the Army to use force, or arrest anyone without warrant, on someone who has committed an offence. No army personnel can be tried without permission from the Central Government.

What is Sharmila protesting against? It is the AFSPA which she wants to be repealed. The Prime Minister Manmohan Singh when he visited Manipur had made two commitments - one to hand over Kangla to the people of Manipur and second the AFSPA would be reviewed to a more humane law. The people of Manipur felt possibly the life of one girl could be saved, that is Irom Sharmila. A committee, the Jeevan Reddy Commission, was set up and their report also felt the same, that the AFSPA should be repealed. However, nothing has been implemented.

The decision to go on a long fast was not planned earlier as Sharmila had joined the anti-AFSPA group just about two weeks before she went on the '*satyagraha*'. Sharmila greatly respects Mahatma Gandhi and prefers to follow the path of non-violence. A three-member team of Indian People's Inquiring Committee which was headed by Justice H Suresh, had gone to Manipur to hold discussions with human rights lawyers, journalists, academics and people from different walks of life. This was Sharmila's first political participation. Some of what she heard from young girls against the army had really shaken up Sharmila.

The 'fast' started on 5th November 2000, three days after the Malom incident at the very place where the massacre took place. Second November saw ten innocent people dead after firing from the Assam Rifles soldiers; they were retaliating to insurgent attacks on 1st November 2000 to an Army column. Among the ten dead civilians was an 18-year old S. Chandramani, a National Bravery Award winner. He was four-years-old, when he saved another child from drowning. Chandramani was at the bus stop seeing off an aunt. It was this Malom incident which made Sharmila begin her fast. It was a Thursday and Sharmila had always fasted on Thursdays since childhood and that day she was fasting too, she just continued with her fast.

Before starting her fast she sought her mother's blessings to work for 'betterment of humanity' and left home. And this was the last time she saw her mother, however the pledge was broken later. Her brother says when Sharmila started the fast her mother had promised her that she would see her only when she had achieved her goal. But sadly this was broken as her mother had fallen sick and was hospitalized last year; Sharmila had to go to see her. Her mother, Sakhi Devi, was very upset and asked Sharmila why had she come; this at that time had upset Sharmila a lot. Sharmila's mother Irom Sakhi Devi did not know what was in store for her youngest daughter. Sharmila straight away went to the very spot where the massacre had occurred and started her fast unto death. Irom Sharmila's protest started with no fanfare, no media hype; it was totally a peaceful way of fasting to tell the people 'we must live without fear'. At first, people made fun of her that how a young girl could take on the mighty army and said that it was a passing fancy. But Irom Sharmila proved all of them wrong; she stood steadfast in her resolution of fasting till the AFSPA was removed. This simple '*satyagraha*', the Gandhian way of fasting stirred the people of Manipur, they all were on Sharmila's side, and this epic protest seems 'one of a kind' in history. Sharmila has been mentioned in the Guinness Book of World Record for her fast, 'the longest protest on a social cause by a single individual anywhere in the world'.

Sharmila was arrested after a few days when she went on a hunger strike on 2nd November 2000 for attempted suicide. The laws of the land say if a person is arrested for attempting suicide, he/she can be imprisoned only for a year. So at the end of a year she was released and again rearrested on the same charges and kept at the hospital to be fed through the nose. Ironically every year she is released on 'International Women's Day' and rearrested a day later as she refuses to go off her fast. They say the cost of her hospital stay is over a lakh for a year. This use of the taxpayer's money also troubles Sharmila, she says "this hunger strike is the only way I can achieve my goal of getting AFPSA withdrawn from Manipur. I am a revolutionary, a social reformer, but only through peaceful means".

The Prime Minister Manmohan Singh in November 2004 had requested to review the laws of the AFSPA that had been imposed to fight the insurgents, they said the AFSPA could be removed in Imphal, but Sharmila's views remained unchanged. She wanted the whole state to be free from AFSPA.

Sharmila has not eaten a morsel of food or taken a sip of water since November 2000. Today her body weight is about thirty seven kilograms; her weight and age are almost the same. She is forcibly kept alive by a mixture of vitamins, nutrients and laxatives forcibly fed through her nose by a tube. Her body is ruined from inside, the bones have become brittle and her menstrual cycle has stopped. But nothing can be a deterrent for her for achieving her goals. Sharmila keeps her teeth clean by rubbing dry cotton over it and her lips are cleaned with dry spirit so that her fast is not spoilt. When you visit her in hospital you find Sharmila a frail fair woman, and no wonder she is sometimes lovingly called '*menghaboi*' or the 'fair one' by the people. Her hair is black and curly and slightly unkempt as they have not been combed for some time. Her hands are clean and her voice halting, she takes a while to speak as her body seems to be tired and in pain.

After her stay in Jawaharlal Nehru Hospital in Imphal, Manipur, and her supporters took advantage of the release from custody after serving a 'year long custody' at the hospital, they literally smuggled her out of Imphal to reach Delhi to turn her "regional" campaign into a "national" one. Sharmila was smuggled out by her brother Singhajit and two friends Babloo Loitangbam from Human Rights Alert, Manipur and Kangloipal to Delhi. In October 2006 Sharmila left Manipur for Delhi. Like all other years, this time also the government did the same that is release and rearrest Sharmila. Embarrassed police officials later admitted that they had no inkling of the plan to "smuggle out" Sharmila.

The 'satyagraha' had shifted to Delhi as the six years of fasting in Manipur had yielded very little. The group arrived in October and camped at Jantar Mantar, Delhi. The only place Sharmila has visited in Delhi is Rajghat – Mahatma Gandhi's Samadhi. Within a few days of stay in Delhi, Sharmila was arrested by the Delhi police for her suicide attempt and then admitted to AIIMS. Outside the hospital room was her brother Singhajit who gave up his job to 'look after his sister from outside the door'. There was pain and grief on his face as Sharmila has been refusing the nasal feed at

AIIMS as she wants to be produced before the judicial courts to find out why she has been arrested.

According to her brother Singhajit, "We are in the middle of a battle now, we have to face the trouble, and we have to fight till the end even if it means my sister's death. But if she had told me before she began her fast, I would never have let her do this to her body. We had to learn so much first. How to talk, how to negotiate? We knew nothing. We were poor people. "

Sharmila cannot meet her relatives but she is allowed to meet the media. In hospital Sharmila keeps fit by practicing yoga four to five hours a day, she is self taught. Sharmila is also a naturopath. Yoga helps her keep a balance between mind and body. Sometimes she is allowed to walk the corridors of the hospital but of course with security around her. Sharmila is a voracious reader and has read books on Gandhi, Nelson Mandela and Che Guevara. These books have helped her keep loneliness at bay. Most of the books she has read she passes them on to the library in Imphal.

Sharmila was nominated for the 2005 Nobel Peace Prize; being one of the thousand other women. Shyly she had asked if she could meet the other nine thousand and ninety nine nominees. Sharmila has received support from Naga Women's Organisation and international human rights group too.

In 2007 the Gwanju Prize for Human Rights Committee (Korea) was awarded to Sharmila. Her brother Singhajit accepted the award on Sharmila's behalf as she was unable to travel, she was in hospital under heavy security, or in other words under judicial custody. The money from the prizes she receives goes to the welfare of the people who have suffered losses at the hands of the security forces.

Irom Sharmila's mother waits for her to return to their hut in Imphal. While talking to Delhi-based film maker Kavita Joshi she says she is possibly weak hearted, as if she sees her daughter in her condition she may break down and cry. This will weaken Sharmila's resolve, she feels. Sakhi Devi knows how hard Sharmila's days and nights must be with so little fluid going into her body. She is waiting for the AFSPA to be repealed even if it is for a few days then she will feed her rice water. After that even if Sharmila dies her wish would have been fulfilled.

Sharmila's fast still continues and she remains steadfast in her resolve to not be distracted; nothing will shake her from the path she has taken. Doctors say her fast is a medical miracle. Singhajit also says, "She always had extraordinary will. Maybe that is what made her different. Maybe this is her service to all her mothers". Both her sister Vijanthi and brother Singhajit say Sharmila has had a 'Never say Die' attitude since childhood. At times one wonders what made this young girl from a middle class family, who could not complete her studies, take up such a challenge. Her legendary struggle for human rights has been a hallmark in the history of Manipur. A relay fast was started by the women of Manipur; about sixty women are fasting to save Sharmila.

The literary minded Sharmila is a talented poet and has written hundreds of poems, till date one of her collections 'Imadi Khongdai Setlaroi' has been published.

At times one wonders which the right path is as the Army has also had its own casualties. Is it the lack of political will by our leaders? The Government and politicians seem to be only interested in themselves. Fasting seems to be a minor tool; we need a mass movement by the public, a social consciousness. For this both media and public have to work together, mob fury is something we all fear, only then maybe Sharmila's dream will be fulfilled.

18

K Namrijinpou
The man who was one of the first to be Baptised into Christianity

K Namrijinpou a Rongmai, sometimes in Manipuri called a Maipak became a Christian under tragic circumstances. Namrijinpou was born in Khukiu village of Rongmai Hills in Tamenglong area of Manipur. He with his father moved to a place close to Imphal called Keishamthong after his mother died. Namrijinpou with his father's help was employed in a band party of the king of Manipur. Later because of his good work he was promoted to the rank of a Major in the Manipur Army.

Namrijinpou at a young age married Pantigongliu from his own clan. Their married life was not a happy one as they lost all their children in infancy due to illness. No amount of praying to their Animistic gods helped the couple. It was during this difficult period of their life that Pantigongliu and Namrijinpou met two converted Kukis, Teba and Longhobel from the Ukhrul Christian Mission School. They explained how men committed sins and how Jesus Christ son of Joseph and Mary died for it. During this time a son was born to Namrijinpou and Pantigongliu, they called him Kaphunlong David, meaning 'seed of life'. Both Teba and Longhobel convinced the couple that Christianity was a strong religion and they should follow it and help in its growth.

On 6th December 1914 the couple with four others was baptized by Rev. Fox at Imphal. This brought about the beginning of Christianity in the Zeliangrong Hills.

In 1916, Pettigrew a missionary started a new church at Keishamthong where a small Christian community came up. They had people from the Kukis, Manipuris, Rongmais, Gorkha and Sema Nagas. The Christian group decided they would set up a church near Imphal. Porom Singh the first Manipuri Christian came from Ukhrul to settle here.

Namrijinpou resigned from the Manipur Army in 1919 as he wanted to devote more time to his new religion, Christianity. Namrijinpou started his evangelistic work among the Zeliangrong people with great earnest. In some of the villages he met with stiff opposition from the Animists who were supported by the British government officials who wanted the Nagas to remain primitive and uneducated. The village elders complained to the British government about the Christianized Zeliangrongs disturbing their traditional ways of life and wanted them to be thrown out of the village. Namrijinpou was asked to leave and pay a fine for disturbing the peace of the area.

Namrijinpou went to Semang village as a Christian leader and set up a school for the education of Christian and Animist children. When the Animist Nagas got converted to Christianity they also came in contact with the outside world which possibly broadened their horizons. They realised they could improve their economic conditions like the change from old jhuming cultivation (slash and burn method of cultivation) for paddy and cotton, hunting and trapping of wild animals and forest resources like timber and cinnamon for their livelihood. And they could at the same time devote their time to preaching of Christianity but had to put up with the anger of the Animist Nagas. Christianity progressed in the Zeliangrong Hills and more churches came up, by 1930 eight churches were established in the Kuki villages.

But we find in the Zeliangrong areas Animism still had a strong foothold as the Animist Zeliangrongs did not permit the Christians to preach Christianity in many villages for fear of losing their own faith, Animism. At times Namrijinpou was ordered to be stoned to death if he came preaching the Gospel. What troubled the Animists was that he was working against the law of Animistic life, that any and every man had the right to believe, think and say what he had in mind irrespective of his birth. The Animists felt that Christianity was questioning their very belief in life. Under such trying circumstances Namrijinpou did his best to spread Christianity, he would stand outside the village praying, preaching and reading from the Bible till exhaustion took over. But Namrijinpou and his followers did not give up easily; they went to the villages to preach and sang hymns loudly. By and large the Zeliangrong Hills remained a stronghold of Animism and the Christian Missionaries found the going difficuLt It was apparent the Animistic followers did not permit the Christians to preach Christianity.

Later he had two followers Hurunag and Lalibam. These two met with stiff resistance and this group was thrown out into the jungle where they established a church and got together about twenty families and a small village sprang up around the church. The Animist Nagas complained to the then Sub-Divisional Officer RH Shaw that a church had been built which was against the Naga Animistic traditional style. The SDO (Sub Divisional Officer) Shaw did not favour the emergence of Christianity in this area, as he wanted to favour the Animistic group. So he ordered the church building to be destroyed. It was under such trying circumstances Namrijinpou and his followers preached Christianity in the Zeliangrong Hills without looking for any gains. We find Namrijinpou had to struggle for his new faith but he did not give up easily as this new religion gave him happiness.

19

Major Ralengnao Khating

Ralengnao Khating a Tangkhul Naga was born on 8th February 1912 at Ukhrul in Manipur State. Bob (as he was popularly called) Khating came from a well-to-do family and his primary education was at Ukhrul, followed by Kangpobi Mission School for Class VI, those days passing class VI was a big achievement and it was greatly appreciated by everyone. Bob passed this easily and also won a scholarship from Rev. Pettigrew. Dutiful son that he was, he handed over all the scholarship money to his mother. Bob finished his matriculation examination from Johnstone High School, Imphal. Later he graduated from Calcutta University. He was one of the first graduates among the Manipuri and hill people.

Bob Khating took up teaching as a profession and became the Head Master of MES School, Harsingha, Assam. This was followed by MES School Ukhrul in Manipur. Bob Khating emphasised on girls education as he felt the society would improve with this, Pundit Nehru too shared the same feelings.

In May 1941 the then Political Agent of Manipur C Grimson asked young men to join the War Service. Bob applied for a king's commission in the army and passed through all the tests. Finally, he passed out from Mhow (Military Headquarters of War) in Madhya

Pradesh and was commissioned into the army in 1941. Bob Khating was commissioned into the 19th Hyderabad Regiment (later called the 7th Kumaon Regiment) and was posted at the Regimental Training Centre at Agra. After his posting at Agra he was sent to the General Reserve Force, Jorhat to join the elite 'V' Force. During this time the Second World War was on and the Japanese were advancing very quickly from Burma to Manipur. The 'V' force was formed to recruit local people as volunteers for intelligence gathering, counter-intelligence work and guerilla tactics in war. It was the duty of Capt Khating to recruit these people from Ukhrul, and the Kabaw Valley. Capt Khating went to Ukhrul and met the village elders to explain his mission. He recruited about five thousand men for the 'V' force from Bungpa area where people were coming in from Burma into Tangkhul areas. Bob Khating started a base which covered south-east of Manipur. When the Japanese forces reached Shangshak and Ukhrul it was Capt Khating who was called to guide the British forces to counter the Japanese.

With his 'V' force he mobilised the Tangkhul leaders who organised the intelligence setup, passing on the movement of the Japanese to the Allied Forces. It was with this combined effort the British could contain the Japanese troops. Even after the Japanese troops withdrew the volunteers of the 'V' force continued to work. These volunteers were a dedicated lot of workers who had won many gallantry awards and were a force to reckon with. During May 1942 and May 1945, Capt Khating was awarded the Member of the British Empire (MBE), Chief's Gallantry Certificate, and the Military Cross (MC). All these awards tell us that Bob Khating was totally devoted to his job and the country. Bob Khating was an army man, who throughout his life followed the ethos of the army that is 'service before self'. He stands tall in the annals of Manipur history.

Finally the 'V' force was disbanded in 1943 and Bob Khating was transferred to the Assam Regiment and was posted to the 3rd Battalion at Shillong. The Maharaja of Manipur realised that Bob Khating was a brilliant officer and decided to request him to join the Manipur State. The then Political Agent and the Ukhrul elders also felt the same and repeatedly asked him to come back to Manipur. Finally, Bob Khating resigned from the Army in October 1947 and joined the Government of Manipur State as Minister-in-Charge of the Hills Administration. He stood for elections and won them, but he continued to be Minister-in-Charge of Hills Administration.

Bob Khating also helped raise the Manipur Rifles, the State Armed Police Force. In October 1949, the Manipur State Assembly was dissolved and Manipur became a part of India.

In May 1950 Major Khating joined 2nd Assam Rifles for an interim period as he was supposed to be absorbed by the North East Frontier Administrative Services which came under the External Affairs Ministry. The North East Frontier Administrative Services was called the Indian Frontier Administrative Services. The first batch had people like Nari Rustomji and Ralegnao Khating to name a few. Bob Khating was chosen to work under the NEFA services as an Astt Political Officer. His military acumen helped him to be a successful man here too. One such incident which stands out to show that Bob Khating was an excellent officer was when an earthquake took place and all his supplies and help were cut short as their wireless sets were damaged and all the Mishmi porters had run away to their villages. Major Bob Khating and his men quickly organised restoring groups to help the Mishmi villagers and asked for food supplies to be air dropped for the Assam Rifles soldiers and the local people.

Major Bob Khating visited Tawang on 6th February 1951. He had with him Capt HB Limbu and some soldiers of the 5th Assam Rifles, Captain Menters from the Indian Medical Corps and a peon, his only civilian staff. The journey was a difficult one as the terrain was inhospitable and the mercury at times dipped below zero temperature. Major Khating quickly established his authority over Tawang which had previously been governed by Tibet. The Indian Tri-colour was hoisted on 9th February 1951 and Bob Khating announced that the Tawang region, south of the McMahon Line (formed under the Shimla Treaty of 1914) became a part of India. A permanent site for the Assam Rifles post and the Administrative Headquarters and a civil dispensary was opened. Khating had got house counting of all villagers and the '*gaon burahs*' as interpreters. By August 1951, Indian Administration was in control of the Tawang area. Bob Khating's 'mission impossible' became 'mission possible', for this effort he was honoured with the 'Padamshri'.

In December 1957 Bob Khating was posted to Mokokchoung, Naga Hills as the first Deputy Commissioner of the Mokokchoung District. Later in 1961-1962 he attended NDC (National Defence College), a feather in his cap as a very few get to attend it. After finishing his tenure at NDC, Bob Khating was posted to Sikkim as the

Development Commissioner of the state. The year 1962 was a testing time for Bob Khating as the Chinese troops occupied the border of NEFA, this included Tawang, Bomdilla and Sela. Ralengnao Khating requested the External Affairs Ministry to post him out of Sikkim to NEFA, this was readily granted by the Ministry.

Bob Khating was to report to Headquarters in Tejpur. He worked very tirelessly and helped the people to get back to normal life. He was appointed Security Commissioner and helped the Army and civil authorities to work in harmony. After this Ralengnao Khating became the Chief Secretary of Nagaland.

When he was to retire from the Army, Ralengnao Khating was offered the post of Ambassador to Burma/ Myanmar and he accepted this very graciously and went to Rangoon as the Ambassador of India. After retiring, the Government of Manipur appointed him as the Chairman of the Tribal Law Commission (honorary) and in 1980 as advisor to the Government of Manipur when it was placed under President's Rule.

There are certain tales about Major Khating which makes him liked by all. He enjoyed his liquor like most of others and once when he was hospitalised at Tezpur (Assam) he was asked to stay off alcohol. When visitors went to see him and asked if he needed anything, the answer was if they could smuggle in Hercules XXX Rum for him (Rum is a popular drink of the soldiers). Bob Khating in spite of reaching such high ranks, he always preferred his favourite Hercules Rum, like a common soldier.

On 12th January 1990 this brave soldier left for his heavenly abode. Bob Khating died at his Imphal-Mantripukhri home with his family and friends around him. Huge crowds had come to pay their respect to a man who was never angry; humility and resolve were two facets of his character. Bob Khating was a Naga Tangkhul by birth, cosmopolitan by nature, loved by all who knew him, especially in Nagaland, Manipur and Arunachal Pradesh. Thus came to an end a life well lived.

'*Tagra raho*' (Greeting – meaning "be healthy") as they say in the Assam Regiment.

20

Mary Kom – The Woman's 'World Champion Pugilist'

How many of us know that woman's boxing has come of age here in India? For that matter we have a world champion amongst us. Yes, it is true; it is none other than Mangte Chungneijang Mary Kom. She stands tall in her sport in the world today. Mary Kom as we call her was born to Tonpu Kom and Saneikham Kom. They belong to the Kom tribe of Kangthei Village, Moirang Lamkhai, a small village in rural Manipur. The village has about thirty odd families. Kangthei is thirty-five kilometers away from Imphal. Tonpu her father is a farmer, the family had a small one acre farm to start with and on this the whole family was dependent. Mary Kom laughingly recalls. My father owned one acre of land which was our only source of income. But our village is so poor that we were considered among the wealthier people". Her family background tells us that she had to struggle very hard to reach the level she is today. Being the eldest she helped her parents in the '*jhum*' fields, cut forests to clear the land for cultivation, helped in making charcoal and fishing too. She also helped her mother look after her younger siblings.

Mary Kom took to sports to supplement the families' income. Manipur is the land of polo and sports is loved by one and all.

The people are natural athletes; rarely do you see a young fat Manipuri! Mary Kom has two sisters and one brother, in all they are four siblings. Mary's childhood was similar to most other Manipuri children. She went to the local village school and had a carefree life. Mary Kom was always interested in sports and in school she excelled in athletics. She loved playing football and deep in her heart cherished being a boxer after she saw Dingko Singh – the Manipuri boxer who had made a mark for himself in the boxing arena. She was highly impressed by Dingko Singh. Mary Kom says, "I was initially an all-round athlete, and 400m and javelin were my pet events. When Dingko Singh returned from Bangkok (Asian Games) with gold I thought I should also give it a try. Dingko's success triggered off a revolution in Manipur and surprisingly, I found I was not the only girl who was drawn into boxing. "

Young Mary Kom was a very sincere, determined child and had secretly started active boxing after she saw some boys and girls practicing. She had gone to the local Sports Authority of India (SAI). The coach realised this spunk of a girl had great potential; she had the right fighting spirit. Mary Kom insisted she be trained with the boys and had learnt the basics in a few weeks time. Mary Kom's talent outside academics was noticed by people and in Class IX she shifted to Takel in Imphal under the SAI training facility. It was here that she began her training as an athlete. During her workouts at Khuman she met boxers both boys and girls which inspired her to put on her boxing gloves in the year 2000. The basics were quickly learnt and as Mary Kom says, "I guess I had God given talent".

Very soon Mary Kom won the state championship and her photographs appeared in the local daily. One fine day to his horror Mary Kom's father saw his daughter's photograph in the local daily and being hailed as the 'queen of boxing' in the year 2000. He was furious, understandably so as 'boxing' was a male sport and was taboo for girls. To top it all this had taken place behind his back. He told her, "Your face will be so battered no one will marry you". Looking back she remembers, *"I still remember I was castigated by my father who said with a battered and bruised face, I should not expect to get married. He was furious that I took to boxing - a taboo for women - and he did not have the slightest idea about it. But my passion for the sport had got the better of me and I thank my cousins who coaxed and cajoled my father into eventually giving his nod. I'm happy that I did not let anybody down,"* *Deccan Herald* in 2004.

Undeterred by such happenings, Mary Kom had more important things in mind like 'boxing' and she was determined to prove to the world, she was the best. Mary Kom won the National title the next four years. In the second Asian Women's Championship- Hissar (2003), the Third Asian Women's Championship 2004 in Taiwan, she ruled the world as the best. From 2004 to 2006 Mary Kom won three world titles. 2011 saw Mary Kom, India's 'pocket dynamite' in the 48 kg category beat North Korea's Kim Myong Sim to win the Asian Cup boxing tournament in China. The boxer was going through a tough time as not only was the game on her mind but she also had her young three-year old son going through heart surgery for a hole in the heart. As she puts it, "the determination to win for the nation comes from the mind and to be a perfect mother comes from the heart, but it was not easy", says the young mother.

Mary Kom had never been interested in her studies, she herself says books did not interest her and she has no time for them. It is only recently that she took her Class XII Board Examinations. Mary Kom couldn't get through her HSLC examination from Adimjati High School, Imphal. She did not wish to repeat the year and the National Institute of Open University kept her hopes alive. Possibly her disinterest in academics proved to be a boon for women's boxing. Her low income family background made her more determined to improve. Mary has never taken her position for granted and has invested wisely all her earnings. She has bought a new house and land for her parents, for her brother and sisters she has put away money for their welfare.

Life has not always been a bed of roses for Mary Kom as when she was going for her first Asian Women's Championship, she lost her baggage that contained her passport also. Hearing about the loss her worried parents Tonpu and Saneikham asked her to come back home but Mary Kom was not the one to give up easily. A help came from a local uncle who gave all support to help the young girl. But the trauma of the theft had taken its toll and Mary Kom had to come back empty handed. It was a sad day for Mary Kom but she was not the one to be easily bogged down. So she and other boxers practiced rigorously and soon 'dame fortune' smiled. In 2002, the gold came in Turkey to Mary Kom. Along with the gold medal came $2,500. The medal was the harbinger of a change, a change for the better. Mary Kom returned to a heroes welcome in Imphal. *The North East Sun* has called her the 'Queen of the Ring' after her triumph at Moscow. In 2005 she got another heroes welcome in Sadar Hills Manipur. In the welcome group were gospel singers, Chochan Kongzai, Esther Sitlhou and many more.

Mary Kom is deeply religious and visits the church regularly. Here is one incidence which stands out to show that Mary Kom has a lot of guts and is quick witted. On a Sunday morning when she was on her way to the MB Church service from her SAI colony hostel in Imphal; she had taken a cycle rickshaw. The cycle rickshaw driver thought he would have fun and started teasing her. Mary Kom the fighter that she was, did not take this lying down, she landed a few punches, left, right and centre. The poor rickshaw driver went down crashing before round one ended. He ran for dear life, not waiting for the second round!

Before any bout Mary Kom always prayed to Lord Jesus. According to her, "Seven days without prayer makes one weak". Her life partner K Onkholer, has always supported her in her career and home. When at Hissar, Onkholer had written 'Jesus 100 percent' on Mary Kom's gown as he too feels that God always helps. Mary Kom says, "Jesus is my strength". She always prays before a bout or even after she has knocked someone down.

Mary Kom's positive attitude to life has always helped her to overcome all odds. Her religion, parents, husband and church have always supported her. Often the church and relatives have helped in paying for domestic and international events. At times she has felt low when she has faced international opponents but never to give up easily. Mary Kom has always bounced back; she has full faith in herself and God. As they say when the going gets tough the tough gets going and that is exactly what Mary Kom does?

The World Champion took two years off for her wedding and children. She has twin boys K. Rechungvar Kom and K Khupneivar Kom. When Mary Kom is out of the house on work or training the boys are looked after by the father Onkholer. She definitely misses the two boys but can do her work in peace knowing that they are well looked after. Mary Kom returned to boxing with a will to win. She got her fourth gold medal in AIBA World Championship at Nigboo City in China 2008. Mary Kom defeated her opponent Romania's Stleta Duta by 7-1. The pugilist from India had put all doubts to rest as to who was the champion and to prove it she has also won her fifth gold in 2010. She was definitely the world's best and deserved all the gold she won.

At the National Games, Gauhati Mary Kom was missed. She could not attend the meet due to a tragedy in the family. Her father-in-law, Reikhupthang Kamang Kom, was murdered under mysterious circumstances. He was shot dead by gunmen in a place called Samu Lamlan Kom. He was the village headman and some people whisked him away and afterwards his body was found in Nenglong Tampak. They say a note was found close to the body which said he was given capital punishment as he was going against the interest of the Komrem National Front. Her uncle too died due to cancer somewhere close to the event.

We find that over the years sports people have looked for security in jobs like the banks, railways, police or other public sector undertakings. Today Mary Kom has a job in the police department of Manipur and is an inspector. She lives on the outskirts of Imphal with her husband and two sons. She practices at least four to five hours a day to keep fit. She also coaches young girls from her area. A girl under her care, Nengnei Hat Kom (40 Kg) has won a bronze medal in sub-junior national meet. Mary Kom finds gradually people are coming out to help young boxers. Arzoo. com has offered Mary Kom Rs. 25, 000 per month sponsorship for a year to help for training facilities. She is happy that at last people of the country are taking notice of boxing and recognising her efforts to put India on the world map. She has dreams of setting up a boxing academy for children in Moireng in Manipur. The champion says only a strong body is not enough, we have to have a fighting spirit. And who would know this better than Mary Kom. According to her, her style is to tier out her opponent by making them run around a lot.

The sports people look for recognition of their achievements. Mary Kom too would like the government to appreciate her effort. 'The Boxing Queen' has been awarded the 'Arjuna Award', the prestigious award is given to sportsperson who show outstanding achievements at the international level. However, the 'Khel Ratna' award had been proving to be elusive. Hers is a classic case of official neglect. She says it is only because of ignorance about the sport she is in. The then Arjuna Award Selection Committee Chairman Milkha Singh struck off her name as 'he did not know which sport she competed in'. This has definitely offended the boxer. She almost cries out in pain, "How many more times do I have to win for him and for the country to believe that I deserve the honour"? But finally she did get her Padamshree and the Rajiv Gandhi Khel Ratna award.

Mary Kom was chosen as the 'first ever' amateur boxer to win the "Fighter of the Year" by Women Boxing Archive Network, a premium boxing portal. AIBA, the world governing body for the sports, has got four times women's boxer champion Mary Kom to be one of their brand ambassadors, the others will be from USA and Sweden. This has been done to lend a hand to women's entry in the 2012 Olympic Games. Let us hope and pray that the 2012 Olympics will see Mary Kom with gold, only then will one of her dreams be fulfilled.

21

Ningthou Ching – Thang Khomba and 'Raas-Leela'

Most of us have seen or heard about the *'Raas-Leela'*, the dance story of Krishna with Radha and her *'sakhis'* or friends. *'Raas'* is emotion and *'leela'* is roughly 'play of the dance'. In other words it is 'Dance of Divine Love'.

Ningthou Ching – Thang Khomba (also *Rajarshi Bhagya Chandra, Jai Singh Maharaja*) (1748–1799) was a monarch of the 18th century of Manipur. He is famous for inventing the Raas Leela and bringing in Vaishnavism to Manipur. Bhagya Chandra came to the throne of Manipur in 1759 as his father Samjai Khurai-Lakpa and grandfather Pamheiba who made Hinduism the official religion, were killed by his uncle Chitsai (the villain of the story). Soon after Bhagya Chandra came to the throne in 1762, Manipur was attacked by the Burmese and the Burmese they say were helped by Chitsai to overthrow the throne. Bhagya Chandra had to flee with his Queen and some loyal followers to Assam where they lived under the protection of the Ahom ruler King Rajesvara.

Life was not easy for Bhagya Chandra as his uncle Chitsai wrote to King Rajeshwara that the man taking refuge in his kingdom was a fraud and not the actual Bhagya Chandra. King Rajeshwara got influenced by this letter and doubts started cropping up in his mind. They say King Bhagya Chandra had supernatural powers and King Rajeshwara decided to test him and Bhagya Chandra was asked to capture an elephant unarmed.

Bhagya Chandra prayed to Lord Krishna to help and guide him. Lord Krishna appeared to Bhagya Chandra in his dream and asked him to enter the arena with a garland and 'japa' beads or shall we say 'rosary' beads. Krishna stated that he, Bhagya Chandra would be the sole king of Manipur but after reclaiming the kingdom he would have to put up an idol of Krishna. The deity Krishna would have to be cut from an old jack fruit tree found on the slopes of the Kaina Hills. After installation of the deity the King had to arrange for a performance of *'Raas-Leela'*, in which Krishna would be worshipped with song and dance. In his dreams Bhagya Chandra also received the plan on how to perform the *'Raas-Leela'*.

When Bhagya Chandra went to meet the elephant he found Lord Krishna sitting on the elephant as his 'mahout' or owner, only Bhagya Chandra could see Lord Krishna. The elephant at first charged but the moment he saw King Bhagya Chandra he knelt down and Bhagya Chandra garlanded Lord Krishna which to the others seemed as if he was garlanding the elephant and mounted it and rode through the cheering crowd. King Rajeshvara was amazed to see this and apologised for having doubted King Bhagya Chandra.

Later the Ahom King Rajeshvara helped the Manipuri king to regain his throne. King Rajeshvara sent Ahom soldiers with King Bhagya Chandra to fight the forces of Chitsai and conquer back the throne of Manipur. The first attempt made in 1767 to regain the throne was unsuccessful as they were attacked by Naga tribes and poisonous snakes. The second attempt proved to be successful. King Bhagya Chandra consolidated his empire and brought unity amongst his people. In 1773 Bhagya Chandra was reinstated as *Ningthou* (meaning King) of Manipur.

Bhagya Chandra had not been able to install the idol of Lord Krishna, possibly because of Burmese invasions. He was one day reminded of this. A tribal woman once came to the royal palace and wanted to meet the king as she had a message for the king. The message was that a young boy had come to her and asked her to give the message which was - the boy was very annoyed as King Bhagya Chandra had not kept his promise. The king realised the boy was none other than Lord Krishna. So the king went with the woman to the Kaina Hills to recognise the jackfruit tree Lord Krishna had talked about. The tree was cut and statues were made of Krishna but Bhagya Chandra was not happy as these idols or statues were not exactly the one of his dreams. Though these idols were installed yet the search for the exact idol was still on. Finally, there was one statue which matched the one of his dreams. With a lot of fanfare on a full moon day in 1776 it was installed. The king with his kingdom was dedicated to Krishna. Devotion to Krishna became the cultural life of the Manipuri people. Most became Vaishnavs or devotees of Lord Krishna. Even today they call themselves Manipuri Vaishnavs.

The first performance of *'Raas-Leela'* was held in 1779. After the *'sthapana'* or installation of the *'murti'* or idol of Lord Krishna what was left was the performance of the *'Raas-Leela'*. The planning of the dance, music and costumes had to be done and the King himself took great interest and guided his people. Grace, artistic and spirituality are the hallmarks of the *'Raas-Leela'*. The dance had to be performed in a 'Raas Mandela' or a special theatre where Krishna would be the centre of the dance. During this time there was no idol of Krishna's consort Radha. The problem came as to who would be Radha in the play. Finally, it was decided that it would be the beautiful young princess Bimbavati. Bhagya Chandra himself decided to be one of the 'mridang' or drum players to satisfy Lord Krishna. Even today *'Raas-Leela'* is performed by first praying to Lord Krishna on behalf of Bhagya Chandra. Princess Bimbavati after the *'Raas-Leela'* was so influenced by the dance that she renounced the world and spent the rest of her life singing Lord Krishna's name. She was called 'Sija Lairobi' or the princess who owned the Lord. The golden deity of Radha at the Govindji temple at Kangla resembles her.

In 1798 after ruling for 39 years as the King of Manipur, Bhagya Chandra abdicated the throne to his eldest son Labanya Chandra and went away to Murshidabad (West Bengal) on a pilgrimage. King Bhagya Chandra was a disciple of Srila Narottama Dasa Thakur and was greatly influenced by him. In 1798-1799 he died and his body was cremated in Murshidabad. Bhagya Chandra wanted one portion of his ashes to be brought back to Manipur and the other portion be taken to Navadwip, the native place of Chaitanya Mahaprabhu. Some Brahmins have called him*'Rajarshi'* or a sage in the form of a king.

The dance form of *'Raas-Leela'* which Raja Bhagya Chandra created has become the classical dance form of Manipur. During his reign, there was resurgence of the arts in Manipur and some very glorious art traditions were established then. The art of Manipur was so much a part of the society's tradition, that even members of the royal family took part in these rituals. It was not unusual to see a Queen dance at the same venue as commoners. The people believed that dance and music were offerings to God and position and caste were not barriers, the worship of Vishnu remains vital to the people of Manipur.

Today we have the 'Bhagya Chandra Festival of Classical Dance' at Shri Shri Govindji Temple complex at Kangla between 27th and 30th November every year.

'Govindai Nomo' or my respects to Govinda.

22

Princess Thoibi

"A Tale of Love

He loved too well, but not wisely".

Shakespeare: Othello.

The story of Thoibi and her love Khamba is well-known in Manipur and has occupied centrestage since the 15th century. The tale, they say, was written almost five hundred years before Romeo and Juliet of Europe. The story is as emotional as Romeo and Juliet and as tragic. It is said that about thousand of years ago there was a kingdom in Manipur called Moirang on the banks of the great Logtak lake; the lake lies roughly about ninety kilometers south of Imphal. (The lake is five kilometers wide and eight kilometers long. The name is possibly from the Chinese word Meung-kha-la (Meung=Land; Kha=Lake; La=Wide). Khamba was a prince of the previously routed Khumal Royal family. Khamba fell in love with Thoibi - a princess of the Moirang clan. Thoibi is considered to be the reincarnation of the rice-spirit mother Phou-ouibi, goddess of Manipur, and worshipped as a woman of sustenance.

One of the ministers of the King had a daughter called Khamnu and a son named Khamba. The minister had saved the life of the

Chief Minister from a premature death. As a reward the minister wanted his daughter Khamnu to be married to the Chief Minister's son Feiroijomba. The Chief Minister agreed, but fate had other things in store. Both Feiroijomba and his father, the Chief Minister were struck with amnesia and did not remember the promise.

Very soon the minister died and poor Khamnu and Khamba went through difficult days, after their father's death they were left under the care of their maternal uncle. The uncle was not too happy to see them. Khamba had to leave his studies and had to work as a mil kman. But to the envy of his friends he was an excellent sportsman. Life became so difficult that they had to leave their home and take shelter in the Hills.

A Naga chief took pity on them and gave them shelter. The brother and sister had to work very hard in the forest. Khamba would cut trees in the forest the whole day and Khamnu would go and sell it in the village market. It is during these market trips Khamnu chanced to meet Thoibi. Thoibi was the daughter of the crown prince; she with her maids-in-waiting would often visit the market place to shop.

One day Khamnu loaded with firewood was staggering into the market place when Thoibi saw her. Thoibi being tender hearted took pity on Khamnu and asked her to live with her in her palace. Khamnu was tempted to do so, but when she remembered her brother Khamba who would be all alone in the forest she gave up the idea of a luxurious life in the palace. Thoibi was disappointed at this but decided to give her a few gifts. Among the gifts was an expensive shawl, the shawl was a gift to Thoibi from an admirer, he was Nongban one of the knights of the king. Khamnu went back home and showed the shawl to her brother Khamba who was happy with the gift and the person who had gifted it.

One day Khamnu went with Thoibi and her maids-in-waiting fishing in the Logtak lake. All were very happy and enjoying each others company in the boat as it rocked gently in the water. They could hear someone playing the flute from a distance and gradually the noise of the flute came very close and the girls realised it was Khamba. The boat he was travelling got entangled into the fishing nets spread for Thoibi. Immediately, the maids-in-waiting captured Khamba and his boat. There was a law which said that when a royalty was in the waters of Logtak no one else could come in and Khamba had violated the rules. The scandalised maids tied up

Khamba as he was a law breaker. Khamnu told Thoibi that it was her brother Khamba and not a rogue as they thought him to be. Thoibi ordered his release and as soon as she saw Khamba they both fell madly in love.

Nongban, (the man who had earlier gifted Thoibi a shawl which she had given away to Khamnu) was waiting to woo Thoibi back and got an opportunity to win her back. There was a wrestling match on and Nongban was in full form as he made short work of his opponents. As Nongban was about to see himself the winner he found there was someone who threw down the gauntlet, it was Khamba who stepped into the arena. Khamba's foster father the Naga chief had taught him in life that a challenge had to be met and not to be side stepped. Khamba easily defeated Nongban even though he was very young. Thoibi's father the crown prince was very happy with Khamba and conferred the title of nobility on him. The crown prince asked Khamba his father's name and unfortunately Khamba did not know it as Khamnu had hidden this from Khamba. At this moment of glory Khamnu told all the name of their father and to the Chief Minister reminded him of his promise to wed her to his son. The Chief Minister now remembered the promise he had made to his friend. He called his son and got Khamnu married to him. Finally, a promise had been kept!

Nongban the man who had been spurned by Thoibi was waiting for an opportunity to hit back. He turned into a Maiba, a priestly medium. A Maiba could foretell the future. The message was that a red bull was roaming the Hills and had to be tamed, otherwise famine and death would overtake the land. The bull was caught and brought to the arena. Nongban and Khamba vied with each other to tame him. Nongban won the toss and took the first turn to capture the bull but was defeated and ran away in shame. Khamba came into the arena and lassoed the bull, the bull unused to being tied down charged at Khamba. Khamba did something unusual, he whispered something unusual and a transformation came over the bull. The animal started nuzzling Khamba and Khamnu as if it was happy to see the brother and sister. It so happened that it was the same bull that Khamnu had let loose into the forest when she and her brother had gone away to the jungles. Khamba begged the king to let the animal free and not sacrifice it to propitiate the gods. The king granted the favour, and let it be known to the people that the bull be treated like a 'god' instead of a 'demon'.

Thoibi had started weaving a shawl for Khamba and was lost in her love for Khamba. Her father accompanied by Nongban happened to pass by her Palace and admired it. Her father the Jubaraj or the crown prince asked for the shawl but Thoibi could not give it as this one was meant for her love that is Khamba. She promised to make a better one for her father. After some days, Thoibi met Khamba on the banks of the Logtak Lake at night and presented him the shawl, as she lovingly put it around him the ever watchful Nongban saw this and reported the matter to the crown prince or Thoibi's father. The father at first did not believe him and thought Nongban was plain jealous. At the arrow shooting festival when Khamba met Thoibi's father he had the same shawl on. The angry father felt belittled and in a fit of rage he banished his daughter to Burma (now Myanmar).

The crown prince wanted to dispose off Khamba so he got an elephant to trample him. Fortunes were in Khamba's favour as the elephant turned out to be his old playmate of the Hills, together they had grown up and the elephant remembered their shared memories. He picked up Khamba on his back and rushed to the forests in the darkness of night. Khamba went off to the jungles towards Burma looking for his love; sometimes in loneliness he played his flute. It was this flute which Thoibi heard and ran towards the jungle to meet her beloved Khamba. They met and decided to stay in the jungle in hiding.

In the meantime, Thoibi's father repented his action and sent Nongban to fetch Thoibi, but by that time Thoibi had already fled to the jungles. Nongban had to return empty handed and had to tell the father that Thoibi was nowhere to be found. The crown prince or jubaraj now was a wiser man and appreciated the uniqueness of Khamba. The father realised that if his daughter, a girl from a noble family with high intelligence could love Khamba then Khamba had to be special. He was no common man. The father decided that a duel should take place between Nongban and Khamba and the winner would get Thoibi's hand.

When all this talk was going on about the duel and the decision had been sent to the King there appeared a man-eater, a tiger prowling around the village. The problem seemed to get a solution; it was that whoever killed the tiger would be declared the winner. In the combat between man and tiger Nongban lost and Khamba won. Nongban died a hero's death and accepted the fact that Khamba was a better warrior and definitely deserved Thoibi. The day of the wedding was set and Khamba and Thoibi became husband and wife. For sometime they lived happily together. Khamba's love for Thoibi was so great that often he would flaunt it in front of his friends. One of the friends suggested he should test his love. So after a few years of happiness Khamba decided to test Thoibi's love. He told Thoibi that he had to go away for a few days to Burma on some work. The unsuspecting Thoibi bid farewell to Khamba but could not sleep in the night. Suddenly, she found a man had entered her room and jumping up she caught hold of a spear and pierced his heart. Khamba fell down calling out her name. By the time Thoibi realised this, it was too late and remorse took over, she could not bear the pain and killed herself.

The Khamba-Thoibi story has been told and retold and has seen many changes. No two stories are the same. The story forms one of the most touching ballets. The Khamba-Thoibi dance is a duet of male and female partners, a dance of dedication to the deity 'Thangjing' of Morang. It is believed that Khamba and Thoibi danced in front of the deity for peace and prosperity in the village. The ballad has three parts, *Loi Kum* (exile), *Loi kab* (return) and *the tragedy*. Most often the tragedy is not enacted as the Manipuris feel it brings bad luck.

In the months of May and June the people pray to 'Omang Lai Haraoba', the forest God, with much happiness. All lovers dance the Khamba-Thoibi dance as they feel their desires and wishes will come true. The dance begins and ends with the dancers offering fruits and sweets to the deity. Such is the power of Khamba –Thoibi in the life of the Manipuris.

23

Rev William Pettigrew

William Pettigrew was born in Scotland but at heart was a 'Meitei' or a Manipuri. He loved the land and its people as his own. William was born on 5th January, 1859 and had his education from Livingstone College, London. William Pettigrew was a good Christian who wanted to spread the message of the Lord. Young William started his early career in East Bengal, now Bangladesh under the Arlington Aborigines Mission; and later joined the American Baptist Church at Sibsagar in 1896.

William Pettigrew first arrived in Silchar (Assam) in 1891 at the young age of twenty. He could not go to Manipur as the place was going through turbulent times politically. The British government then thought it prudent to keep him away from Manipur. So for some time he stayed in Silchar. William utilised his time in Silchar well by learning Bengali and Manipuri. After the British conquered Manipur, William Pettigrew was given an opportunity to spread Christianity here. 6th February 1894 saw William Pettigrew landing in Imphal. This became an important day in the history of spreading Christianity in Manipur. He set up a school for the Hindus but met with a lot of resistance from the locals and so had to move out of Imphal. The Political Agent Major Maxwell advised him to leave

Imphal and shift to the North of Manipur and work among the Kukis and Nagas. The chosen place was at Ukhrul where a school came up. The first Kukis (from North Nagaland) were Nehseh Chongloi from Makui followed by Ngulhao Thomsong. Both came from Nagaland but helped set up churches in Ukhrul in Manipur. William Pettigrew was a man with a vision and wanted all the Manipuris to come together through their own language. When you are in a foreign land people really appreciate a person if he knows the local language well. William Pettigrew's knowledge of Bengali and Manipuri came in very handy and soon a rapport developed between the Manipuris and the Englishmen.

A word about the importance of 'Bengali' in the Manipuri language. For many years Bengali was the medium of instruction in Manipur, it was William Pettigrew who realised that Manipuri should be the medium of instruction. He felt that the people of Manipur should have their own script. He tried reviving the ancient Meitei script which today the modern Manipuris find archaic, the archaic Meitei script, is comparable to the Thai script. The Manipuri Language belongs to Kuki-Chin group of Sino-Tibetan languages. With the arrival of the British, the script was modified and Bengali script started being used. The Bengali script is being still used in spite of the efforts by the Meiti loyalist to change to the Meitei script. William Pettigrew was an intelligent and mature person so he did not want to upset the Bengalis by stopping the Bengali medium of instruction. Instead he worked on the Manipuri medium of teaching and he quietly asked the state authorities to allow him to open a school. A lower primary level class was started with Manipuri as the medium of instruction. The school by the river at Morangkhom still bears his name and was a success as two more schools were opened at Tera-keithen and Thangmeiband. William Pettigrew wrote a primary text book which was later followed by other primary text books. He always wanted to excel and was always on the look out for new words in Manipuri and match them with their counterparts in English. In other words he had started compiling for English to Manipuri dictionary. This was followed by English to Manipuri handbook which was much appreciated by the British who wanted to communicate with their subordinates and attendants. The Manipuris also found it convenient to converse with the British. William Pettigrew wrote about the history of the 'Meiteis' which today unfortunately has been lost and cannot be found. William Pettigrew never forgot his education work while trying to improve the linguistic studies.

He continued to open primary schools with Manipuri as the medium of instruction. The Manipuri State Authorities appreciated the good work done by William Pettigrew and appointed him an Honorary Inspector of Schools.

During this period of spreading education the British government decided that only Christianity should be preached among the Hindus. It was later realised that preaching of Christianity was the main motive. Education was only a cover to protect the British, the main motive being to spread Christianity. William Pettigrew's first convert was young boy called Porom Singh and news about this spread like wildfire in the hill areas. Porom Singh was born somewhere around 1885 in the village of Phayeng. His father, Tambour was a doctor or a '*vaid*' as they say, and his mother, Tonu, died when he was still young. The father left the son with William Pettigrew as he was finding it difficult looking after a 'motherless' child. Whatever the reason, Porom Singh lived with the Missionary and went to school from here. When William Pettigrew left Imphal, Porom Singh became his right hand man in Ukhrul, he was more like a son to William Pettigrew. Circumstances had become so bad that William Pettigrew had to leave Imphal and shift to Ukhrul. He was offered Senvon village along with Mao Songsong and Hunphung (Ukhrul). But he did not receive permission to come to the village and preach the gospel from the chief of Senvon and Mao Songsong, so he went to Ukhrul. Porom Singh helped William Pettigrew to raise a labour force for the British army. Later he went to France and worked with dedication there. In 1916 Porom Singh married Kasuni, a Tangkhul Naga. Their son Dr Koireng Singh is a famous name in Manipur. Porom Singh later became a teacher and then the Head Master of the Ukhrul School.

The first inter-tribal marriage took place between Ruichumhao and K Yanghu from Kom tribe and this was encouraged by William Pettigrew. Incidentally Mary Kom the boxer also belongs to the same tribe. In the words of Prof Lal Dena, "Had he (Pettigrew) received that permission from the then chief of Senvon the religious and political history of the Chin-Kuki-Mizo tribes might definitely have taken a different turn".

The conversion of the Manipuri Hindus was the main goal of the British, especially William Pettigrew's. Since the Tangkhul Nagas were mostly animists and technically they did not come under the laws of banning conversion of Hindus, this made things easy for

William Pettigrew as he could continue preaching and progress with his missionary work, specially opening schools which were his passion. The Tangkhul Nagas were mostly head hunters and lived in villages which were mostly bordering Upper Burma. Around 1895, a village was attacked and about one hundred and forty heads were cut off and carried away. It was after this that William Pettigrew in October 1895 landed in Ukhrul and started his Mission School in 1896. This school was called No. 12 as this was the twelfth one. William Pettigrew faced the same problems again and again, that is no children in schools. One day he met Raihao, the village chief, and requested permission to open a school in his area. The chief was a little unwilling as he was superstitious and did not want to send the children to school. He told the Rev that the Tangkhul script was written on animal skin and a dog had taken it away. Since the script was not available it was foolish to even think of education, was the village chief's opinion. The quick-witted clergy man replied that he had just met the dog and had brought back the animal script to them. The chief realised that there was no way out and very reluctantly gave permission. The villagers with a lot of vacillation sent their children to school but attendance was poor and all requests made by the clergy man fell on deaf ears. So the Political Agent's help was sought and by order thirty students had to be sent to school. However chief Raihao controlled the school and also was the interpreter for the children as without the chief, the children refused to go to school. In 1896 William Pettigrew taught his first class of thirty students in a hut in Ukhrul. This was of great historical importance as it marked the beginning of modern education in the history of Tangkhul Nagas. William Pettigrew's pioneering work has left a mark on the Tangkhul Nagas and has helped change many a life in Manipur.

It was only in 1899 that the students of Ukhrul Mission School started learning English.

But it was found that the Political Agents had to use force many a times and punish the chiefs of villages if the children did not come. Sometimes the chiefs themselves would enroll to help the school. But in spite of all these efforts regular attendance could not be had. At times William Pettigrew had to cajole them with sweets, clothes and sometimes with pictures. This seemed to be a regular feature to attract students. Even today we sometimes find the same method being followed in areas where the school drop out rate is high, for example a snack or a midday meal like a 'samosa' or 'aloo-puri' attracts students especially in the Primary sections.

In 1897 William Pettigrew went to Calcutta to get married. He married Alice Gorehome in the Lower Baptist Church. By the time William Pettigrew returned to Ukhrul he found it had undergone many changes, the tribals were protesting against the spread of Christianity, fearing their own animistic religion was fading away. News about this spread to Imphal and the Political Agent ordered the chief to give up coming to school everyday, instead he should look into the administration of the village. But this did not mean the number of children would go down. Two teachers were employed, one a Meitei and the other an Assamese. The state gave financial support to help in the running of the school and to ensure that the work did not suffer. From 1896 to 1916, that is for almost twenty years the Reverend and his wife lived in isolation praying and singing the hymn, 'send the light, the gospel light' hoping that people would come into their fold. Up to 1915 the only church at Ukhrul had about sixty to sixty-three members, the bulk being Tangkhul Nagas. These people who lived in isolation somewhat prospered in agriculture. It was William Pettigrew who brought in the cultivation of the humble potatoes in the Hills here.

The year 1913-1914 saw William Pettigrew and his wife take long leave. When they came back in 1915, their school in Ukhrul had petitions for them to come and set up schools and help organise them. Both the clergy man and his wife felt that their prayers had been answered, after a wait of almost twenty years that finally people had started coming to church. In 1917 the Kukis, Kon, Anal and Kabui Nagas sent a petition to allow the headquarters of the Mission Church to be shifted from Ukhrul to a more central part of the state. It is presently located at Kangpokpi on the outskirts of Imphal, the capital. So in this way the whole of the North East was opened to Christianity.

William Pettigrew was also made the administrator and gradually education progressed in the Hills. In 1910 -1911 William Pettigrew was made the Superintendent of Enumeration in the Ukhrul area for the country's first census. No one else knew the Tangkhul dialect as well as William Pettigrew – an outsider! The Reverend, who had a flair for languages, had written two books in Tangkhul, a primer for children and a Bible in the Tangkhul dialect. Later he wrote a Bible in Thado, the Kuki dialect too.

During World War I William Pettigrew, a loyal British citizen helped the motherland that is England in as many ways as he could. He had the tribal people enlisted to work for the labour force. He himself joined the army as a Captain. When William Pettigrew came back to Manipur after the War the Maharaja allowed him to shift to Kangpokpi which is about twenty five miles north of Imphal. This was close to Ukhrul. Later the Reverend started a dispensary which today has grown into a hospital. William Pettigrew's Christian heart made him open a leper asylum too.

William Pettigrew spent all his life in learning new languages and writing about the history of the places and people he lived with. His endeavours were appreciated by the Asiatic Society of Bengal and in 1930, he was made a member of the organisation. In 1933 the General Secretary of the Society called his work a 'priceless accomplishment' which if not recorded would be a loss to the linguistic world. The Director of Linguistic Research, Grierson encouraged William Pettigrew to do intense research in the Meitei script. He was helped by a Meitei, Yamjao Singh from the Imphal Press. William Pettigrew first found the Meitei script on ancient coins, stone slabs and copper plates and started collecting material for his work on the 'Metei' script.

All this had to be left as Lady Pettigrew fell sick and in 1943, the couple had to leave for America for medical support. She did not recover and after all this William Pettigrew never returned to Manipur. The Meteis have never forgotten William Pettigrew; even in 1965 when the Kukis were celebrating the 'Golden jubilee' of the Baptist Church, they remembered William Pettigrew. Some village elders had fond memories of him and had the same respect for him as we have for Mahatma Gandhi. The Manipuris remember him for reviving the Meitei language. He became a true Meitei without any political biases. This is the life story of William Pettigrew a man born with a vision, a man who thought of others first. He was instrumental in bringing the Manipuri people together with his linguistic skills and his efforts are still appreciated.

Meghalaya

Abode of the Clouds

Meghalaya, or translating into Sanskrit means 'Abode of the clouds' stands up to its name. The Britishers called it 'Scotland of the east'. When I first saw the place, nature seemed to be at her the best. Geographically, Meghalaya has the Brahmaputra valley in the north and Bangladesh in the south. It is also called the Shillong or Meghalaya plateau, belonging to the oldest rock formations of India. The Shillong plateau is an extension of the Peninsular India. The state gets abundant rainfall; one of the highest rainfall areas is Cherrapunjee. Meghalaya has rivers, plateaus, Hills and a climate worth envying. Such a beautiful place also has interesting myths about itself. Most of these are transmitted orally from generation to generation. Some of them are like fairy tales. Most of these myths centre on the creation of the earth and water and the origin of tribes. Some of the Khasi and Jaintia stories are about celestial origin. Shillong, the capital has many legends about its name, some say it originated from a handsome man called Shylong.

Some of the stories go like this.

- Long, long time ago, there were sixteen families in heaven, who had the privilege of coming down to earth by a golden staircase on 'Sohpetheng' or the 'the navel of heaven', the place they came to watch the Umiam lake. Seven of these families wanted to live on earth in the Hills and God granted their wish, and the staircase was removed and so the seven families had to live on earth. They say the Khasis Pnar originated from these seven families. The nine families that remained in Heaven are still remembered by the Khasis.

- They say the name Shillong - the capital city - came from a woman who frequently came out of a cave called 'Krem Marai' which is not very far from Shillong Peak. One day a young man dared to go and meet her, he was scared so he put in a pole with a bouquet of flowers tied to it. The young girl came out of the cave to smell the flowers and the young man could catch her hand, the maiden was the daughter of the Shillong deity. Her name was '*Pahsyntiew*' or 'Lured by Flowers'. She married the young man and two boys and a girl were born to them.
- The Jaintias folklores say that God first created three sisters who were the sun, water and air. Next came 'Fire' who was the brother to these sisters. Another Jaintia story says that goddess 'Bei Rymnaw' requested God to make the earth a place worthy of living and it became so beautiful that servants of God became jealous and sent down animals to fight with each other. To bring peace and harmony the 'Seven Families' from the sky were sent to rule the animals on earth.
- Garos believe that at first the earth was a watery planet completely dark. God then made the Sun and the Moon and sent in air to fill the empty space, later came the clouds and vegetation. Animals followed and the monkey was the first one to arrive. With the help of the Sun the water was dried up at first. Later the rivers were made to flow and next came the rain. After all this God created 'Sani'and 'Muni' or man and woman. The Garos are descendents of 'Sani' and 'Muni'.

Meghalaya is the home to the Khasis, the Jaintias and the Garos. The place is also known to be the earliest known group of settlers in the Indian sub- continent; they were the Austroloid Monkhemer race. The Khasis are based in central Meghalaya, the Garos in the western and the Jaintias on the eastern side. The Jaintias are also known as Pnars, the Khasis living in the footHills are called Bhois. The Khasis, Jaintia, Bhoi, were jointly known as the Hynniewtrep people and they live in east Meghalaya, they are from the Austroloid Monkhmer group. The Garos from the Garo Hills belong to the Bodo group of the Tibeto-Burman group. The Garos like being called Achiks and the area they stay is called Achik land. All three tribes, the Khasi, Garo and Jaintia earlier had their own kingdoms, it was only later they came under the British rule in the 19th century; Meghalaya became a part of Assam in 1835. When Bengal was portioned into two in 1905 by Lord Curzon, the then Governor General of India, Meghalaya became a part of 'East Bengal and Assam', later in 1912 the partition was reversed and Meghalaya became a part of Assam. After independence in 1947 Meghalaya was given independent autonomous state within Assam, the people of Meghalaya were not too happy with the state of affairs and were longing for complete statehood. Things got worse when Assam introduced Assamese as the state language which the tribal people of Meghalaya did not know. The centre realised the situation and finally on 21st January, 1972, Meghalaya became an independent state. It was a victory which was done amicably, only through peaceful negotiations.

The Khasis earlier had twenty-five or so independent kingdoms in the 16th century; they came under the control of the British later. There was constant fighting amongst the different chiefdoms, and so it was easy for the British to take control over these areas and soon the British stopped all trading activities amongst the tribes and fortified their positions. The enmity ended when a road was built to connect Calcutta with the Brahamaputra valley. Treaties were signed which allowed the Khasi kingdom autonomy freedom from paying taxes. In 1947, the tribal region autonomous body was answerable only to the Governor of Assam.

The Garos originally came from Tibet; they travelled to Cooch Bihar and Dhubri in Assam, and settled along the Brahamaputra valley. The first Garo kingdom started here and the first king was Abrasen. In the later part of the 18th century the British East India Company established contact with the Garos after getting the Diwani of Bengal from the Mughals. The British took over all the small states but their internal administration was not disturbed. Later on after independence in 1979 the Garo Hills was made into two districts, the East and West Garo Hills.

The Jaintias belong to the Jaintia Hills and are also known as Stunga Kingdom. The villages of a particular area were also called '*elekas*'. The chief of such '*elakas*' was called 'Doloi', the 'Doloi' was elected by the older villagers, the 'Doloi' could be removed from office if found inefficient or immoral. A group of such '*elakas*' made a kingdom, the 'Jaintia Syiemship'. The chief of such kingdom was the Raja. The 'Doloi' of different areas represented the people in the Raja's Durbar. This old setup still exists without the Raja of course. Earlier, the Jaintia Hills were called '*Ka Ri Khadar Doloi.*' or the 'Land of the Twelve Tribal Chiefs'. The British abolished the 'Syiemship' or 'Kingship' of the Jaintia Hills but kept the concept of 'Doloi' and village headman or 'Waheh Chonong'. The British brought the whole area of the Jaintia Hills under their control. In 1952, the 'District Council' concept was introduced in these hilly regions, both the Khasi and Jaintia Hills were given different district councils. In 1972 when Meghalaya became a state the whole area came under one administrative unit. The most important town of the Jaintia Hills is Jowai. Driving from Shillong to Jowai one passes through green meadows, forests of oak and pine trees, with meandering river Myntdu to give you company.

The Khasis, the Jaintias and the Garos have a matrilineal society where descent is traced through the mother; the father also has an important role to play in the material life of the people. David Roy, the then political agent had this to say about the Khasis, "A man is the defender of the woman, but the woman is the keeper of his trust". Inheritance of property in the Khasi society goes to the youngest daughter or 'Ka Khadduh', if she dies without a daughter then the ancestral property goes to the next elder sister. Amongst the 'War Khasis' the property is divided amongst the children equally, but amongst the 'War Jaintias' only the female children get the property.

The staple food of the Khasis is rice with fish and meat. The Garos' main meal is of rice with onions, capsicum and salt. The Garos also like eating meat. Most of the hill areas brew their own spirits, either from rice or other foodgrains. Most of the Khasis of today are Christians but earlier they believed in the Supreme Being or the Creator 'U Blei Nongthaw' and under him were other deities like water, mountains or Mother Nature. Marriage within the clan is taboo and in the traditional marriage rings and betel-nuts are exchanged but in Christian families marriage is a civil contract. Death is mourned not only by the family but the entire community, earlier the bodies were cremated but with the coming of Christianity they are now buried. Meghalaya has agriculture as main occupation, the people are mostly farmers. Though it has deposits of minerals like coal, limestone and granite there are not too many industries as yet.

Meghalaya is a tourist's paradise and is famous for various kinds of butterflies; the most beautiful species is called the 'Kaiser-i-Hind'. Shillong has many parks and lakes in and around the city. Cherrapunjee has historic past as it was the first outpost of the British, Sohra is the original Khasi name for Cherrapunjee, it is one of the rainiest place in the world and is sixty odd kilometres away from Shillong. Cherrapunjee has deep gorges and massive water falls, 'Hohsngithiang Falls' being the famous one. Cherrapunjee also has limestone caves. As one drives around the state, we find a number of monoliths and table stones, they are memorials for the ashes of the dead or commemorating important events. The upright stones or monoliths that we see are those of men, sometimes they are about six meters in height.

24

U Kiang Nongbah

"Freedom is the most important factor of a human's life, and a country without freedom cannot be claimed to be even alive".

– U Kiang Nongbah

U Kiangn Nongbah was a Jaintia martyr who fought against the British in what is called India's first war of independence, and gave up his life for his people.

Some incidents which led to the uprising were the following:

Raja Ram Singh from the Jaintia Hills had entered into an agreement with the British run East India Company, but unfortunately died in 1832. His grand-nephew Rajendra Singh, a young boy of seventeen years succeeded him to the throne. The British Governor General's Agent TC Robertson saw this change of kings as an opportunity to take over the kingdom. He insisted the agreement had become invalid with the death of the old king Raja Ram Singh. Robertson now suggested that a sum of Rs. 10,000/ be taken from the new Raja, but the new Raja refused to pay as he felt it was a 'breach of contract'. Rajendra Singh said that the revenue which came to him was not too much as according to the Khasi tradition; the King could not levy taxes on the people. Robertson tried to take up the issue with the Calcutta authorities but it seems he did not become successful as Raja Rajendra Singh stood his ground and refused to give in. All Robertson could do was to wait for an opportunity to hit back. And such an opportunity did come. They say in 1832 four people of the British government were captured by the Raja of Goba, who was a petty Chieftain supported by the Jaintia Raja. According to the legend three of these men were sacrificed at the altar of Goddess Kali, the temple was within the territory of the Raja of Goba, and the fourth man managed to escape and informed the British about the horrible incident.

Robertson's opportune moment to take revenge had come; he at once held the Jaintia Raja responsible for the heinous crime as the Raja of Goba was under the protection of the Jaintia kings. Robertson now insisted Rajendra Singh, arrest those involved in the killing of the British subjects and that the Raja of Goba be arrested and handed over to the British government. Robertson suggested that the British government should arrest Rajendra Singh in case he failed to apprehend the culprits. Robertson even had a replacement ready to replace Raja Rajendra Singh. A lot of letters kept going up and down until one fine day the British took an unjustified step of confiscating the Jaintia Raja's property in the plains of Surma Valley which was also known as the Jaintia Parganas. The Jaintia Raja was successful in capturing the offenders who had committed the crime and delivered them to the British but the British refused to let go the opportune moment. Rajendra Singh refused to give up his territory in the plains and retire to the Hills, finally all his property was confiscated by the British. After this there was a lull for a short while. A young man who was greatly affected by these stories was U Kiang Nongbah. Though indirectly related to the uprising, the fact that their Raja was wrongly deposed left a deep impression on the minds of the people. In the first rebellion U Kiang Nongbah kept his identity a secret as he was a shrewd organiser.

The 'Doloiship' type of government was allowed by the British and all they wanted initially as a token was a 'he goat'. Very soon of course the peace all around was disturbed as the Synteng people broke into open rebellion. One of the immediate causes was a house tax levied by the British and it was followed by an income tax imposed by the Department of Imperial Finance, British India.

The major rebellion that followed was of 1862-1864, the people of the Jaintia Hills took up arms to expel the British. It was a planned movement by the Hill tribe groups, these people wanted to protect their identity and U Kiang Nongbah was the chosen leader, he was a commoner without any formal education, but he had the presence of mind to get the people together. The Chieftains also joined in and supported U Kiang Nongbah. In 1861 at a meeting of the tribes at Syntu Ksiar near Jowai, the tribal people decided to throw out the British and install the Raja back to the throne. When it was decided that U Kiang Nongbah would be their leader someone from the crowd asked whether he, U Kiang Nongbah could show why he was to be their leader, U Kiang Nongbah without thinking dived into the cold waters of Syntu Kisar and came up with a plant which had three branches, the Oracles found this auspicious and said that U Kiang Nongbah was the right choice. So after consultations the priests and oracles were definite it was U Kiang Nongbah who was the chosen one and once this important decision was taken U Kiang Nongbah started his work. He went from village to village talking about the situation and to protest against the British rule, he had to organise a military force to tackle the British. Soon durbars were held secretly and so forth the Jaintia Hills were abuzz with the news that U Kiang Nongbah had started a movement, the Dolois too joined in, messengers were sent in different directions to far off areas. Though swords and shields were banned by the British it was U Kiang Nongbah's insistence the people armed themselves with traditional materials. He realised that a disciplined fighting force was the need of the hour. U Kiang Nongbah and his men started 'guerrilla' tactics through ambushes. U Kiang Nongbah, being an intelligent man, realised that their failure was due to lack of a leader and organisation skills.

At the annual dancing festival, held on 28th December 1861 preparation was on in full swing and this became a cover for the battle preparation. The Jaintia's participated in a dance called the 'Pastieh' in which the dancers had swords and shields and were depicting a theme of warriors returning home from a raid. The British had got to know about it and had sent forces as a preventive measure. The British sent a Khasi officer from the British side - U Solomon took away all the weapons and closed down the dancing. U Kiang Nongbah asked the people not to react as soon the moment to strike back would come, so a disaster was averted.

Another incident which took place was a cremation procession that was stopped near a police station and this angered the people as religious sentiments were hurt. A funeral was stopped as cremation of bodies in the old cremation ground was banned. U K Nongbah's prediction that the British were out to destroy the tribal culture was coming to be true. Now an attack on the police station took place and both parties met with damages. The British found the enemies very tenacious and the fights continued for some time. This uprising was called the 'Synteng Rebellion' and was a result of the taxes and the religious practices being stopped by the police. Time had come to retaliate so the villagers put up barricades outside the village, the grains were carefully stored away and women, children and the old men sent into the jungles. The men were now ready to attack. On 17th January 1862 about six hundred odd Jaintias attacked a military post at Jowai and burnt a few Christian houses, roads were blocked to Cherrapunjee, the headquarters of the United Khasi and Jaintia Hills. Very soon the British took over the control of the area and passages to these Hills were blocked, the British troops when they occupied these areas found villages had been deserted and realised this was a planned effort. The people of the Jaintia Hills fought bravely, they were more determined now and relied heavily on their bows and arrows, swords and indigenous guns called 'suloi tynsah' and the Jaintias were successful in keeping the areas free for a long time. Time was running out for these brave Jaintia warriors as they could not match up with the British army. There were casualties on both sides but comparatively the Brtish loss was much less.

An Act XVI of 1857 came into being which stated, "Anyone harbouring the rebels, supplying them with arms and supplies would be punished". Raja Rabon Singh of Khyrim and Raja Ram Singh of Cherra in the Khasi Hills were sent by the British government to start negotiations with the 'rebel leaders'. U Kiang Nongbah now demanded that all taxes be removed and that there should be no interference with religious rites. U Kiang Nongbah moved from hill to hill to keep the morals high and ensuring no taxes were paid. The Raja was put under surveillance and a reward of one thousand rupees (a big amount those days) was offered as capture money for U Kiang Nongbah. Soon the British troops were combing the Hills for the rebels, the rebels on their part kept troubling the British with their guerrilla tactics, with their bows and arrows. The British realised that U Kiang Nongbah had to be taken in to stop the rebellion and so a plan was made and a few local men were taken in to work for them, a man whose name often comes up was a gentleman called U Sinmon who at times was nicknamed U Sinmon Phareng or U Sinmon, the foreigner. The British had been looking for U Kiang Nongbah to finish off the war when the news came that U Kiang Nongbah was lying seriously injured at a friend's place in Mynso.

During this period of war, agriculture had been neglected as the men were out fighting; a stage came when women, children and the old were dying of starvation. U Daloi Tyngker a trusted man of U Kiang Nongbah could not take this any more so he went to the British with the thought of making peace, while U Kiang Nongbah was unaware of all this. U Daloi Tyngker took the British at face value and believed them when he was told no harm would come to U Kiang Nongbah if he surrendered. So U Tyngker gave away the secret of his hideout. The British quickly planned to draw away the soldier's guarding U Kiang Nongbah by attacking a place called Shangpung, the bulk of the Jaintia warriors went to defend Shangpung and only a few were left to look after their leader U Kiang Nongbah. The Jaintia's suffered a setback on 27th November 1862 when U Kiang Nongbah was captured from his hideout by Lt Sadler of the British army. The British wanted him to say that he had surrendered but U Kiang Nongbah refused to comply. A mock trial was set up and U Kiang Nongbah was sentenced to be hanged publicly on 30th December 1862. The people were forced to go to watch the hanging; this was a warning to others that similar fate was in store for them if they dared to disobey the British. U Kiang Nongbah was allowed to address his people, the people who hung down their head in sadness as he stood on the scaffolds, and his last words to his people were, "If my face turns eastward when I die on the rope, we shall be free again within a hundred years. If it turns westwards, we shall be enslaved forever". U Kiang Nongbah's words came true as freedom finally came to us in 1947. The people of the Jaintia Hills could hold on for another year but by 1863 all the leaders were forced to surrender, a brave warrior's effort had to come to an end.

Near the banks of the river Myntdu we have a large field called 'Madiah kmai Blai' and at its centre there is a monument of U Kiang Nongbah, it is a tower like structure with Jaintia designs. It is the same field where Jaintia leaders had met to fight the British.

Every year on 30th December, Meghalaya observes this day in memory of U Kiang Nongbah, the martyr. The present Governor

RS Mooshahary had this to say at a function, "We should be proud of inheriting the legacy, principles and ideals of these martyrs and they should be an inspiration to us to fight against injustice, exploitation and corruption. These are the qualities we inherit from our forefathers which clearly showed that we will not let sufferings come to us, and we should live up with it in this present world".

25

U Tirot Sing

During the time of U Tirot Sing, the Khasi Hills were divided into small areas ruled by a Syiem or King. It is said that U Tirot Sing was a man of medium height with one hand maimed or disabled, but being a man with a lion heart he had become well-known for his valour. U Tirot Sing's nerves of steel had made him good at combat from early childhood; he was also good at archery, a sport still very popular in Meghalaya.

The British interest in the Khasi Hills started when they first got the 'diwani' in 1765 or shall we say revenue of Sylhet from the Mughals and so were on the borders of the Khasi territory. They realised that there were possibilities of getting minerals like limestone, iron, coal, wax and honey from these areas. Very soon 'lime stone and coal' became a British monopoly, it is not that the British were not troubled by the Khasis, sometimes the Khasis went down to the plains when they found the traders from the plains were unfair to them. David Scott was made the Agent of the Governor General and was responsible for looking after the North East Frontier. The British so far had followed a policy of non-intervention with the Khasis, but soon things were to change because of trade. David Scott felt that a more permanent solution to the trade had to be made and the British Government of Bengal agreed to it. David Scott an intelligent man realised the importance of keeping a healthy relationship with the Khasis as he saw there was a requirement of having a postal system for communications between Gauhati and Sylhet, and for that in those days a good road was required. Good roads were also required for setting up cantonments and sanatoriums; they would also reduce marching time for soldiers. The road would also allow the British to keep a watch on the Khasis. In return the Khasis were told the road would allow the Khasis easy access to the markets of the plains to sell their goods. David Scott to achieve his goals first stopped the Khasi traders access to the markets in the plains because he wanted to annexe Bordwar which belonged to the Syiem of Nongkhlaw, but indicated to U Tirot Sing that Bordwar would remain his if he permitted the East India Company to construct the road linking Sylhet to Gauhati. U Tirot Sing was further asked by David Scott to get permission from other Syiems to allow the right of passage as the road would pass through other kingdoms.

The Nongkhlaw Syiem was also known as Khadsawphra in which there were fourteen ministers or as they were called 'Myntries'. U Tirot Sing's loyal ministers were – U Monbhut, Larson Jarain, Khein Kongor Ka Phan Nonglait who fought against the British. The place is now called Mairang, it has open fields and a history to offer to visitors. Mairang also has the U Tirot Sing Monument; the place is about forty kilometres away from Shillong. In the early nineteenth century U Tirot Sing was famous for his fight against the British Empire. End of the eighteenth century saw the Ahom power declining due to internal frictions and external Burmese threats and this disturbed the British. Two wars were fought and soon the British had full control over the Ahom territory and later lower Assam. Earlier the British had control over Sylhet and later Assam came into their hands. The British apart from the road were also interested in the Hills as they wanted to set up a cantonment in the cool Khasi Hills for their soldiers and officers to relax.

Before the British came in 1835 there were a few roads, amongst them the most well-known was the 'royal road' linking Jaintiapur (the capital of Jaintia kingdom) to the southern plains, with Nartiang the summer capital and also the ancestral property of the royals. The road can still be seen today, parts of it were used by travellers till motorable roads came up. The road was paved with stones and needed very little maintenance. David Scott did utilise it and also improved it but because it was circuitous he had to look for a road through the Khasi Hills.

The thought of a road connecting the areas was but natural and the road proposed was the one passing through the Khasi Hills. The British required a road from Gauhati to Sylhet, a long journey time could be shortened. The new route through the Khasi Hills would make life easier was in David Scott's mind, who was Agent to the Governor General for the northern territory. Hearing this plan U Tirot Sing, Syiem/ King of Nongkhlaw became interested as it would mean regaining possession of portions of the 'duar' land; it was fertile land his people owned before the British came. David Scott, shrewd man laid bait for U Tirot Sing saying he could have the land back if he made some concessions for the British. David Scott at that time did not know a Khasi King did not have absolute power like other Indian kings. A Khasi king shared the powers with representatives of his clan. Probably they had a more democratic form of government than us even in those days. U Tirot Sing had to call for a meeting of the leaders to discuss this important matter and U Tirot Sing offered David Scott to come as an observer. A British officer who had accompanied David Scott on this special meeting held on 1st November 1826 said there was a lot of difference of opinion and so the meeting extended to the next day when finally permission for the road was given. That fateful day started the end of Nongkhlaw Syiemship. Initially U Tirot Sing did not realise this as his thoughts were 'my people have benefited', but things were not what it seemed to be like.

Soon work on the road started and both the Khasi and British groups were happy. When the road was being built two houses were also built by the British, one for the British officer on duty and the other a police post. But happiness was not in store for U Tirot Sing as he was to discover later. U Tirot Sing found in the plains his rival Raja Balaram Singh staking claim on the 'Duar' land as his ('duar' land is fertile land between two rivers), this upset U Tirot Sing and he went to the British thinking his problem would be solved. When he was on his way to get the land back he found some British Company sepoys blocking the way, there was a tussle and lives were lost on both sides. When an inquiry was set up U Tirot Sing had this to say to the Assamese official, Mahador Barooah, "Mr Scott had promised the Borduar Revenue, he has not done it and now has a wish to give his troops to the Raja of Ranee, who is my rival. Mr Scott had promised saying your enemy is the Company's enemy".

U Tirot's behaviour was now very arrogant and out of sheer anger there was bloodshed. On 4th April 1829, U Tirot Sing's soldier, a group of about five hundred odd Khasi men killed two British officers, they were Lt Burton and Bedingsfield as David Scott could not be found. The Khasi warriors after killing the two British officers burnt down the bungalows and released the convicts working on the road. Soon news of his victory spread to the Hills all around and Syeims from all over came forward to help U Tirot Sing. Finally, a tired David Scott offered peace treaty but no one was willing to listen to him as U Tirot Sing had gone under cover, he preferred living the life of a commoner.

So the wrath of the British army now fell on the hapless Khasi chief. Thus started the Anglo Khasi war, it was from 1829-1833 and the Khasis were defeated badly, the military superior power was the winner. But for four years the guerrilla warfare continued and the Khasis gave the British a tough time. Initially U Tirot Sing could not be caught as he went into hiding in the caves and the guerrilla warfare continued, this upset the British and they decided to get help from people who knew the area of Khasi Hills well. David Scott had asked for help and reinforcements came in plenty, Capt Lister of the 44th Sylhet Light Infantry moved in from the Sylhet side, Lt Vetch from Kamrup. The Khasis too were prepared and hordes of them were ready to attack, from all over Khasi warriors had joined in as word about the Nongkhlaw flare up had spread like wildfire. Lt Vetch met with stiff resistance as both the armies met at a place called Jirang. The Khasi army was led by U Tirot's maternal uncle U Jidor Singh who gave tough resistance to Lt Vetch and the British army had to retreat to Gauhati. On the way back the frustrated man burnt down a few Khasi villages. Capt Lister's priority was to rescue David Scott from Cherra in the Khasi Hills as U Tirot's men were hounding him from all over, after rescuing him he left him in Sylhet and then went on to Nongkhlaw, U Tirot Sing's kingdom. Capt Lister in the fight was somewhat injured as an arrow had pierced his thigh. But this did not deter the captain and the very next day he attacked again and was successful in breaking into the Khasi army. But the Khasis were still not defeated as they kept putting up resistance. They say that Dr Beadon went out to help in offering the peace treaty by David Scott but was met with an arrow on his nose and had to beat a hasty retreat. The offer of peace treaty was not acceptable to U Tirot Sing. He moved from hill to hill trying to encourage the people not to give up so easily, even women joined in this fight for freedom, one such woman was Ka Phan Nonglait. These women had killed many British soldiers and stolen arms from the camps. U Tirot Sing tried seeking help from the Ahom King Chandrakanta, the Singhpos. His messengers went to the neighbouring kingdoms of the area and people who supported him were the Syiems of Myriaw, Jirang Mawsynram, Bhowal, some were neutral like Cherrapungee, Langrin and Nongston. The Syiem of Cherra U Duwan Singh played an active role in supporting the British; it is here David Scott took refuge from U Tirot's men. Some helped U Tirot Sing secretly, they were Peoli Phukan and Maniram Dewan who tried to smuggle in rice into the Khasi Hills when the economic blockade was put to weaken the Khasi struggle.

The British now wanted to capture U Tirot Sing and for this they turned towards Manipur for support. The Manipuri support was given by Maharajas Gambhir and Nara Singh. According to the *Manipuri Royal Chronicle* the two kings had to support the British as they were helped by them when the Burmese marauders were attacking them, so a favour had to be returned. Both the British and Manipuri armies met at Sylhet and it was decided they would attack U Tirot Sing from two directions. Earlier the British had tried blocking all supplies to the Hills and the depleting resources may have been a factor for U Tirot Sing falling for the bait which was a peace talk, his thoughts must have been for his people. The British announced a peaceful meeting and U Tirot Sing was captured as he came out of hiding. The Manipuris were successful in capturing U Tirot Sing and soon they handed him over to the British and the Manipuri soldiers returned back to their own areas as their was no enmity between the Khasis and Manipuris. It was first thought U Tirot Sing would be sent to Burma but decisions changed and he was sent to jail in Dhaka. He was offered freedom if he agreed to come under British Administration. Proud man that he was he refused, his reply was, "I would rather die as a king in jail rather than become a slave king". He died in jail on 17th July 1835. His message to his people was "Go back home and tell them U Tirot Sing lived and died like a king". That was years before the Revolt of 1857.

Today he is remembered for his courage and leadership qualities, a great tribal freedom fighter who stands out in history.

Mizoram

The Land of the Highlanders

Mizoram was formerly called the Lushai Hills, the word 'lu' in Lushai language means head and 'shai' means cutter, this was only one interpretation. Shakespeare suggests it means a person with long head, referring to Lushais tying up their hair in knots at the back of their heads. Mizoram attained statehood in 1987. The state lies between the Chin Hills of Burma (Myanmar) and the Chittagong Hill Tracts of Bangladesh.

The state has great natural beauty of Hills, rivers, numerous brooks and the verdant jungles are a botanist's paradise with bamboo and orchid growing aplenty. The Lushai Hills run from north to south and from east to west. The height of the Hills ranges from 1200m – 2,500m. Some of the mountain peaks are Phawngpui (the highest) Lengteng and Tantlang. These Hills are interspersed by rivers and brooks. The rivers are not often used for navigation because of the terrain. Only rivers like Tlawng, Tuiral, Karnaphuli and Kolodyne are navigable. There are some plains scattered along the Hills. The largest is the Champai Plains. Most of these plains are used for cultivation. Mizoram also has a number of beautiful lakes. The Palak Lake is in Chimtuipui district. It is the only abode of aquatic birds found in Mizoram. The other lakes include Tamdil,

Rungdil and Rengdil. Mizoram gets a fair amount of rain and the rivers bring down the top soil, due to leaching the soil is not very fertile.

The word 'Mizo' means a highlander (it could possibly be related to these people living on a higher area); the people are a group of tribes who started moving into the state from the Chin Hills of Burma. The Lushai are the most dominant tribe and were the first ones to arrive, they were followed by Hmars, the Pawis, the Raltes, the Paites, the Thadous, the Lakhers and finally the Chakmas from the Chittagong Hill tract. The Lushais are clever and a determined group of people, sometimes to the point of obstinacy. A Lushai in the olden days was a wizard in jungle arts and was capable of the greatest physical endurance and achievement. Even today the Mizos follow a special code of chivalry/or conduct called Tlwmnaigna, (explained in detail later), a Mizo at all times must be considerate towards others and follow the spirit of mutual help, this is the view they all have. We do not have a caste based society in Mizoram. The Mizos have very little distinction between the high and low order in society. Though earlier, the chief had full political authority over his subjects but in social life he was as much a commoner as others. This may be the reason why it is not uncommon to see a minister or chief minister sharing the same table with his driver or guard for dinner.

There are many legends about the Mizos origin – there are no written records for lack of a script. Earlier only oral traditions were followed. According to one such tradition they say they helped in construction of a long and thick wall in China. As the work progressed life became difficult so the Mizos decided to look for a new and healthy home, it was this thought which brought them to the North East or Assam. Life was not easy for the Mizos as they had to fight their way through to make a place for themselves in Assam.

The Mizos are from the same stock as Chins of Burma. They at one time lived in Burma and before leaving the place they had planted a tree to commemorate their existence in this area. They believed that when the branches touched the ground they would return. Sometimes in 1912 some of the group did come back and they were welcomed by the Burmese. The Mizos say the place was Khampat in Upper Burma. We also sometimes hear of a few folk songs which tell the tale of the beautiful Hills of Burma.

Another story says they were brought into this world by a big stone called 'Chin Lung'. Some Mizos believe they originally came from inside the earth. The forefathers came out of a cave called Chinlung. The story may mean that Chinlung is not a cave but the name of a Chinese prince Chin Lung. The Prince, they say, displeased his father and so was banished from the empire, who later settled in Burma with his faithful followers. This event in the oral tradition or transmission lost the historical aspect and became a legend.

The history of Mizos is shrouded in mystery beyond Burma. The Ahoms also have not mentioned anything about the Mizos in their well preserved chronicles or '*Buranjis*'. The Ahom Buranjis do mention tiffs with the Nagas, Monpas and Sherdukens but the Mizos have not been mentioned. It was only in 1826 AD that the British administrators have talked about the Mizos. 1893 AD saw two Christian missionaries Savidge and Lorrain in the Mizo Hills. They spread Christianity, opened schools and dispensaries. Savidge also compiled the Lushai-English and English-Lushai dictionaries. Gradually, the Mizos fell in line with the British administration; some later joined the British army as they were a brave, hardy race.

Today peace prevails in the area and literacy has spread to most parts of the state, literacy has possibly led the state to prosperity. Even in very remote areas we have schools, quite often related to the church. It is a common early morning sight in the villages to see children neatly dressed and going to school.

26

Mary Winchester – Zoluti

Mary Winchester or Zoluti (meaning the one who came to the Mizos) as she was called by the Mizo people was only six when she was brought to Mizoram and left a huge impact on the life of the people here. She was the one responsible for bringing Christianity to Mizoram; this was not planned but by chance. Mary Winchester we are sure did not realise the impact she had made on the Lushai Hills, not only did she bring in Christianity but also the light of education here. Early morning in villages and the cities one can see every Mizo child going to school, can't be said for the rest of the country.

Mary's father was a Scotish tea planter, the tea garden manager of Alexanderapore Tea Estate. Alexanderapore lies in the Cachar district of Assam. Mary's mother Jatly Kangmeiza was a Meiti girl from Manipur, she died at child birth and that maybe the reason why very little is known about her. Mary came into prominence because of a certain incident in the tea gardens. Those were the days the British were looking for areas to begin their tea plantations and the jungles were cleared for the tea estates. In the early 19th century, the Mizos came in contact with the British in Assam, most of them were British tea planters, and the Mizos felt threatened as the hunting grounds were being encroached by the White men.

There was no clear cut demarcation of the boundaries of the tea estates and the hunting grounds which also led to the Mizos feeling threatened by the British. The Mizos did protest to all this as they felt their hunting grounds would soon disappear, but it fell on deaf ears as the British were interested in only getting what they wanted. So to stop the encroachment, the Mizos started killing and plundering the White men.

Sometimes the native workers were also killed or taken away as booty. Very often young men from the 'Zawlbuks' (boys dormitory), would be used by the Chiefs for such attacks, the young boys were unpredictable and people feared them as the tea gardens did not have much wherewithal for such an attack. The second reason for such attacks might have been that the Mizos were looking for arms, ammunition and metal tools which could be easily found in these tea estates.

One such attack changed the life of the area completely; it was the attack on Alexanderapore Tea Garden. The Mizo Chief Benkhuia Sailo had sent his warriors down to Cachar to ward off the British or as a warning to them to not encroach on Mizo hunting grounds. Benkhuia ruled over the villages Serchip, Sailam, Kawlri and Thenzawl. Benkhuia was a popular chief who looked after his people well. It so happened that, on that particular day a planter named Dr James Winchester manager of Alexandrapore tea gardens, was visiting an old school friend called George Sellar. James Winchester had thought of taking long leave to go back to Scotland after twelve long years in the tea estates as manager. He had thought of leaving Mary with her grandparents so that she could go to school and get educated but that was not to be, life had something else in store for her. The Winchesters had spent the night at Alexandrapore and the next morning at breakfast a sudden commotion was heard, before people could react there were a large number of Mizo hunters on them. George Sellar was lucky; he managed to escape on his horse. James Winchester was not as fortunate as he had to pick up his daughter Mary and run to his horse, he was too late, and the Mizos had struck James Winchester. He could not even pick up his revolver or gun to defend himself. James Winchester lay wounded with Mary in his arms. His last words were, "I am shot, and God only knows what will happen to you". Dr James Winchester a true Christian had always felt that, "Wherever she (Mary) went, Jesus would go with her". This came so true later as the British and Christianity had a close relationship in the Lushai Hills. The Mizos left James Winchester to die and they picked up Mary and a few workers, quickly running off into the thick jungles. Very soon the news of the killing reached London and a painting appeared in the English dailies showing a frightened child in a thick dense jungle looking petrified and lost, this stirred the English mind. A rich millionaire Robert Arthington was so effected by this picture that he decided to do something to help the 'poor hapless soul'. So Robert Arthington immediately started the Arthington Aborigines Mission to help the little girl. Arthington used all his influence to get help from the British government to rescue Mary from Chief Benkhuia. It was in 1871 Chief Benkhuia's men took away Mary to his village Sailam, for about a year Mary was with them.

During this period the British were trying to extend their areas to the Assam-Mizoram region. The British government sent three groups from three directions to rescue the little girl Mary; the first one came from Burma, the second from the north and the third from the south. The column responsible for the Lushai Hills was the Chittagong one and had mainly Gurkha troops under the command of General Brownlow. The main objective of this group was to recover Mary Winchester who had been taken from Alexandrapore Tea Estate in 1871 and to avenge the murder of Dr James Winchester. The expedition did not have an easy task as difficult terrain had to be crossed. The Gurkha troops were successful in subduing Chief Vanhuliana Sailo and now the British had a toe hold into this area. The Southern column was led by Col Thomas Lewin and he set his base three miles away from Benkhuia's camp at Serchip. Lt Colonel Thomas H Lewin was ably supported by Chief Rothangpuia who agreed to negotiate with the Howlong group for the release of Mary Winchester and he was successful in this. Lewin met Benkhuia unarmed on the banks of river Chal and came to an agreement that Mary would be released and a dog was also sacrificed to mark the occasion. Legend had it that when Azim Subdar Sahib of the Police went to get Mary, she refused to let go of her Mizo guardian's hand, but when she was offered a sweet she could not resist herself, 'would you like a sweetie' was all that was required to be done. Mary had settled down into the Mizo way of living and when her rescuers found her she happened to be playing with other children outside the Chief's house. Pi Tluangi an old lady who looked after Mary had become very fond of her and looked after her very well,

Mary of course called her Piklawangi in her childish way. She did not want to leave the motherly Pi Tluangi and she wept bitterly when she had to go. The old lady gave her some hard boiled eggs as a parting gift and Mary in return cut off her golden locks as a parting gift for Pi Tluangi. Later there was a restraining order on the Mizos; they could not leave their land without permission of the British and this they violently resented.

Pi Tluangi's grandson Vanchhunga, later became one of the three Christian Evangelists, whose family later moved to Aizawl. Mary was indeed fortunate to have Pi Tluangi to shelter her, it could have been that had Mary not been rescued by Col Lewin and his troops she may have become a Mizo bride to some young Mizo man! After she was rescued Mary was sent to Calcutta from where she went to London to live with her relatives in Scotland. Ten years later her name appeared in the list of Royal Moray College of students who had creditably passed an examination. Mary had come a long way from her Mizoram days. Col Lewin later met Mary Winchester who had married and become Mary Innes Howie in London, but was not very happy with the meeting as he called her "a stuck up little half caste woman". The same can't be said of Savidge or Sap Upa who at a later date had taken a few Christian from Mizoram to London and they met Mary who was happy to meet them.

In her old age Mary 'Zoluti' wrote an account of what happened, this gives us a good idea about all the incidents. A page from her diary:

"He lifted me up, a girl of five, and tried to run towards his horse tethered a little way off, but alas it was too late. The Lushais were on us. My father was shot from the back, fell, and I was extricated from his arms. He was conscious for he spoke to me. I was taken with my ayah and many coolies, and he was left to die. "I am shot, God only knows what will happen to you" were his last words. Thanks to my ayah who made good her escape, the terrible news was carried to other Planters, and by persistent demand for better protection, my release was afterwards gained

"I have a mixed recollection of the journey into Lushai country, the huge fires at night in the jungle to protect us from wild animals, the upward journey passing through the various villages, with pigs and bantam cocks and hens, and then a resting place, and then a chief, and finally a bungalow with a dear old motherly woman who was so good and kind to me. There was a younger man of whom I was afraid as he threatened to kill me, but the old woman would not let him have anything to do with me. Often has it been said I romanced when I spoke of the old woman, but I am glad to have lived to prove that it was no stretch of imagination but a fact, for she was no other than Piklwangi, the grandmother of Vanchhunga, one of your native preachers at Aijal. She wove me garments, a blue striped skirt and a red tartan shawl made of silk, which I treasure not only as a relic of my life there, but of the love, Divine given, that prompted the weaving of them.

"Then came troublous times. I was threatened to be killed as being the cause of it all, but the old woman shielded me. One could see villages being burnt lower down the slopes and a general uneasiness prevailed where I was. Then I was fetched and with grief left my friends and felt far from happy or settled till I had been six months in Elgin [Scotland], where my old grandparents begat confidence in my then suspectful and rebellious heart. It took many years before I could recognise the hand of God in my life, but now when I see the workings of His omniscient powers I can today say "Thy will be done" as it is best.

"My father had been father and mother to me from almost my birth, and nothing on earth has replaced him. My grandparents were devoted to me and gave me all that money and love could give, and I was glad to have been of comfort to them in their old age.

"I was given up on the 21st of January, 1872 one year except six days after being taken prisoner. "

Today a memory stone or as they say in Mizo 'Zoluti Hriatrengna Lung' has been placed at the spot Mary was handed over to the British, it is at Kawlri Tlang close to Serchip, Kawnpui. We have had the Kristian Thalai Pawl (Christian Youth Fellowship) Branch erect a stone in memory of Zoluti (Mary) daughter of Dr Winchester.

27

Pu Buanga and Sap Upa

The men who helped in bringing Christianity and the written script to Mizoram

Mizoram follows Christianity as a religion as almost ninety five percent of its population are Christians. What brought in the change, a change from animistic beliefs to followers of Jesus Christ? A 'Missionary Day' on 11th January is observed where people from all denominations of Christianity observe this day, the special day where two priests from United Kingdom set foot on Mizoram soil at Sairung village which is about 23 km from Aizawl. The two missionaries were JH Lorrain and FW Savidge, they were popularly called Pu / Mr Buanga (Lorrain) and Sap Upa (Savidge). On 11th January all churches and state government offices remain closed so that special services in praise of the two priests can be held. The year was 2010 and it was the 117th anniversary. In the 21st century many denomination of the Church have come up like the Roman Catholic, Salvation Army, Methodist, Pentacosta and the Assembles of God and all remember Lorrain and Savidge as the harbinger of Christianity.

It is interesting to note how Lorrain and Savidge reached Mizoram; a certain Arthington felt the need to spread the message of Jesus Christ to those who had never heard of him. Arthington started the Indian Aborigines Mission or Arthington's Mission and his plan was to recruit people for two years in groups of two to go out and spread the message of our Lord. Two Baptist Church Members, James Herbert Lorrain and his good friend Fedrick W Savidge joined the Arthington Mission in London and were sent out to India. It was Lorrain who first came to India and first landed at Agartala (Tripura) in January 1891, Savidge followed in 1891 and landed in Bengal. Both the missionaries initially were not given permission to go to Mizoram. Their friendship was strengthened when together they went to Chittagong (now in Bangladesh) and from there they went to Kassalong in the Chittagong Hill Tracts and they presumed it would be now easier to reach the Mizo Hills. But their plans failed as Savidge went down with the 'Indian belly' or dysentery and both had to return to Calcutta. When Savidge regained his health he and Lorrain tried going to Tripura but the Maharaja did not oblige them. Both then thought of going to the Welsh Mission in Silchar (Assam) where they met a few Mizos in the markets. Lorrain and Savidge did pick up a few words of the Mizo tongue when they met a few men from the Mizo Hills. Unfortunately, most of these people did not stay too long with Lorrain and Savidge to teach the language to them. Only one person they say helped, he was Chawngkhuma or popularly called Chawngi Pa.

After waiting for a year Lorrain and Savidge were given permission by the Political Officer of North Lushai Hills to go to Aizawl (the capital city today). Both the missionaries were very excited and did not want to lose time on coolies to take their luggage so they made bundles which had tents and a few clothes and off they left Silchar in December 1893 and reached Aizawl in January 1894. Both men caused quite a stir in the bazaars of Aizawl as Mizos had never seen a White man carrying his own baggage. They were called the 'Wandering Sahibs' or 'Mad Sahibs' or in Mizo 'sap vakyai' (wandering White men) by the Mizos. Lorrain and Savidge were given permission to put up their tents in the parade ground and not to venture out too much as the Mizos were not used to blue eyed men! The years between 1894 and 1897 were important years for Lorrain and Savidge as they laid the foundation for many things new to the Mizos. People said that these men were very cultured and one habit of theirs which stood out was being frugal; 'waste not, want not' as they say was their policy.

Both were very keen to learn the language and Lorrain had a natural flair for languages as wherever he went he could pick up the local languages. While in Bengal he learnt Bengali enough to preach, while in the then Assam, now Arunachal Pradesh, Lorrain learnt the Abor Miri dialect enough to preach and write a book on 'Grammar'. While in Aizawl they learnt the language and practised writing out small books in Mizo and of course translating the Bible.

The Mizo forefathers said that there were a few written documents on animal skin but one day a dog came and took it away as it was hungry! Basically there were no written documents till the last part of the 19th century, though Mizos have rich tradition of oral literature. It was these two Brititsh missionaries who brought the written script to Mizos. Before this there have been attempts to write the Mizo script with Bengali alphabets, but this did not prove to be very successful. The credit for codifying the language were the effort of JH Lorrain and FW Savidge who reached the banks of the river Tlawng without any coolies to carry their baggage and since they had very little authority like the British administrators the Mizos did not feel there was any danger from them. To top it all they could speak asmattering of Mizo tongue which both had learnt from Thomas Herbert Lewin's book (1839- 1916). Thomas H Lewin at that time was the Deputy Commissioner of the Chittagong Hill Tracts and was a popular man with the Mizos and the Mizos called him Thangliana, perhaps a corrupt version of Tom Lewin. Lewin had written a number of informative books about the Mizos like the Progressive Colloquial Exercise in the Lushai Dialect in 1874. Lorrain and Savidge started making the alphabets required for the Mizo language and said that the work of Lewin was extremely useful to them but could not be used by the locals. Lorrain writes that, "It therefore fell to our lot to reduce the language to writing in such a way that our system could be readily adopted by the people themselves. For this purpose we chose the simple Roman script, with a phonetic form of the spelling based on the Hunterian system". What turned out was a very simple form of language which was easy to read and write, for example 'futbol' instead of football. So if one could speak and understand the language writing became a simple task. Lorrain and Savidge had made the language so easy that a Mizo chief, called Thamliana, came to the priests and learnt the language in two weeks. Children too, learnt to read the language very quickly and the Mizo script could be typed on the English typewriter. Mizos were fortunate to have a script of their very own, possibly the first amongst the 'Seven Sisters'. Savidge before he came to India had been a teacher in London so his interests in school made him open a school near Thangpunga's village. The school had a thatch roof, sun baked mud floor with three sides open and a few very unwilling children from the village. To attract a few students they started a Sunday school and gave away sweets, sometimes a picture or a rosary as incentive. A young boy called Chawnga remembered this and later became the first teacher of Mission Veng Primary School; he stayed there till he retired in 1946. On Sundays the two priests would venture out to nearby villages to see if they could attract more people to the church. Sometimes people who came to the church were given medicine and this at times won their trust. Though no one was baptised in these four years the Mizos were educated about Christ and most importantly their trust won. The Census of 1901 saw about 1000 educated men in Mizoram, the power of the print became a passion and this has finally led to the state having one of the highest literacy rates in the country.

Pu Buanga and Sap Upa when they arrived in Mizoram remembered that they had to finish as much work as they could as they knew they would have to shift out due to Mr Arthington's policy of moving people after a few years of work. So throughout 1897, they concentrated on translating the books of St Luke, St John and The Acts of the Apostle from the New Testament, they wanted to finish the translation as quickly as possible and place it with the printers, all this in case they had to leave in a hurry. The translation of the Old Testament was finally done in 1955. A Mizo 'Grammar and Dictionary' was written by Pu Buanga and published in 1946. The first book to be published in Mizo (Lushai) was a "Child's Primer", printed and published by the Assam Government in 1895. Lorrain or Pu Buanga was responsible for putting together the Lushai Dictionary and Savidge or Sap Upa, the grammar book. Pu Buanga before his death in 1940 had collected a large number of words, almost thirty three thousand words, which was later published by the Royal Asiatic Society of Bengal. Sap Upa also had translated a number of hymns and had brought out a small book which the Mizos called 'The Old Catechism'.

Having learnt to read and write the Mizos now craved for more and more books, so the missionaries took care of that by getting books published in Mizo. It was Lorrain and Savidge who visualised that before they started teaching Jesus Christ's message they must do something to make the Mizo tongue come out in print. After publication of the Mizo Bible (over the years very few changes have been made) a number of translations of hymns and other stories became published to cater to the demands of the new literates. These two priests opened the eyes of the Mizo people to a new world. They now saw their life and death from a different perspective. Some Mizos were not satisfied with reading translations so we had poets and story tellers with their own versions in Mizo talking about Christianity, such songs in Mizo are called 'Lengkhawm Zai' and are sung with a drum. These songs contribute a lot to Mizo literature.

Lorrain and Savidge's fear of being recalled came true as Arthington became restless and asked them to move on, both had been in Mizoram for only eighteen months and desperately wanted to stay back so they wrote to the American Baptist Missionary Union if they could take over, but the reply was negative, Arthington asked the Welsh Mission to take over from them. Arthington's short term approach made Lorrian and Savidge severe their ties from him, but God had other plans. Arthington died in 1900 leaving a large sum of money almost five hundred thousand pounds to the Baptist Missionary Society. Lorrain and Savidge started the Assam Frontier Mission to pave their way for a second coming back to Mizoram.

It was in 1901 the Baptist Missionary Society decided to enter South Lushai Hills/ and everyone felt Lorrain and Savidge should return, so in 1903 they came back as missionaries of the Baptist Missionary Society. Both landed at Tlabung and were greeted by fellow Christians, there were about a total of one hundred and twenty five Christians and from these men twenty five went to Demagiri the riverine port of the river Karnaphuli to welcome Lorrain and Savidge and escort them back to Lunglei. Both missionaries were happily welcomed as they spoke the Mizo tongue. Lorrain and Savidge no longer had to carry their baggage as many helping hands came forward. Pu Buanga and Savidge finally settled down in Serkawn, Lunglei. Serkawn became an important place as the Baptist Church of Mizoram took off from this place. The first group of the Christian faith to be baptised was on 20th January 1904. Rev. JH Lorrain/ Pu Buanga baptised twelve men and FW Savidge/ Sap Upa eleven people. The first communion service was on 25th January 1904 at Sethlun Church.

While working here in Serkawn, Pu Buanga felt the need of a spiritual leader in South Mizoram so he wrote to his younger brother Rev. RA Lorrain to come to Mizoram. RA Lorrain started the Evangelical Church of Maraland. The Mara or Lakher's live close to the borders of Mizoram and Burma (Myanmar) RA Lorrain started the Lakher Pioneer Mission in 1905 and together with his wife started the Evangilical Church of Maraland, it is interesting to note that RA Lorrain's granddaughter lives here with her Mara husband in Lorrain Villa, Saikao.

The arrival of Pu Buanga and Sap Upa have made significant changes in the Mizo society and education as they did the ground work for the systematic documentation of the facts and the language spoken in the area. The first series of elementary books for beginners was started by these two in Lushai in Roman Script and of course 'The Bible' in Mizo. Christian Missionaries when they came to India had a purpose, spread the word of Jesus and educate the masses. It is through them, that many languages developed and so did Mizo.

The two pioneer missionaries worked in Mizoram for thirty-three years and Pu Buanga left Mizoram on 17th February 1932. From Tlabung Bungalow he wrote, "Going home to England perhaps never to return to these beautiful Hills where so many happy years of our lives have been spent, " speaks volumes about their love for the land.

28

Ropuiliani

Pi/Ms Ropuiliani was perhaps the first Mizo woman to become a chieftan after the death of her husband Vandula. Ropuiliani became the regent after her husband's death as her son was young. Mizo society normally is a patriarchal society and so the son inherited the property. Ropuiliani was the daughter of the great Chief Lalsuvunga and had got married to Chief Vandula, but in the case of Ropuiliani she inherited her father's property too. A dedicated person, she loved her land and people. Wherever there was an uprising against the British, Ropuiliani directly or indirectly was involved. The year 1870-1871 saw her giving full support to her husband Vandula who was trying to fight the British and his Mizo pride did not allow him to bow down.

Ropuiliani's clan were ruthlessly victimised during the anti-British rising, her experiences had left Ropuiliani very unhappy but she put up a brave fight in spite of her advancing years. Most of the chiefs were surrendering to the British but Ropuiliani and her son Lalthuama did not give in to the British demands and Lalthuama was perhaps the only chief to continue his chiefdom.

The year 1888-1889 saw the British trying to subjugate the Mizos and they had thought success was easy as there was an unnatural calm. But the peace was lost with the killing of Lt JF Stewart and his two bodyguards, plus a sepoy at Rangamati in the Chittagong Hill Tracts. The incident that sparked off the trouble was because of a chief, Howsata, he had quarrelled with his wife who left his house for her father's. Jabuta, the father-in-law of Howsata agreed to send his daughter back if Howsata could bring back the heads of two foreigners. Howsata the desperate husband went looking for the heads of two White men, it was unfortunate that at that very time Lt LF Stewart with his troops was out trying to reconnaissance the area near Demagiri. Before Lt Stewart and his group could realise what had happened their heads were off and Howsata was speeding away with his booty towards his in-laws place. The headless bodies were left behind for the British. But it was a warning for the British to strengthen themselves. A massive assault was launched under the command of Col FVW Tregear. Captain Shakespear, Murray and Walker were sent in to meet the chiefs and get their support for peace. On the way they visited Howsata's village but found it deserted, Howsata had died before they could reach and when his grave was opened up they found his grave had weapons and food as is customary in Mizoram, this was to help the dead on his journey to the other world. Beneath the corpse was the gun which belonged to Lt Stewart. While returning the British troops burnt the village of Jabuta, Howsata's father-in-law. Lalthuama, Ropuiliani's son came under suspicion as the British felt he was responsible for the crime. Some of this may have been true as both mother and son wanted the British to leave Mizoram for good.

During the winter months an additional post was set up near Lalthuama's village at Lunglei so that a strict watch could be kept over the movements of Ropuiliani and Lalthuama. Both mother and son could upset any plans of the British as at times they could be ruthless. So the British called for a meeting of the chiefs on 3rd April 1889, the meeting was presided over by the then Political Officer D Lyall and the Intelligent officer was Capt J Shakespear. John Shakespear became the Superintendent of the South Lushai Hills in April 1891. Ropuiliani as expected rose in revolt and did not attend the meeting. In 1891 the northern Chiefs rose against the British but were subdued. Ropuiliani's nephew Chief Lalbora in the east took up the cause of the Mizo's but met with stiff resistance from McCabe and his forces, he came into Lalbora's village and was forced into subjugation to come under the British.

The British imposed fines and introduced bonded labour, all this was very much disliked by the Mizos but most of the Howlong chiefs surrendered except for Ropuiliani and her son Lalthuama, the British hesitated to take in Ropuiliani and her son as they were both respected and loved in their own community. When a house tax was introduced, true to her people Ropuiliani reacted and the following words said by her grandson speak her mind, "Our people would never contribute any labour or taxes to foreign people. We are the owners of the land and we will drive the foreigners away from our territory". Even when all other Howlong chiefs had surrendered she did not give in nor did she allow her son Lalthuama to bow down. It was now time for Ropuiliani to gather all her people to come together and make a concerted effort to fight back. She got in touch with the Northern chiefs to come together and make a final assauLt The summer of 1893 found the village of Denlung very active and this made the British become suspicious. Ropuiliani had planned her attack well - they would be (a) destroy all means of communication, (b) destroy all bridges and boats, thereby hampering the movements of supplies of rations and arms, (c) ambushing the British troops whenever possible. But the mission did not prove to be successful as the information about the activities were leaked by the coolies and interpreters to the British, nothing abnormal as the British had a good network of spies. So some troops under Capt Shakespear were dispatched from Lunglei to surprise Ropuiliani and her son Lalthuma. Taking no chances Capt Shakespear when he reached Denlung said that since all was not according to regulations he imposed a heavy fine on guns, animals and rice. Ropuiliani and Lalthuama as usual refused to comply with the demand and now were more determined than ever to fight back. They were now waiting for the northern chiefs to join in. The British sensing trouble decided to arrest Ropuiliani and her son before the northern chiefs could join in. They reached Denlung and took Ropuiliani completely by surprise. She was captured along with her son and the Mizos were all disarmed. Capt Shakespear remained the Superintendent from 1891- 1897, but most important task was the capture of Ropuiliani, a sad day for the Mizos.

Proud Ropuiliani even after her arrest refused to walk, and like a Chieftain she wanted a palanquin to be brought in. Capt Shakespear had to bow down to her wishes and Ropuiliani went out in a regal style with her head held high! Both mother and son were jailed, first they were kept in Mizoram and later sent to Rangamati jail as it was the headquarters of the Chittagong Hill Tracts. Even in jail, mother and son were given the respect of state prisoners as special guards were kept to watch over them and not police constables as was the norm those days. Ropuiliani could not take in the humiliation and within a year died in prison in January 1895. The British with great reluctance agreed to send the body of Ropuiliani to her homeland, Mizoram. Her body was embalmed and her son brought her body back to her village Denlung "Home they brought the warrior dead". She lies buried there amongst her people and the land she loved so much. Denlung is 2 km away from Hnaithal town and it is believed her grave still exists. Ropuiliani finally had arrived home, close to those she loved so dearly like a mother loves her children. Lalthuama, the son was also allowed to settle down close to his home.

Even today people talk about her courage and lovc for her land, Mizos have named town halls and roads after her. In May 1988 at Champhai, Mizoram the Zo Reunification Organisation in their meeting started the 'Ropuiliani Award' and Rani Gaidinliu (Naga Freedom Fighter) was its first recipient. Such is the legacy of a woman who defied the British and lived life on her terms.

29

Tlawmnagaihna
Followed even - Now

Tlawmnagaihna is a code of conduct which all Mizos follow even today, a code which they hold very dear in their hearts. Tlawmnagaihna - the word has no equivalent in English, one can only say it means all the good qualities in life. Here is an example of tlawmnagaihna, when a group of people went hunting for a week in the olden days; there was always a moral competition among the young men that one should do more than the others, like take less food, getting things ready before the others got up in the morning, asking one's friend to shoot first. The moral code which dealt with male was called 'mipa tlawmnagaihna'.

The girls had a code where they were measured by the way they welcomed their suitors. In spite of working at home, doing household chores and then working in the 'jhum' (cultivation area), they must at all times have a smile on their faces.

Those who possessed this strict moral discipline were always rewarded. The Valupas' or guardians who kept a watchful eye on the young men later at a special ceremony offered a cup of rice beer called 'tlawmnagaihna no' in a cup made out of horn. This was first offered to the young men who had followed tlawmnagaihna. The 'no' was the highest 'award' in the olden days.

I was fortunate to see tlawmnagaihna being observed even today, though the incident was a sad one. A few years back which seems only the other day, a tragic accident had happened on the road to Aizawl (the capital). A bus had rolled down the Hillside having lost control of the wheel. A number of people died and many were injured. A large number of dead belonged to the village of Vairengte, where we had lived for some time. We were enveloped by the gloom of tragedy and shared the sorrow of the affected families. The next morning we found a lot of new faces in the village, very curiously I asked my friend Parthangi (or Pari) "What happened"? "Oh! they have all come to help". Able-bodied people from far and near had all come to assist the village people with all the requirements of the funeral. All the men were busy either digging the graves or making coffins; the older ones were making wreaths; the girls and women were helping out cooking, making tea. The affected families did not have to take on any of the work load. This is the norm, this is the tradition, and this is "tlawmnagaihna".

One thought that comes to my mind, 'such camaraderie' was only seen in the army. This is something all Mizos revered and lived by. In fact it is 'unMizo' not to follow tlawmnagaihna. This unique code teaches the Mizos to be kind, hospitable, unselfish, and brave; to respect equality of status and be of energetic habit. As per the 'hnatlang' (social work) system the Mizos contribute their labour for the welfare of the community by helping to construct inter village paths, community halls, water points and so on. According to this system the Mizos extend their help to one in need (be it a death in the family, or a house destroyed by a storm, or a wedding feast, virtually anything) as their social obligation. It is a treat to see the young keeping this code of conduct alive all over Mizoram and always helping the old and the weak.

Pu (the Mizo equivalent of Mr) Rokunga, a famous poet wrote:

Hallowed Tlawmnagaihna

Precious flower of life

Pray bloom and grow

In our beautiful highland forever and forever......

Tlawmnagaihna is an age-old code in the Mizo system or should one say way of life. It means 'service before self' (interestingly that is the credo of the National Defence Academy) and that is a code a Mizo holds very dear and follows very strictly. This helping attitude, this philosophy of sharing, this concept of concern has become virtually unknown elsewhere, especially in our so-called sophisticated (?) and civilised (?) urban societies. Aping the west we are losing our roots; we avoid the good (being punctual, being courteous) and follow the bad (chewing gum, poor language, aggressive showmanship and the like) not wanting to stop and think about where we are headed.

Vana Pa (a renown chief) is the one who made Tlawmangainha popular among the Mizos.

Pu Buanga (Re. JH Lorrain was called by this name because, though an Englishman, he identified with the locals and lived like one) describes this unique code as 'unselfishness and self-sacrifice'. But, honestly, there is no equivalent word or words in the English language that can quite sum up this code of conduct. Vanapa, when he went out on hunting expeditions, would carefully preserve his camp leaving sufficient firewood and drinking water so that other hunters who may come there could use them. Grandma's stories indicate that Vanapa did not take a morsel of food until all the members of his group had had their fill. When a bison or some such animal came into view the privilege of using the first arrow would always go to someone else though Vanapa was well-known for his never failing aim and hunting prowess.

One legendary figure not to be forgotten is Taitsena, possibly the idol of all young Mizos. The tenacity of Taitsena's mind and fortitude under extreme difficulties and hardships were unsurpassed.

The only near equivalent that comes to mind where observing such a code of conduct is still in vogue is the Army...... remember Latur or the Bihar floods or any recent tragedy they seem to be there first, work quickly, earn the gratitude of the affected people and carry on to some other job without making any great show about assisting.

But individually speaking, Tlawmnagaihna can teach all of us a thing or two about ourselves. Tlawmnagaihna is a value system, a culture an attitude deeply embedded in the Mizo psyche. Even today (unaffected by selfish competition) it is zealously sought to be promoted to fit in with the modern social swings. This inculcates a 'never say die' attitude; a kind of quality not to give up but surpass others. The acid test of Tlawmnagaihna is to follow it under difficult circumstances (in fact extremely difficult); when you have to up the last drop of water to someone else; when you go down a hill to fetch water at the end of a tiring day for someone else; when you travel for hours in the rain through leech infested forests to bring to the hospital an ailing old person; and so on the list would run. It is not an easy or comfortable code of conduct to follow; it is not something you can buy; it is not, in a way, meant for the weak willed; but the joy of doing things for others, of sharing, of giving, will pay (if you like that exchange) you back in kind… in peace and happiness. Love live Tlawmnagaihna.

30

Tlawmnagaihna

Followed even - Then

Taitesena

Tlawmnagaihna is an age-old code in the Mizo system or should one say way of life. It means 'service before self' (interestingly that is the credo of the National Defence Academy) and that is a code a Mizo holds very dear and follows very strictly. This helping attitude, this philosophy of sharing, this concept of concern has become virtually unknown elsewhere, especially in our so-called sophisticated (?) and civilised (?) urban societies. Aping the west we are losing our roots; we avoid the good (being punctual, being courteous) and follow the bad (chewing gum, poor language, aggressive showmanship and the like) not wanting to stop and think about where we are headed.

Vana Pa (a renown chief) is another one who made Tlawmangainha popular among the Mizos.

The name Taitsena is held in respect by the Mizo youth as he is also famous for following 'Tlawmnaghaina'. All Mizo youths love him; he has remained an idol to them down the centuries. Taitsena's real name was Khalvunga and he belonged to village Hrangvunga in Serhmun. No task was difficult for Taitsena and he could withstand any work no matter what the situation was. Never did he complain about any difficulty nor was he angry at any given time.

While going out on a hunt Taitsena ate very little rice. He always wanted to be alert and ready for any eventualities. Taitsena excelled in javelin throw, shotput and wrestling, a popular sport in the olden days. They say the chief of Taitsena's village wanted to find out who was the strongest man on whom the chief of village Hrangvunga could depend on. He sent one of the village elders to the Zawlbuk saying, "Go to the nearest Zawlbuks and tell the young men there that I have an important message to send to my brother chief who lives on the other side of the river. Much as I would like to wait till the morning the message is so important that I cannot pass it on till the morning. I will not be able to sleep. The night is dark and it is raining heavily. I am not sure if you will be able to find a volunteer to go on this errand; but I must have one person". The man who took the message himself did not know what the exact requirement was of the chief. The elder was a little shy of asking any question. He went to the Zawlbuk and asked the young men if anyone was willing to take on the responsibility, but no one was willing to budge out of the Zawlbuk at that odd hour. It was only Taitsena who was sleeping on one side of the Zawlbuk who quickly got up and dressed himself, ready to take on his duties. Taitsena asked the village elder what the task was but the older man said since he was not clear of the message, a good idea would be to go to the chief and find out. When Taitsena went to the chief he said, "I have no need of an errand boy tonight. We have too many enemies around and at all times need to be prepared. I only wanted to see how many I could trust". After this the chief invited Taitsena to a drink, but Taitsena initially refused and requested the chief to retire for the day as it was late in the night. But the chief insisted and so both the chief and Taitsena drank rice beer and talked all through the night as if they were old friends. This was a rare honour for Taitsena as the chief rarely requested even his own village elders to drink with him. Though Taitsena drank with the chief that night he was never heard of getting drunk.

The life of the people was difficult those days as there was danger from the wild beasts and nature's wrath. So the situation was of survival of the fittest. It was during such a fight with wild animals that Taitsena lost his life. In Serhum, the village of Taitsena there were a few brave warriors like Zingkela Ralte, Vungtawna Palian and Dozika Ralte and of course Taitsena. One year a ferocious tiger came to the village and soon the villagers had laid traps for him, unfortunately the tiger fell into one and the villagers thought it had been killed but only to find it had been injured and had managed to escape. The four braves rushed in to overpower the tiger but in the process became injured. Taitsena was caught by the tiger and in the tussle Taitsena broke his thigh bone. Finally, the other villagers overpowered the tiger and killed it. All the four braves they say did not take any help and walked back home. Later all four died, one tiger had been killed but so were four braves lost.

(A word about the Zalbuks, they are basically bachelor dormitories of the pre-British days as today with the coming of Christianity it has disappeared. It was earlier mandatory for all Mizo young men, over the age of fifteen years to join a Zawlbuk. It is here training was given in wrestling, hunting and village government. The young boys who were trained in the Zawlbuks came out as confident young men, ready to face the world. The importance of these Zawlbuks can be compared to the '*Guru Shisaya*' system found in the northern parts of India. As they say the simple forms of education as evolved from the Zawlbuk with the 'code of conduct' teachings remained for life for any Mizo man).

31

Vana Pa

What is it that compels us to remember a man who lived in the 18th century, a man whom people still respect and it is because of that roads and town halls have been named after him.

Vana Pa's real name was Thanazachhina from the Chawngthu Vanchiau clan; he is still remembered for following the Mizo code of conduct or Tlawmnagaihna to the ultimate. While hunting they say he would offer food and water to all first and then have it himself. But Vana Pa had not always been like this. Earlier he had been an ill-tempered man and it is due to this he could not get a wife when he was young. His bad temper most often got him into trouble and he became the butt of many jokes. It was almost at forty he could get married. Vana Pa they say was good at basket weaving and earned his living through that as manual work was difficult for him.

One day he thought that his ill-temper was getting him nowhere, so he decided to change himself. It was with great difficulty he succeeded, but his life in the village was not easy. Vana Pa would find his baskets broken or his precious necklace taken away and hidden. Vana Pa took all this in his stride and learnt to control his temper. Later his famous temper had gone and even the tone of his voice had become soft. A new man had emerged whom the people hardly recognised. They now respected the new Vana Pa.

Vana Pa belonged to Hilmen, the same village as of Chief Lalsuvunga. Lalsuvunga was responsible for giving orders that allowed a man with a gun to go hunting. The 'jhum' (slash and burn) cultivation areas could also be used for hunting. (In the North East, the Hills are used for cultivation and for that the mountain side is cleared by cutting the jungle and then burning it down. The burning is done so that the ash is used as fertilisers. Cultivation in these areas is done for two to three years and after that the land is left fallow for it to get back its fertility. It is being discouraged now as there is a lot of soil erosion due to this type of farming. Most often it leads to landslides. Mizos down the ages have loved hunting and it is because of this possibly we find very few animals around. Now of course the younger generations are trying to change this habit).

Vana Pa worked very hard to save enough to buy a gun, the gun was a prized possession as it is found everywhere. Though initially he was not known for his valour but being a skilful artisan he became successful in tactics and was a good counsellor. Chief Lalsuvunga was happy with him and so were his fellow warriors. Soon Vana Pa found he had become indispensable to Chief Lalsuvunga as the neighbouring chiefs were subdued by him. 'Never say die' attitude helped Vana Pa to attain his goals in life. He chased the Hmars right up to Manipur and was successful in capturing a large number of arms and ammunition. One variety of the gun was a breech loading gun and was popularly called 'Manipuri' by the Mizos.

Vana Pa is still remembered for his strict adherence to the Mizo code of conduct or 'Tlawmnagaihna'. Reverend JH Lorrain or Pu Buanga as he is lovingly called calls it 'self-sacrifice or unselfishness', perhaps we can say it is more than this as it has humility, no class distinction and devotion to duty. Tlawmnagaihna is something all Mizos hold very dear in their lives.

There are many stories about Vana Pa and his Tlawmnagaihna. Whenever he went out hunting or 'shikar' and had to spend the night at the 'jhum huts' he would leave the place neat and tidy, with sufficient firewood and drinking water for other hunters who may use the 'jhum huts' while hunting. Sometimes when Vana Pa and his hunters while returning from such a hunting expeditions had nothing to eat as all rations had been finished and the hunters had to go to the forest looking for berries and roots of plants, Vana Pa would wait for all to eat, it is only after everyone had had their fill would he eat. Another story has this to say, after a successful hunt when all the members of Vana Pa's group had all bagged a wild beast, Vana Pa was the last one to try his luck. As he was about to shoot a big bison a young man tried to shoo away the animal to a nearby bush by mistake. Vana Pa almost lost his shirt as they say and was about to reprimand the man when he remembered his pledge of not losing his temper. In the evening he complimented the young man for the fine meat for dinner.

Chief Lalsuvunga found Vana Pa a wise guide and an intelligent man and offered him chieftainship of one of his village but Vana Pa refused as he preferred being a councillor of the village. Though, he did ask the chief to allow his son to take his place after he was no more. They say Vana Pa lived a life following 'Tlawmnagaihna' and is remembered for this even today.

Nagaland

Verdant Hills and Fierce Warriors

Nestled among the ranges of the Northeast India, Nagaland has always aroused an awe-inspiring mysticism, primarily because of its remote geographical location. Nagaland as a state of India was born on 1st December 1963. It has no written history and the early history of Nagaland is largely not documented. The Nagas have a legend which explains why there are no written records. It is said that in the beginning of creation God gave the knowledge of reading and writing both to the hill men and the plains men. The plains men were given paper to write upon and the hill men skin. The hill men ate the skin as it tasted good. That is why we have no written records about the Nagas, is the old saying. The Nagas are a proud race and have many stories of valour which their forefathers have handed down through oral literature, song and dance. Nagas have a classless society and do not care about the social hierarchy. Women enjoy equality of status with men from time immemorial. Naga society is patrilineal and the descendents are from the eldest male member of the family. Nagas do respect their elders, something which is diminishing in today's world.

The Nagas are said to belong to the Indo-Mongoloid stock, a race whose presence was first noted 1,000 years before Christ.

Sanskrit literature describes them as 'kiratas' or hill men "living on Nature's gifts, warlike and possessing formidable weapons". The meaning of the word 'Naga' is obscure. Some say it is derived from the Sanskrit word 'Naga', meaning mountain, so 'mountain man'. Yet others say it means a warrior. Some thought 'Naga' is related to 'nanga' meaning naked. Possibly it is derived from '*Nok*', which in some dialect means 'people. ' The name Naga they say was given by the plains men.

We hear about the Nagas in the epic Mahabharata, Princess Ulupi was a Zeliang princess who fell in love with Arjuna and took him to Nagalok. The Rakshasa Princess Hidimba and her son Ghatotkoch by the second Pandava brother was a Kachari princess and the Kachar kings had their seat in Dimapur in today's Nagaland. Ptolemy the historian has also made a brief mention about the Nagas in his work. The Ahom *Buranjis* (Chronicles) also mention the Nagas and their coming in contact with the Aos and Lothas. There were frequent clashes between the Ahoms and Nagas but the Nagas were kept under control by the Ahoms as they were made to pay tributes, the Nagas paid tribute to the Ahom Kings with mithuns. The Naga tribes had socio-economic and political links with tribes in Assam and Myanmar, even today large population of Nagas inhabit Assam. After 1816, the area along with Assam came under direct rule of the British and this period was a difficult time for Nagaland and Assam. The British East India Company took control of Assam in 1826; they steadily expanded their domain over modern Nagaland. By 1892, all of modern Nagaland except the Tuensang area in the northeast was governed by the British. They stopped inter-tribal conflicts, and put an end to the practice of head-hunting by the use of force and diplomacy. But it was largely due to the work of Christian missionaries in the area that transformed Nagaland. Many Naga tribes embraced Christianity, in particular the Baptist faith, the state has now ninety percent Christian. However, there are a small group of tribes who continued to practice the animist religious traditions that existed before the arrival of the British.

The 16 major tribes inhabiting this small state speak a number of languages including Ao, Konyak, Angami, Sema and Lotha. Each tribe has its own dialect. In the olden days as people were always at war with each other so the need for a common 'lingua franca' did not arise. But with the increase in inter-tribal communication, the lack of a common language was feLt Out of this need a 'pidgin' Assamese came into being, today we call it 'Nagamese' which uses the local dialect, Assamese and sometimes a few Sanskrit words. Nagamese has proved to be a successful link language and today we can hear it on All India Radio too. Nagamese does not belong to a particular group or tribe nor does it have a written script. The missionaries rendered a great service to the Naga languages as they wrote the first grammar books and compiled vocabularies. The missionaries used the Roman script.

Various myths have been handed down through ages about the origin of the Nagas. The Aos believe that the first of their forefathers were created out of a rock – 'Lungthurok' or shall we say the 'great rock' on the Chongliemdi Hills. Another story says that every person has to cross a great river to go to the next world. When people die relatives put in some money into the palm of the dead one, this is to be given to the boat man to row him/her across the river. The different tribes have different myths but there are common themes which all believe in, it is the Supreme Being. Most Nagas talk of a good and bad spirit. The disturbance in our life is brought by the evil spirit; it is felt not only in this world but also in death. All unnatural deaths like drowning, killing by a wild animal are the work of an evil spirit. The Naga Hills had a variety of wild life, like the tigers, leopard, elephants, deer, bear and monkeys. These animals are connected to the life of the people. It is here the concept of lycanthropy comes in amongst the Nagas. Generally it was believed that a lycanthropes soul would enter the body of a tiger or leopard at night and returned to the human body during the day. It was felt if a soul remained out for a few days; the human being would be lethargic for that period. JP Mills had recorded the case of a person called Hillo Rengma, who died in 1927. His widow told him that Hillo became violent when his tiger was killing at night, during the day he would sleep or was very lethargic when the tiger's belly was full. Sometimes Hillo's buttock would have a wound, it was almost like a sympathetic wound when the tiger was wounded or shot at by a hunter. They say the last known lycanthropist was an old woman who when she was asleep her body was in her place or house but her soul roamed about the forest in a tiger's form. In today's world all this may seem unnatural, yet we do hear of 'werewolves' in Europe.

The state is divided into seven districts, Kohima, Phek, Mokokchung, Wokha, Zunheloto, Twensang and Mon. The terrain is hilly, rugged and mountainous. The highest peak is Saramati in the Twensang district which is 3840 metres above sea-level. The average height of the peaks is between 900 and 1200 metres. The main rivers that flow through the state are Dhansiri, Doyang, Dikhu, Tizu and Melak. There is no waterfall in Nagaland. The only well-known lake is Lacham to the east of Mehiri. The hill sides are covered with green forests. In the Angami region, the terraced fields are a feast to the eyes. Life for the Nagas who have been hill dwellers, has never been easy. They had to work hard on the mountainous terrain. They live in a beautiful land and are very proud of it. A large number of people are tillers who are attached to the soil. Most of the tillers of the land practice 'jhum' cultivation.

The Nagas love hunting and are attached to their weapons, though much of the game is extinct now. Dogs are sometimes used to track the animals. Elephant hunting is a thrilling sport to them. The Nagas are great meat eaters; the most popular meat is pork, beef and chicken. One rarely finds a vegetarian Naga, at least not by choice!

32

Rani Gaidinliu

Gaidinliu the beautiful daughter of Lothonang and Kocotlenliu was born on 26th January, 1915 at Lungkao in Rongmai, a Naga village. The village was in north-western part of Manipur. The family belonged to the Pamei clan of the village. From early childhood Gaidinliu showed signs of spiritualism and learnt her Animistic religion, traditions and practices well. Though formally not educated as there were no schools, she had learnt the dialects of other Naga tribes. At that time, the British were only interesred in educating the people who were turning towards Christianity. The Christian missionaries were working hard to convert and educate the Nagas. The very thought that the Nagas were turning away from their own religion towards Christianity upset Gaidinliu.

So when Gaidinliu heard about Jadonang and his new religion, 'the reasserted Naga Animistic belief', she was drawn towards the movement. In 1927, she went to meet Jadonang at Bhuvan Cave and was greatly impressed by him, she later became an ardent follower of his teachings and beliefs. Gaidinliu became a priestess or '*maibi*' of Jadonang's religion. Gaidinliu with other priests or '*maibas*' and priestesses or '*maibis*' preached the new religion, which was called 'Haraka' (meaning 'Pure' in Zeliangrong language). Gaidinliu chose this difficult life with her eyes open. Some of this we find reflected in her speech to Indira Gandhi. She said that like all young girls she dreamt of a family with children but she had to sacrifice all this and take up the leadership to liberate her people from the foreign powers. Though a difficult decision, she chose the path of liberating her people.

Gaidinliu and Jadonang seemed to have developed a bond of trust and friendship. Gaidinliu when in Kambrion used to pray at Jadonang's temple, Jadonang also visited Gaidinliu's village to preach Animism. It pained Gaidinliu to see her Naga people drifting away from their own religion. She called on her people to be strong and follow their own religion. The villagers of Lungkao took Gaidinliu as their own leader and built a temple for her. At the inauguration ceremony, Jadonang also joined in the feast. Gaidinliu tried to hold the attention of her people with her ability, her very sincerity attracted people towards her and her Animistic beliefs. She asked the people to draw strength from their inner reserves and awaken from their slumber. Gaidinliu joined Jadonang's movement wholeheartedly. Now with support from her people she asked them not to pay house tax to the British, the Britishers who gave no protection to them against the Kukis. Her followers obeyed her by not paying tax, not lifting luggage and doing other lowly jobs for the British government officials. Her protests were so successful that she invited the wrath of the Britishers. Gaidinliu also told her people about what she had heard about Jadonang, Mahatma Gandhi, Jawaharlal Nehru and other great leaders. It was about Nationalism and to boycott the Britishers in all possible ways. Gaidinliu told her people that a day would come when a free 'Naga Government' would be established. Co-incidentally it was during this time Mahatma Gandhi's civil disobedience movement was on in full swing. She told her people about this and advised them to disobey all British orders.

Jadonang's imprisonment and finally execution shifted the mantle of leadership on Gaidinliu and she bore the responsibility well. The Britishers realised that the movement was gaining momentum and had to be curbed. So the Assam Government placed it under the control of the Deputy Commissioner of Naga Hills. Gaidinliu was declared a 'wanted' person and an arrest warrant was issued to put her under trial. The Britishers said she was the priestess of a cult who believed in human sacrifice.

To avoid arrest Gaidinliu moved from village to village preaching her faith. During this time a lot of Naga traditional stories and songs were passed down orally. The theme being all men are equal and they should be able to give their life for their belief. The soldiers of the Assam Rifles tried their best to catch her and at times destroyed villages to scare the people, but the Nagas a very loyal and trusted people never gave her away. Gaidinliu moved eastwards towards the Angami areas and asked the people to fight for the Nagas. The slogan heard everywhere was, 'the day of the Naga is coming'. The ever elusive Gaidinliu went underground and through the jungles visited remote Zeliangrong villages. At times she seemed to be like a ghost. Her most staunch follower was her Army Commander -Masang from Keplo village. He also looked after her security.

During this time there were some Nagas who had been educated in British and American Missionary schools, these people did not support the Animistic movement. Some of these people felt the Nagas were not ready for freedom. Such Nagas were used to hunt down Gaidinliu and her followers. Dr Haralu from Pulomi village gave full support to the British to track down Gaidinliu. Dr Haralu firmly believed that western education and Christianity would help in the uplift of the Nagas. Ironically, Dr Haralu's younger brother Jenyi was a strong follower of Gaidinliu. Jenyi used to interpret Gaidinliu's sayings and predictions and read scripts which Jadonang had invented.

Once while Gaidinliu was hiding in Puloni village the British tracked her down with the help of Naga spies. Gaidinliu was captured, 'the most wanted Naga woman' by Bir Bahadur Thapa, a Nepalese Naik working under the British. Gaidinliu and her brother Marang were brought in chains to Imphal jail. A trial was conducted by JC Higgins – the Political Agent of Manipur. She was convicted and sentenced to deportation for life at the tender age of seventeen. Her brother was set free as he was very young.

The movement seemed to go down but to the Nagas she was still their leader.

The consequences of trying to be free and daring to go against the British were drastic. They were: One, the British stopped all aids and development works in the Zeliangrong Hills, as a result the Zeliangrong people remained illiterate and backward. Two, the policy of divide and rule made the Zeliangrong people come under three administrative units - Manipur, Kachar and the Naga Hills. Three, most of the Zeliangrong hills people; the Rongmais were brought to Imphal to be night soil workers to the British, Bengalis and Marwaris. Possibly because of this most 'safaiwallahs' of today in Manipur and Kachhar are Kabuis.

Even when in jail Gaidinliu had her followers meeting her and following her orders. Gaidinliu was kept in Shillong jail and then shifted to Jorhat jail by the Assam Government. It was in 1937, Jawaharlal Nehru while in Assam heard of Gaidinliu - how she fought to free her people. She dreamed of freedom for her people and because of this was put behind bars for six long years. Nehru wanted to bring her out of jail and went to meet her. He was moved by her story and rightfully called her 'Rani'. The Rani was set free in 1947 from Tura Jail in the Garo Hills, but her movements were restricted. In 1950 the Rani went back to working for the Zeliangrong people, it is in this connection she met a number of Indian National Congress leaders and told them about the problems she was facing. In 1951 at Tuensang she heard about the good work done by the Christian missionaries and realised that Christ was a good man and his teachings helped in the uplift of her people, the Nagas, but all the same she did not get baptised.

In 1955 there were violent clashes between the Indian Army and the Nagas who wanted a separate Nagaland. Rani Gaidinliu had problems facing her as the educated Christian Nagas criticised her faith, they took the Animistic beliefs as Satanic. She was also criticised for only thinking of uniting the Zeliangrong people - the Zemai, Liangmai and Rongmai areas. During such trying situations the Rani for her own security and to defend her religious movement went underground with her private army. Her army commander was a Rangma - a staunch Zemai Animist. Gaidinliu's followers opposed Zapu Phizo and his group because Phizo's group wanted a Christian independent Nagaland. Rani Gaidinliu and her followers had problems from all quarters, the Indian Army and the Federal Nagas. Some of the Naga Christian converts had completely moved away from Animism to Christianity and at times called Gaidinliu and Jadonang 'Khampai' in the derogatory sense. 'Khampai' meaning polemical (a person who strongly advocates an idea or speech forcefully and with conviction). At times the Animists burnt down churches and Christian houses to stop Christianity spreading. Gaidinliu firmly believed in Animism and integration of Zeliangrong people but the Assam Government felt it was a grim cult and so kept a watch over it, later combing operations in suspected villages took place. The Assam Government tried to tempt them to come out of hiding as they found Gaidinliu and her followers as objectionable as Zapu Phizo's group. Phizo by then had escaped to London and settled there.

The Deputy Commissioner of Police Subodh Chandra Dev was asked by the Chief Minister of Nagaland Shilu Ao to persuade the Rani to surrender or shift out from that area. SC Dev decided to choose the first that is request Gaidinliu to surrender and so sent out a letter to her. Initially, Gaidinliu did not agree to meet Dev but later finally did. People called this meeting historical. In the *Assam Tribune*, Kelakini Sekhose wrote about SC Dev, "Somebody else in his place might have shivered even at the thought of meeting the woman who was considered to be an evil spirit and said to be thirsty for human blood". SC Dev's journey was back breaking as the Rani's hideout was tucked away on a hill side, it was well-fortified too. SC Dev had possibly imagined the Rani to be very ferocious looking as she had become a near mythical figure. When the Rani finally did appear, SC Dev found her to be an old woman, the Rani was dressed in the traditional Naga dress and she welcomed him with a "Jai Hind". Quietly she said in Bengali, "*Chalaki korben na*" meaning "no tricks please". The Rani asked SC Dev if he was scared of meeting her and SC Dev's answer to this was that he had come to meet her like a son; this moved the Rani and made the meeting an easy one. The Rani insisted she was an Indian and a Naga too and talking of their separations was madness.

Before surrendering Rani wanted to meet the Prime Minister and if talks failed she should be permitted to go back to her jungle domain. Gaidinliu asked SC Dev to put this down in writing in his own blood, Dev readily agreed to this archaic tradition as he realised this was the only blood that would flow if he did what was asked. The Rani's meeting with the Prime Minister also ended on a happy note.

On 16th January 1966, Rani Gaidinliu formally agreed to lay down her arms with her men and work overground for the betterment of the Zeliangrong people. The men from her army were later absorbed in the Nagaland Armed Police. The Rani later on lived in Kohima- Forest Colony. She was given a pension and '*tamrapatra*' by the Government of India. In 1988 the Mizoram state also honoured her with the 'Ropuiliani award 'for her struggle to free her beloved land.

Today the Rani is no more in flesh. Rani Gaidinliu died on 17th February, 1993 but her spirit lives in the hearts of her people.

Thus came to an end the story of a near mythical figure, the priestess of Haraka faith, follower of Tingwa (God) who celebrate each night of the full moon with rituals similar to the Hindu Tantrik cuLt No account of insurgency can be complete without the story of Rani Gaidinliu. She stands out bold and bright in Nagaland's blood soaked history. Her dedication and sacrifice will always be respected and remembered by her people.

33

Haipou Jadonang

To understand why Haipou Jadonang is an important historical figure in Nagaland, one must know a little about Naga Animism. Traditional Animism believed in the existence of one Supreme God, who is all powerful. There were subordinate gods who were both good and evil; they also included angels ruling over human beings, animals, the sun, the moon and the earth. Worship, offerings, ceremonies and rites were absolutely necessary when an occasion rose, be it good or bad in the people's Animistic life. It is during this time the Naga Animistic group and Christianity were struggling for survival in the Zeliangrong Hills. Christianity was progressing at a good speed possibly because the Nagas believed in a Higher Being without the identification with any object or idols. This could have helped in the acceptance of Christianity. On the other hand, the Animists were trying to survive. Christianity preached about Jesus Christ, it did not talk of gods and goddess. It is during this time there emerged a young man called Haipou Jadonang. Jadonang did not refute the teachings of Jesus Christ as he found them to be good, ethical and with moral values. He was intelligent enough to realise that Christian missionaries carried with them something brilliant, 'The English Language'. The Nagas were divided into sixteen major tribes, with each tribe having its own dialects or languages.

Earlier since they were continuously at war with each other, the need for a common 'lingua franca' arose. The English language had become a common language of the Nagas, Nagamese as a language came into being.

What Jadonang was against was not Christianity but Christian missionaries' denouncement of Naga Animism. Jadonang emerged as a 'Messiah' for the Nagas. Haipou Jadonang was a thin, short-statured man. His date of birth is not known due to lack of written records but people generally say it is 1900 AD. His parents, Thiudai and Taboliu, were farmers. Jadonang was only a year old when his father died. Taboliu his mother brought up her sons by tilling the land. Jadonag was his mother's favourite child; he was also looked after by his elder brother Mundnnang. Right from early childhood Jadonang was a deeply religious man and would pray to God for hours. Though he had no formal education he was well-versed with Animistic laws, traditions, culture and social etiquette. Being very religious he had visited all the religious places like Bhuvon Cave and Zelad Lake where the Animists believed God resided. At a young age, he went through trance or communicating with gods or divine spirits. In the presence of spirits Jadonang saw visions of people and their doings of far and near. Like other Nagas, in villages under trance he could prescribe correct medicines. When the spirits left the body he would become an ordinary human being. The Nagas felt such men were messengers of God. Jadonang won the confidence of his villagers with his mystic powers. Once when the villagers were facing drought, Jadonang suggested a mithun be sacrificed for a good harvest. The Kambrion villagers did this with hesitation but were later blessed with a good harvest. After this they took Jadonang as their spiritual leader. Through the spiritual powers Jadonang won the confidence of his people. He claimed to be the 'Messiah King' of the Nagas and wanted to free them from the British.

Jadonang married twice. His first wife could not bear any children and a childless woman to the Nagas is a bad omen. So Jadonang married again and the second wife gave birth to a son called Kapindammano. Some old people say he joined the British Army and had gone to Mesopotamia during the Second World War. Jadonang started the practice of Animism on a more modernised fashion; he called his new religion or reasserted Animism as 'Haraka'. In Zeliangrong language it means 'pure'. For this he built a temple close to his home and preached from this temple. At times she would heal people with his supernatural powers. All this attracted people to his faith, people from Zemai, Liangmai, Rongmai tribes living in Tamenglang areas of Manipur, the Naga Hills and the Kachar Hills flocked to his temple. He also had a number of priests '*Maibas*' and priestess '*Maibis*' among who Gaidinliu was the chief priestess.

Jadonang to keep his Naga language going invented his own script for the use of the Nagas: it was crude and unintelligible but some say it still remains in use. During those days this invention was wonderful as the Nagas found a unique alternative to their script less language. Jadonang wrote down his ideas and songs in his new language in a book. This made the young man happy and proud. Jadonang proudly wrote a letter to the SDO at Tamenalang SC Booth in his new language to show off his wonderful invention. Unfortunately, SC Booth could not appreciate this young man's invention and tore up the letter taking this as something stupid, an illiterate man's idea of a script.

Jadonang who had by now become famous amongst his people resented the British policy of house tax of Rs. 3/- and supply of free labour and food to visiting government officials on tour. Jadonang rebelled against this and the Zeliangrongs gave support to him with heart and soul. He planned to form an army of freedom fighters in 1927. He sent his followers to different areas and among them was Miss Gaidinliu spreading the message, 'overthrow the British Raj and restore Naga sovereignty'. He got together young men to join the freedom struggle. In shaping his political career, he was greatly influenced by Mahatma Gandhi and praised him for his heroic deeds and in 1927AD even wrote a song,

"Oh! Mighty Gandhi
Come to rule upon us.
You are the leader,
You are the great
Come to rule us"

In 1927, Mahatma Gandhi was supposed to visit Silchar and Jadonang had come down with Naga boys and girls to welcome him. Unfortunately, Mahatma Gandhi could not come and Jadonang's dream of meeting the Mahatma could not be fulfilled.

Jadonang wanted to show the British that they were in no way superior to the Nagas as God had created all men equal. His anti-British movement gained momentum and it became a serious threat to the British Government. The Manipur and Assam government under British took all possible steps to stop the movement. There are certain instances which irked the British. Jadonang refused to remove his hat in front of the SDO or dismount from his horse. SDO Booth arrested him but had to let him go with a warning, all this did not have any effect on Jadonang. Another time Jadonang's followers were observing '*Genna* 'or 'taboo' day from any work for the worship of Earth. The Earth Goddess forbade any manual work and on such a special day outsiders were not allowed to come in as is the Animistic custom. It was during such a time four betel nut traders from Manipur wanted to come to Kambrion village. They were requested not to enter but they forced their way in. The Nagas felt they were spies as the travellers wanted to know where Jadonang was. The Nagas asked the travellers to be quiet and remain in their allocated areas. The Manipuri travellers did not obey the orders and cooked food for them. The Nagas felt the Manipuris were disrespectful to their Gods and in their anger killed the travellers. The British called the killing as human sacrifice and Jadonang was blamed for this as he was their leader. Once when he was coming back from Bhuvan Cave after praying Jadonang was waylaid by a police constable in plain clothes. The police constable invited him home for food and rest. It was here Jadonang was arrested, caught unawares, he could not even resist. He was tied in ropes and chains and taken around Lungkao, Kambrion and Kamenglong areas to show to the people that their leader was captured. On 13th June, 1931 he was tried for the murders and he did not have any legal help. Though Jadonang kept insisting that he was innocent and had done no wrong, all this fell on deaf ears. Jadonang was put into Imphal jail and after a mock trial was hanged by the British government. The dead hero lay humiliated and defeated; he left behind years of struggle.

Later with reluctance the British government permitted the body to be taken home and buried according to Animistic beliefs in his own house in Tamenglong. The British Government were worried that Jadonang's death would stir the revenge feelings and revive the freedom struggle. As a preventive measure they burnt all his belonging that included his books in his own script. Jadonang became a martyr for the Naga nationalism in the struggle against the British rule in India. His death made his followers more determined to fight the British in the freedom struggle. Thus, came to an end the life of a religious leader, a social worker, a pioneer of anti-colonial movement in the Naga Hills.

The 79th death anniversary of Jadonang, the great freedom fighter of Zeliangrong Hills was observed on 29th August, 2010 in Imphal. People paid floral tributes to his statue.

34

Natwar Thakkar

What makes a man who is Gujarati by birth go to Nagaland, that too to a remote village called Chu-Chu-Yuilang? Here is a living legend of Nagaland, who loves the place and is working towards national integration. He is more a Naga than a Naga by birth.

Natwarbhai Thakkar was born to Chabidas and Leelawati on 9th October, 1932 in Dahanu – a small town of Maharashtra. Though born in Maharashtra he was from a Gujarati speaking background. As a young boy he was influenced by Mahatma Gandhi. After Matriculation Natwar decided to work for the country, and its people. He was groomed by Acharya Kakasaheb Kalelkar, a Gandhian worker. Natwar Thakkar wanted to do something for the country so Acharya Kakasaheb Kalelkar motivated him to go to Nagaland. At the young age of twenty-three in 1955, Natwar Thakkar arrived in Nagaland. During those days, Nagaland was going through great tension as the Naga leader AZ Phizo had launched his movement for a free Nagaland. Nagaland during that period had motorable 'kutcha' roads or unsurfaced roads; there were no bus services. There were no water supply, no medical facility and of course no electricity. In these difficult times Natwar Thakkar started his social work and continues to do so after five decades and more. He shuns publicity and has silently helped the people to improve their lives and become independent.

Natwar Thakkar has a Naga wife; Lentina supports him in all his work. Lentina and Natwar have five children, three sons and two daughters. She is the first Naga to be trained as a Gandhian worker at Sarnia Ashram Gauhati; this Ashram was first set up by Amalprova Das. Mahatma Gandhi himself inaugurated the Ashram in, 1946.

Some of the Nagas had heard about Gandhi but since most of them had not intimately been involved in the freedom struggle they looked at Natwar Thakkar with suspicion. Social service centres with a secular background were unknown those days. The only social service till then was done by the American Baptist Christian Missionaries. Incidentally, there were no foreign missionaries in Nagaland when Natwar first went there. The mission centers were run by Nagas entirely in the fifties. So when Natwar started his work he was eyed with misgiving. The Naga missionaries felt that he had come to spread Hinduism and militants felt he was a Government of India agent. On both sides, Natwar was faced with opposition and life had become quite difficult for him.

A reign of terror had been let loose by the extremists in Nagaland. Many people were murdered and villagers lived in fear and tension. The army had to be called to maintain peace; there were clashes with the underground rebels and the army. Nagaland was almost converted into a battlefield. Natwar Thakkar true to his idealism went from village to village preaching peace and friendship. Natwar was also responsible for removing misunderstandings between the government officials and village folks. The army was happy at this but the extremists were unhappy as they felt he was weaning away their support. Natwar's name was their on the hit list of the extremists. A well-organised raid was conducted by the extremists on Natwar's hut in 1957, but he escaped unhurt with his family. All the villagers protested to the extremists at this unfair attack. Later on there was no such incident but life for Natwar had become unsafe.

The Central Government sent Natwar to Nagaland with their blessings. Eminent leaders like Pandit Nehru and Dr Rajendra Prasad appreciated this young social worker's efforts. Natwar Thakkar started socio-economic projects too; he started vocational training centres for school dropouts and physically handicapped people. Courses like carpentry and tailoring were started, medical centers had started functioning. Pre-primary schools or Balwadis as in Maharashtra were opened to educate the young. National days like Gandhi Jayanti and Republic Day celebrations were started by Natwar Thakkar. Later it was taken over by the state government. Mahatma Gandhi was known and respected in Nagaland even before Nagaland Gandhi Ashram was established. But as the Naga society had remained somewhat isolated from rest of the country during the British regime, it was not involved in the country's freedom struggle in a major way.

Natwar Thakkar founded the Nagaland Gandhi Ashram (NGA) at the Ao Naga village of Chuchuyimlang in 1955 under the auspices of the Bharatiya Adimjati Sevak Sangh (The society of servants of the tribal communities of India). According to tradition the Ao Nagas when they take over the responsibility of looking after an individual in their midst, it is formally accepted by the elders of the village council (Putu), they become the guardians. The village has remained true to its tradition and has faithfully acted as the guardian of the Ashram during difficult times. The Ashram in turn, true to its commitment, has also served the village to the best of its ability in various ways. The Ashram and the village, both are rightly proud of each other. He has since been working at the Ashram. The objectives set before the NGA or the Nagaland Gandhi Ashram were to work for all round development of the Naga society through constructive work and to promote emotional integration. The Ashram here is essentially a modest grassroot level service centre. The activities are related to rural development and promoting healthy human relationships. The most significant achievement in the socio-economic field has been the popularisation of bee keeping throughout the state.

Chu-Chu-Yimlang is a sleepy mountainous village. Today this tiny village has a telephone exchange, post office, state bank, high school and a small hospital. All the praises go to Natwar Thakkar for his effort; it has been a Herculean task for him. Most Gandhian social workers perhaps have worked in Hindu dominated localities; Natwar Thakkar is one of the few, who have been working in a tribal society which was predominantly a Christian region.

Nagaland Gandhi Ashram (NGA) has maintained a long-standing tradition of observing Gandhi Jayanti at Chuchuyimlang village on its campus. Second October is also a day the Ashram observes as its Founder's day. The Gandhi Jayanti 2007, however, had greater or special significance. The General Assembly of United Nations by an unanimous resolution had determined to celebrate Gandhi's birthday as the International Day of non-violence all over the world from 2007 onwards. This is an important development for India and a landmark in the progress of human civilization and NGA wanted this new resolution to exist in the minds of the people.

Natwar Thakkar also started the Khadi and Village Industries and today Khadi clothing displayed by the Khadi and Village Industries Sangh, Dimapur the town which had the highest number of buyers. There had been displays of various products which will definitely draw great demand in the market if the right platforms and avenues are provided to the village people of Chu-Chu-Yimlang.

Natwar Thakkar has been awarded a number of times by the Government for his good work. Some of them are:

1. Jamnalal Bajaj Award- 1987 for constructive work.
2. Indira Gandhi Award - 1994 for National Integration.
3. Mahatma Gandhi Award- 1996 by the Government of Meghalaya in recognition of services to Naga people.

The legend carries on working for his people, the Nagas he loves so dearly.

Tripura

Heritage of Bir Bikram Kishore

Tripura is landlocked and lies to the south-eastern side of the 'Seven Sisters.' It has borders with Bangladesh on three sides that is north, south and west. Assam and Mizoram lies to its east. The capital city is Agartala. The people speak Bengali and Kokborok. During the British period it was also called 'Hills of Tippera' and has a history of 2500 years and one eighty- six kings. Topographically, the land is divided into Hills, plains, Valleys and river basins. The hill ranges loose height gradually and merge into the plains of Bangladesh. The hill ranges earlier had thick forests but today have become sparse due to land settlements and 'jhum' or 'slash and burn' method of farming. There are a number of rivers which rise from these Hills and are seasonal in nature. One of the most important rivers is river Gumati on whose bank lies the old capital of Udaipur. The place was named after Maharaja Udai Manyikya.

About the history of Tripura not much is known, the first mention is found in the Ashokan pillars of 3rd century BC. In the olden times, Tripura was also called 'Kirat Desh'. Tripura, the descendent of King Druya and Babru, contemporary of Yudhistir was the ruler after whom Tripura is named. In 1300 AD, Tripura came under the control of the Manikya dynasty of Indo-Mongolian origin.

The earliest known recorded history is the 'Rajmala' or the chronicle of the kings, it was written in Bengali, the Rajmala was written by Brahmins in the court. According to tradition King Tugral Khan of Bengal gave the title of 'Manikya' to the king in return of a costly gem which was found, they say, on the head of a frog. It is said that since then the title has been in use. The history of Tripura is divided into two parts – one the traditional legendary part and the second 1431-1462 under Dharma Manikya, Tripura was a generous state which looked after its people well. History says that around the 7th century the kings took on the title of 'pha' or father and the first king was Ratna Pha. In early 17th century Tripura came under the control of the Mughals, but some of the powers were under the control of the Manikya dynasty. The British when they came did not force authority over the people of Tripura, the Maharajas had enough independence to rule, and only when a new king had to come to the throne it needed British approval. The monarchy came to an end on 9th September 1947 when Maharaja Kirit Bikram Kishore, Manikya Bahadur from Agartala (1947-1949) accepted that Tripura should become a part of India. It officially became a part of India on 15th October 1949, a Union Territory on 1st November 1956 and finally a state on 1st January 1972.

Bir Chandra Manikya Bahadur was a man with vision, he wanted Tripura to prosper, and it was he, who modernised Tripura's administration. The Maharaja Bir Bikram Kishore's interest in military affairs came in handy when the Japanese threatened invasion, he could guide his troops to serve the country with honour. However, his early death left a void, it was the time when the British withdrew and the birth of East Pakistan brought in refugee problems, the people found the going difficult as there was severe strain on the administration since the resources of the state were depleting. Maharaja Bir Bikram Kishore's wife Maharani Kanchan Prabha Devi who had become the Regent of her young son Kirit Bikram after her husband's death found it difficult to look after the land and had to merge the state with India, thus ended the independent existence of a powerful state called Twipra or Tripura.

Development in Tripura has not been as much as it should have been; this was largely due to poor economic conditions. In the last quarter of the 19th century Maharaja Bir Chandra Kishore started the reforms and so development began. The Maharaja reformed the revenue system, police, army and built roads. He sent his sons out for education in modern institution. It was Maharaja Bir Bikram Kishore who brought in major changes in Tripura. He succeeded his father at the age of fifteen in 1923 and reigned under a Council of Regents. Education, communications and infrastructure improved and very soon the state of Tripura was at par with other states.

There are different theories about the name given to Tripura-

- Legend says, Tripur was the 39th descendent of Druhya, a descendent of Yayati, belonging to the lunar or 'chandravanshi' race kings. The king was a tyrant and ordered his people to worship him as God. Most of his people fled to Hiramba (Cachar) today's Assam.
- The word Tripura came from the presiding deity of the land Tripurasundari, followers of 'Shakti' believe in her.
- The historian Kailash Chandra Singha says the word Tripura comes from two different Kokborok words 'twi' meaning water and 'pra' meaning near. This could possibly be true as in the olden times as Tripura stretched upto Bay of Bengal, the kingdom stretched from the Garo Hills to the Arakan mountains.
- Tripura may have got its name from the temple at Udaipur of Goddess Tripureshwari, the wife of Lord Shiva.

Earlier the Tripura or Tipra kingdom had stretched from Sylhet, Dhaka and Chittagong (now in Bangladesh), Cachar in Assam and parts of Mizoram. Today Bengalis comprise about 70 percent of the population and the rest 30 percent is made up of native tribal. A large part of the tribal population speak Kokborok, today there are some differences between the Bengali and tribal population. The bulk of the population are Hindus, they comprise about 85 percent, Muslims are about 8 percent, Christians 3 percent and Buddhist 3 percent. Hinduism is the state religion in Tripura and Tripureshwari is the patron goddess.

The Tripura Tiger Force are a part of the tribal groups which was formed in 1990, later in 1992 it became a formal group. These were a group which worked in the Hills of Tripura, recruiting young men, this group met with a crisis when about 1600 group members laid down their arms to the government in 1994, the group works to get the tribal population their land back which had been taken away by the Bengali immigrants who settled in Tripura. The Tripura Tiger Force was banned in 1997. The main aim of the organisation was to get the tribal population their rightful land back and to drive out the Bengalis. The Tripura Tiger Force is headed by Ranjit Deb Burman who has taken refuge in Taragaon in Bangladesh from where he runs the organisation.

The people belong to the Indo-Aryan group, the Bengalis belong to this group and the Indo-Mongoloid group has the Tripuris, Reangs, Cha kmas, Kukis, Mogh and the Lushais. The Tripuris are the original inhabitants of the place and today some have been influenced by the Bengali culture. The Tripura festivals have both religious and cultural elements in them. Some of the festivals are Durga Puja, Kharchi Puja and Garia Puja.

Agartala is the state capital, what we see today is the effort of Maharaja Bir Bikram Manikya Bahadur who turned the place into a planned city with strong roads and a market building. The major attractions of the state are Kamalasagar Lake, Dumboor Lake near Agartala, Neermahal, Trishna and Sepahijala Wildlife Sanctuary. The tourists are not too many in number due to internal strife's and being so far flung away. The climate of Tripura is monsoonal and varies from subtropical to temperate zones.

35

Bir Bikram Kishore Manikya

Maharaja Bir Bikram Kishore Manikya Bahadur of Tripura was the last king and after his death in May 1947, Tripura merged with Independent India and the monarchy ended on 9th September 1947. For one of the world's oldest monarchy finally the curtains were drawn. It was Ratna Pha, the king in the 14th century, who took the title of Manikya and after him all the kings had Manikya as superlative to their name. The Tripuri kings had an Indo-Mongolian origin and the dynasty ruled for almost 3000 years. This was the most glorious period for Tripura. Maharaja Bir Bikram was born on 19th August 1908, with Leo as sun sign, he was a true ruler. Bir Bikram was born a year before his grandfather Radhakishore Manikya died in an accident in 1909. His early death in 1947 at the age of thirty-nine was a setback to the development of Tripura, especially to the people.

Bir Bikram loved his people and was getting ready to shoulder his responsibilities when destiny had other plans. Bir Bikram lost his father Birendra Kishore Manikya at a very young age. Birendra Kishore Manikya was responsible for bringing the tea industry into Tripura, he invited the British tea planters to come and start tea plantations in Tripura. Birendra Kishore was also supposed to have started the foundation of civil services; he had taken great interest in educating his people too. Coming from such background, it is but natural that he would start new things which would benefit his people. Bir Bikram had a normal life of a prince in those days, happy and carefree. Before the start of World War II, the young prince went on a world tour and met some important world leaders like Mussolini, the Fascist leader of Italy, Hitler of Germany, and Roosevelt of USA. The tour broadened the young king's mind and also gave him an insight into world politics, the king came back with his mind open to new ideas, and he had definite plans about the layout of the town of Agartala, and decided that it would have wide roads with a market building.

The Maharaja succeeded his father at the young age of fifteen on 5th December, 1923 and ruled with the help of his uncles. For a number of years he ruled under a Council of Regency, a form of government advocated by the British. He was installed by the Governor General of Bengal Sir Francis Jackson at Agartala in 1927; his investiture ceremony took place with great pomp and show. During the reign of Bir Bikram, Tripura flourished and it was at par with other states of the North East. Bir Bikram right from his childhood had a compassionate heart and this was apparent from an incident during his childhood. When he was a young boy a man had been given the death sentence by his father, the young prince was very upset with this and kept pleading with his father to forgive the man. A king's order could not be reversed and the father King Birendra Kishore tried telling his son the orders could not be revoked. As a last resort young Bir Bikram decided to take the path of 'Gandhi' that is fast unto death. The father Birendra Kishore initially did not give in and kept himself busy in painting and other art work, but things got serious as Bir Bikram refused to break his fast and in the end Birendra Kishore relented but with the condition that he, Bir Bikram would have to take the message of revoking the orders. Bir Bikram immediately galloped out on his horse and was in time to take the man down from the gallows. The convict fell at the feet of Bir Bikram in stunned silence, a life had been saved. Another instance that stands out to show he was a people's king was when he came out of the palace to show he cared for his people. They say after he came to the throne one night while it was dark and the streets were empty as those days electricity had not reached Tripura. A peculiar sound was heard by the people of Agartala outside their homes, no one dared to venture out in the dark.

People thought like on other day's elephants had come to destroy their villages. The bravest of the brave stepped out to see their young king standing on a motor vehicle in full glory to his subjects with a gun and two attendants with torch lights. The Maharaja assured his men that he was always there for their safety and fired a few rounds in the air to confirm his words.

Maharaja Bir Bikram was always interested in military affairs and was commissioned on 29th January, 1928 into the British Army and attached to the Rajput Regiment IA, later he became the Col-in-Chief of Tripura Bir Bikram Manikya Rifles. His knowledge about the army came in good use during World War II; he supported the British in all aspects. He made war committees with its headquarters at Agartala. He started a war fund to meet the war expenses. Bir Bikram's soldiers won fame in the battlefields of Burma when the Japanese army was at our door step. The small Tripura army won gallantry awards and Bir Bikram's brother was among the awardees. He was in an unenviable position as he could not displease the British in the pre-independence days, but at the same time wanted to support the freedom fighters and his method of supporting the freedom fighters was to turn a blind eye to their activities. His superficial support was misconstrued by Pandit Nehru. Nehru felt he was ill-treating the freedom fighters but that was not the case as he was on India's side. Bir Bikram realised India would be partitioned and he had decided Tripura would join India, which is why he had appointed barrister Girija Shankar Guha to be Tripura's representative at the Constituent Assembly on 28th April 1947, nineteen days before his death.

The Maharaja brought in changes in the Tripuri society, the first amongst many was agriculture as he tried to discourage 'jhum' cultivation (a method where forests were cleared by cutting and then burning the area. After cultivation for a few years when the land lost its fertility, people moved to another part. This has led to deforestation of large areas). Bir Bikram encouraged people to take up the plough to cultivate. The Tenancy Act of Tripura encouraged people to take up settled cultivation. With his initiative the land reforms started, Bir Bikram being forward thinking reserved land for the indigenous people of Tripura, later the Tripra Tribal Area Autonomous District Council came up. Bir Bikram realised that with war and migration of people the indigenous people of the state would face problems so between 1931, and 1945 he kept putting away land for the tribal, which post-independence the government could not look after the welfare of the tribal people is a different story. He had visualised a change coming and as far as he could he tried to democratise the administration. Being a just ruler he, as far as possible, protected the interests of the tribal and non-tribal. With the riots of 1941, the Hindus flocked to Tripura from Raipura which is close to Dhaka, Bir Bikram not only gave them food and cash but also tried to settle them in his area. This was an act which won him praise from all parts of the country.

Bir Bikram toured his kingdom right from Tripura to Sylhet and Comilla (now in Bangladesh) to assess his land and improve the life of his subjects. Bir Bikram, a people's man wanted to bring in a responsible government and so in 1939, declared a few administrative reforms. Some of them were the setting up of a 'Privy Council' which would advise the Maharaja on executive and judicial matters. Next was the improvement in the 'Khas Adalat'or High Court which existed as the highest independent judicial tribunal of the state. Bir Bikram also started a Council of Ministers with a chief minister as the head who was supported by other ministers and in the villages '*mandalis*' or groups looked after agriculture related problems. The concept of 'Village Panchayat' or 'Village administration' had started. It is to the credit of Bir Bikram who started the first election of the Agartala municipality by a secret ballot and the first one was held in 1945.

Bir Bikram set up the first higher educational institution – the Maharaja Bir Bikram College. Under his guidance a college and a rural university was to come up under the 'Vidyapathan Plan' or the Educational plan. For this land was given by Maharaja and he called this area College 'Tilla'/ hill, the land lies close to the city of Agartala. Unfortunately, Bir Bikram did not live to see the fruits of his labour. His widow Maharani Kanchan Prabha Devi did fulfill his dreams by starting a college named after her husband. Bir Bikram had planned to create a system where there would be compulsory education for children till the age of fourteen. The money would come from the state and through vocational training given to the children to make them self-reliant. This plan did not see the dawn of day as World War II had started and Tripura became very involved in the war activities.

Early in life he showed interest in architecture and engineering and experimenting on things by himself. Bir Bikram an intelligent man possibly realised that Tripura one day may become landlocked so he thought of an airport and he designed the layout and expansion of Agartala Airport. Today Tripura Airport is one of the busiest airports of the North East. His ancestors had given art patronage and Bir Bikram also gave support to Rabindranath Tagore and his 'Shanti Niketan' by giving generous grants including special grants for a hospital and a library. The poet's 80th birthday was celebrated all across Tripura and a few days before the poet's death, Bir Bikram honored the poet by giving him the title of 'Bharat Bhasker' or 'Sun of India' at a special function held at Shanti Niketan, the poet too reciprocated by thanking the Tripura royalty for generations of kingly support. Bir Bikram wrote a number of poems and plays among them were '*Chand Kumudini*' and 'Sri Radha Krishner Lila *Vilas*' which were staged at Calcutta. He also wrote a play called '*Jayabati*' which was staged at Agartala.

India has a few palaces in the middle of a water body, Lake Palace in Udaipur (Rajasthan) and in the North East, in Tripura we have the '*Neer Mahal*'. In 1930 a palace titled the '*Neer Mahal*' or Water Palace came up on the middle of Rudra Sagar Lake, something not common in those days. Rudra Sagar lies fifty odd kilometers away from Agartala. Maharaja Bir Bikram a man who had an artistic bent of mind thought of building a palace in the middle of a lake. He contacted a British Company 'Martin and Burn' to build this palace and it took the company nine long years to complete. The palace has architecture of both Hindu and Muslim type and had different sections, one each for the king, queen and the staff. It was so designed that you could row into your own room. Today for visitors boats are available to take you from the mainland to the island palace. Tourists can take boats from the side of Rudra Sagar Lake. Thousands of fishermen make a living from the lake but today it seems to be shrinking due to pollution and silting. With a little support from authorities the lake can possibly get back its past glory.

The Reang unrest in 1942-43 was one of the most important happenings during the reign of Maharaja Bir Bikram Singh. It was a religious and anti-feudal movement led by Ratnamoni. Ratnamoni was protesting against the oppressive land taxes the Reangs had to pay. In those days, Reang villages had a Choudhury as village headman. These Choudhurys' were supposed to collect taxes for the king but they themselves were exempted from paying taxes because of the work they did. At times the Choudhurys' were harsh and cruel and it was this people were objecting to. The Reangs had to pay the maximum taxes and the Tripuris the least. The Reangs had to pay house tax and taxes on bamboo and cane. The reason given by the government for the excessive taxes was that the Reangs did not prepare their bills for the land produce properly. The government also felt the Reangs were illegally exporting cotton, mustard and other produce to British India, hence the heavy taxation. It is because of these problems the Reangs approached Ratnamoni a religious preacher who preached from the Mahabharata and Ramayanaa. For the funeral rites money was collected by the Reangs, later there were arguments and after complaints from the people, the King gave orders for Ratnamoni's arrest but he managed to escape. World War II had started and there was a food shortage so the government of Tripura bought all the paddy fields to feed the army and the people of Agartala. Ratnamoni's disciples had taken preventive measures and had collected rice for distribution and kept at the 'Dharma Gola'/ storage space. Some Choudhurys' had also started hoarding to make money and as a result there was famine in some Reang areas. The followers of Ratnamoni were increasing at a rapid pace as they got food from his 'Dharma Gola'. Due to the World War II soldiers were needed and Bir Bikram wanted to recruit some soldiers from the Reang community and ordered the Choudhurys' to get the soldiers but they failed as the Reang men refused to go, instead they revolted. The king sent a large force to quell the Reang rebels and they were defeated badly. Ratnamoni fled to the Chittagong Hill Tracts but he was arrested by the British police and put into Rangamati jail from where he was brought to Agartala jail. Ratnamoni finally was brought to Maharaja Bir Bikram's palace. He died under mysterious circumstances, some say he died of cholera. His followers made a cane chair or throne as they called it, some even referred to him as Maharaja. That Ratnamoni had started a socio-religious movement for the tribal society which cannot be ignored.

Bir Bikram's untimely death in 1947 was a great loss to Tripura and its people. Had he lived the Tripura state might not have had to see such turbulent times as it is going through even today? Tripura is perhaps one of the states which was affected badly by the partition, as frequently it sees demographic changes and insurgency today. If the land could talk I am sure it would say, "We miss you Maharaja Bir Bikram Kishore Manikya".

36

Sachin Dev Burman

Can one ever forget the lilting tunes of Sachin Dev Burman's music? Sachin Dev Burman or SD Burman or Sachin Karta (as he was known to the Tripura royal family) was a musical genius so to say. Sachin Dev sang for forty three years and has about one hundred and sixty songs to his credit.

Sachin Dev was born to Nabadip Chandra Burman and Nirmal Devi on 1st October 1906. (Nabadip Chandra was the second son of Ishana Chandra Dev Burman, the Rajah of Tripura). Sachin was the youngest of the five sons his parents had, in all they were nine siblings. Nabadip Chandra and his elder brother were excluded from the throne of Tripura by their paternal uncle Bir Chandra. Father Nabadip Chandra was a cultured man and Sachin Dev remembered his father as, "I was cast in the mould of my father. His education was my backbone. It is through his teachings that I have developed the little skills of a fine artist. Father excelled in Sitar, Drupad songs (Indian classical), painting and sculpture. During Saraswati, Kali and Durga Puja, he was the one, who would make the statues in our house. "

Sachin Dev Burman had his first lessons in classical music from his father Nabadip Chandra. His formal music training came from

KC Dey (1925-1930) who was uncle of Manna Dey. Manna Dey remembers Sachin Dev visiting his house in Kolkata. He was very impressed with Sachin Dev's singing and often would sing his songs trying to imitate the nasal twang of Sachin Dev. One day KC Dey had to tell Manna Dey that it was alright singing Sachin Dev's song but he need not copy the nasal twang, he must sing in his own tone. In 1932, Sachin Dev got trained under Bhismadev Chatopadhya, this was followed by Badal Khan a sarangi player, later under Ustad Allaudin Khan. KC Dey, Ustad Badal Khan, Allaudin Khan came to Agartala to visit Sachin Dev. Many a night and day were spent in singing and getting completely immersed in music. He was also trained under Ustad Aftabuddin Khan and became a master flutist. It is no wonder that many of Sachin Dev's song had the lilting music of the flute in a number of his compositions. Kazi Nazrul Islam the Bengali poet and lyricist also visited Sachin Dev Burman's ancestral home 'Comilla House' at Agartala. The training Sachin Dev received in classical music helped him get a firm footing to the music, he was to compose later on in life. After his father died, grief stricken Sachin Dev travelled the jungles of Assam and Tripura absorbing the rich folk music which almost became a trade mark of Sachin Dev. He also started his own school called the 'Sur Mandir' in Calcutta somewhere in the 1930s.

Two other people who influenced Sachin Dev in his early years are Madhav and Anwar, the two domestic help in his Tripura house. Madhav the older of the two, after finishing lunch would sit down to recite and sing the Ramayana. These renderings impressed Sachin Dev a lot as they were simple in language and easy to sing. Anwar, they say was great at fishing and taught him the nuances of fishing. Anwar would sing him the famous 'Bhatiyali' or songs sung on the 'river' by boatmen. Anwar would sing accompanied by the 'dotara' (two string instrument) the haunting melodies of a boatman. Both sang from the heart, Sachin Dev would spend many nights listening to Anwar's songs but as a result his grammar lessons suffered. The grammar teacher was not at all happy and protested, Sachin Dev had to shift his study hours to overcome the problem. During those days Sachin Dev had many visitors to his ancestral home – beggars, minstrels and faqirs who sang in their own way. It is these people who made him interested in folk music. He has always acknowledged that in folk music Madhav and Anwar were his 'gurus'.

Sachin Dev in his 'Reflections' (presented by Salil Ghosh) remembered the days when he was in Class V had sung during the Durga Puja festival some of the songs learnt from Madhav and Anwar. It was a big hit and he became the hero of the class. Quite often during breaks the boys would sit out under the trees and Sachin Dev would entertain them.

An incident which stood out in his memory: Sachin Dev had gone to Kamal Sagar which is about ten miles from Comila (Bangladesh) to a village fair with his friends. They all had a lot of fun and time just flew, they did not realise how much time had gone past. It was only when people were leaving and the 'mela' was closing did the boys realise the time, that it was so late. Somehow the boys managed to get into a train and reached their home station. In their hurry, they had forgotten to buy tickets. As bad luck would have it they were halted by the ticket-checker while going out. No amount of pleading helped and very soon they were locked up in a room. Out of sheer fright Sachin started crying and as he asks, "what else could I do"? Mohit, one of the boys suddenly remembered that the station master's mother had recently visited their house and loved the 'bhatiali' songs Sachin had been singing. So Mohit asked Sachin Dev to sing. Sachin Dev somehow controlled himself and started singing. After some time the door opened and lo and behold! the station master's mother was standing there. She asked the station master to let the boys go, and 'wonder of wonders she even gave us sweets to eat', remembers Sachin Dev. Sachin Dev from early childhood had a great sense of humour and made every one laugh with his tales, which held his audience spell bound. This good sense of humour carried on throughout his life. Once according to Anu Malik (Music Director) Sachin Dev went to Kishore Kumar's house dressed as a mil kman to get him out of the house as he had a recording of songs session with him. Kishore Kumar was very grateful to Sachin Dev for reviving his career to give super hit songs to the film '*Aradhana*'.

Sachin Dev could grasp any music around him. The Agartala Royal family supported Tagore's Vishwa Bharati University financially. His voice may not have been as strong as those of some classical singers but he had something very valuable in his style of singing, it was the power to sing songs in a simple yet sophisticated manner which caught the attention of listeners, specially the 'bhatiali' songs.

Sachin Dev served in the court of Maharaja of Tripura for some time. In 1932, he sang on the Calcutta radio station, he made popular East Bengal (Bangladesh) and Tripuri folk songs. 1934 saw him signing a small role in an Urdu film called *Selima*. The same year saw Sachin Dev releasing his first record (Hindustan Musical Record), it had 'E Pathey Aaj Eso Priyo' it meant 'today come this way my dear' on one side. The other side had 'Dakle Kokil Roj Bihane' meaning 'the cuckoo sings in the morning'. The following ten years saw Sachin Dev reach his peak as a singer; he cut as many as one hundred and thirty one songs in Bengali and sang for composers like Himanshu Dutta, RC Boral and Nazrul Islam. In 1934, Sachin Dev attended the All India Music Conference and presented his Bengali 'thumri' (classical song) to an illustrious audience like Vijaya Lakshmi Pandit. Later he was invited to the Bengal Music Conference in Kolkata which was inaugurated by Rabindranath Tagore. Sachin Karta as he was called by the royalty of Tripura sang in Bengali a number of songs and his singing of modern Bengali songs seems like poetry through music. He remains an institution by himself as far as Bengali music is concerned. Sachin Karta's art and craft are truly divine, they are definitely God gifted. Anyone who has heard him 'live' was completely mesmerized by the singing. As they say only Sachin Dev could bring 'flowers to bloom'.

In Calcutta, he built a house in South End Park, Ballygung. In 1937 at Allahabad he met Meera Dasgupta a student of Rabindranath Tagore's Shantiniketan. She became his student and cupid struck, later she married him in 1938. Sachin Dev's marrying a non-royal or a commoner so to say became a problem for the royal family, he had to severe all ties with his family and also give up his inheritance. A son was born to Sachin Dev and Meera in 1939. They named him Rahul Dev; who kept high the traditions of the Dev Burman family. He was a musical genius of his time.

In 1944 he moved to Bombay at the request of Sashadhar Mukherjee from the Filmistan studio. He was to compose music for two films *Shikari* and *Aath Din*. He gave music to a number of films but still was not on centre stage, he did not get his due. Disheartened Sachin Dev wanted to go back to Calcutta but it was here the actor Ashok Kumar insisted he finish his music for *Mashal* and then leave if he wanted to. *Mashal* was a super hit and the song *Upar Gagan Vishal* or 'above is the vast sky' went on to become a super hit. The song introduced Manna Dey as a singer.

Dev Anand by this time had started his own production house called Navketan and signed Sachin Dev with *Jaal, Ladki* and *Bahar*. Manna Dey worked with Sachin Dev as assistant director. Manna Dey remembers working with Sachin Dev was always a pleasure. He was different from other music composers as he could think for himself and visualise situations. Sachin Dev was particular about who would sing the song he was composing. Manna Dey was his all time favourite. Manna Dey's rendering of 'mata mat ro mata lal bahutere' is an all time favourite.

Sachin Dev loved sports and his two favourites were fishing and tennis. Sachin Dev after passing his graduation had joined his master's classes. Those days at YMCA he used to play cricket and also wanted to play tennis. The Anglo-Indians were not at all keen to play with Sachin Dev and made fun of him. Not to be taken lighly, Sachin Dev started playing with the 'marker' every afternoon by paying eight annas or today's fifty paisa to him. Very soon his game improved so much that everyone wanted to play with him, including the Anglo-Indians. Fishing is the only sport that went with him to Bombay from Tripura. Mukul Bose and Guru Dutt were two of his companions who went fishing with him. Once while Manna Dey was working with Sachin Dev he asked him to come with him. "Where to"? asked Manna Dey and prompt came the reply "Of course to watch a football match". Many times the two went out together to watch matches, the trips always made them feel happy. Very often Manna Dey would also be treated to lunch too at wayside small hotels.

Despite so much of success Sachin Dev did not get many awards and it pained him, though he never showed this. Manna Dey remembers that once when Sachin Dev was in hospital with one eye operated the results were awaited for the song *Meri Surat Teri Ankhen*. The results as usual were not in his favour and all Manna Dey saw was a tear roll down from his other eye. But this did not affect his work, Sachin Dev always felt he had to do what was required of him and do that as best as he could do. Music was his religion. He would often say, "Music is my brother, son and friend too".

Sachin Dev has the highest average of hit songs amongst the composers of Hindi film songs. He also changed the theory of the lyrics being set to the tune of music directors in Bombay. It was now the tune first, then the lyrics. Sachin Dev's music had a strong flavour of folk and classical. He discovered the success formula by chance. One day he heard one of the servants singing a Naushad number from a film *Ratan* (1944) 'jab tum hi chale pardes lagakar thes o pritam pyare' and scolded him for singing someone else's composition. Late he realised it was the simple tune which caught the attention of people. This became the *mantra* for him, play tunes which everyone can sing. From then on he would hum the tunes to his large group of servants and get their approval. The music was so simple that anyone could sing them.

Sachin Dev has been awarded the prestigious Sangeet Natak Academy Award and the Padamshree for his contribution to music. Sachin Dev left for his heavenly abode on October 31, 1975. Even when he was lying ill in hospital bed he composed the music of *Mili - Maine kaha phulon se*. Here was a man who did not give up easily; he lived life according to his own terms. On his 100th birthday the royal palace of Tripura was lit up to celebrate the birth of a musical genius. A stamp was released on the 101st birth anniversary of Sachin Dev Burman by the Ministry of Communication and Information Technology. The Government of Tripura has started the Sachin Dev Burman Memorial Award in 2006. This award is presented to famous musicians and singers for their contribution to Indian Music.

37

Rahul Dev Burman –
Percussion Guru

Rahul Dev Burman or RD Pancham was a generationless music composer. People belonging to any age or era were enthralled by his music. He gave us some of Bollywood's greatest danceable numbers. The hottest cabaret numbers came from RD. Even today we do not tire of listening to his music which is ever fresh, it is no wonder people are still trying to remix them or shall we say reinvent them. It was an inherited talent that had come into his genes! After all he was the grandson of Nawadip Chandra Burman, who excelled in Sitar, Drupad songs (Indian classical), painting and sculpting. (Nawadip Chandra was the second son of Ishana Chandra Dev Burman, the Rajah of Tripura).

Rahul Dev Burman was born with a silver spoon or shall we say a 'musical spoon' on 27th June 1939 to Sachin Dev Burman and his wife Meera. As we all know Sachin Dev Burman belonged to the royal family of Tripura. Rahul Dev was born in Calcutta (some say Comilla in Bangladesh). He was however brought up in Calcutta by his grandmother. It is interesting to note that he was nicknamed 'Pancham' by the acter Ashok Kumar. During his babyhood days he would keep saying 'pa...pa' and 'pa' is the fifth syllable in Hindustani music, so Pancham he remained. Rahul Dev was a master of the 'Saat Sur' or the seven syllable of Hindustani music. People say perhaps he should have been called 'Saptam'.

His early childhood was spent in Calcutta while his father Sachin Dev was in Bombay trying to get a foothold into the Bombay film industry. Rahul Dev learnt to play the harmonica very early in life on his own. One day he played the harmonica in school assembly with his father in attendance. It is then Sachin Dev realised how talented his son was. The next day he asked his son for how long had he been practicing and pat came the reply "I have been practicing for the last eight months and want to become a better musician than you". After this Sachin Dev took great interest in Rahul Dev's musical education. A sound grounding was given to the son in Hindustani classical music. Even in his pre-teen years he had learnt to play the 'tabla', the drums and 'sarod' – a difficult string instrument. Rahul Dev or RD as he was also called trained under Ali Akbar Khan and Ashish Khan; both are India's finest classical musicians. RD or Pancham had also started writing songs which were popular in the Hindi film world. He could play the fifteen songs he had written at that time. Sachin Dev wanted to take his son to Bombay to train him in Hindi film music composition. This met with stiff opposition from the grandmother, who felt the big bad world of Bombay film society would corrupt young Rahul Dev who was already very rebellious towards his studies. It was only after his class 10th that he went to Bombay.

A year later Pancham saw *Funtoosh,* a film whose music composition was by Sachin Dev. While watching the picture he realised that the music was familiar, he then remembered it was his lyrics. Immediate reaction was, "My God it is my tune". Rahul Dev then wrote to his father saying he had stolen his musical work and Sachin Dev acknowledged he had indeed stolen it. The song "*Aa meri topi palat ke aa*" became a super hit. This strengthened Pancham's idea of becoming a music composer.

Rahul Dev started working in films as assistant to his father and earned a credit on the film *Pyasa* in 1955. The famous song '*Sar jo tera chakraye*' from Guru Dutt's film *Pyasa* was composed by RD when he was a child. Sachin Dev started coaching him in the finer nuances of film composition and also credited him as assistant music director on films scored by Sachin Dev Burman in the late 1950s. Both father and son appreciated each other and Rahul Dev could hone his skills working under his father. RD or Pancham could play several instruments and the movie *Pyasa* saw this actually happening. *Chote Nawab* was the first movie that had his name as music director. RD continued working with his father too, till the 1960s. RD sometimes accompanied his friends for recordings. The 'twist dance' brought in the western pop music to the Bollywood film industry. RD had been greatly influenced by the American vocalist Chubby Checker and RD's "Ao twist karen" from the film *Bhoot Bangla* in 1956 was similar to Chubby Checker's "Let's twist again". RD at times has been accused of copying illegally western tunes. Of course, RD refuted these charges and said that he had only improvised. "If you copy in toto, you will have trouble" was what he had to say. 1972 saw a peak in RD's career as he composed 19 scores for movies that year.

RD was also a good singer and sometimes was heard singing on his own sound tracks. He sang solo in *Sholay*, the songs "*Mehbooba Mehbooba*" cannot be forgotten easily or "*Duniya Mein*" from *Apna Desh*. In 1987 Gulzar the lyricist, Asha Bhosle and RD Burman brought out an album called '*Dil Padosi Hai*'; this was released on Asha Bhosle's birthday, 8th September. He has produced an album based on the 'samba' and has also worked with Boy George.

It is but natural that RD Burman had many fans and one such ardent admirer was Rita Patel whom he met in Darjeeling. Once they were back in Bombay RD Burman invited her to movie date. Rita had had a bet with her friends that she would go out on a movie date with RD. Half way through the movie, Rita disappeared and poor RD kept waiting for her. Later on she married him in 1960. The marriage lasted till 1971. RD married Asha Bhosle in 1980. Finally, RD had met his soul mate in music and life, theirs was a happy life. Asha Bhosle's association with RD went back as early as 1966 with the film *Teesri Manzil* when he was still working under his father, Sachin Dev. RD was a humble man and while working under his father would never take credit for his work. Asha Bhosle remembers when she was working for Sachin Dev she would often be asked by Sachin Dev to learn the music from RD. This would most often irritate her as she thought Sachin Dev was the music composer. It is only later she realised that the music composition was actually RD's. In the film *Aradhana* in 1969 the music composition was started by Sachin Dev Burman but due to illness could not be completed, RD stepped in and completed the unfinished work.

Rahul Dev had his own band of musicians, almost 35 odd people worked together in the orchestra. The group still meets, especially on RD's birthday, they play the old numbers and they still are a big hit. Manohari Singh who plays the saxophone had worked with RD for four decades and had very fond memories of him. He has also worked under Sachin Dev and other musicians. Manohari used to polish his brass saxophone very carefully before a show, while relating anecdotes on RD sometimes one could see tears roll down his cheeks. Manohari sometimes doubled up as RD's assistant too. Pancham's other musicians were, for tabla Janardan Abhyaankar and Homi Mullah. Trilok Gurtu and Leslie Vaz played the drums. Bhanu Gupta who has worked with RD in all his films has this to say, "Pancham's compositions were unorthodox, but every instrument could be heard. That gave great satisfaction to the musicians and was a major reason why no musician left him. RD made his music in style and everyone gave their best, no one felt left out". Gupta fondly remembers the special care RD took with his musicians, once Nasir Hussain the director had given the music composer's work to RD and asked him to play some of the work. RD played two tunes. The first one was rejected and the second one was accepted. RD's immediate reaction was "Didn't I tell you, the second one would be good. This is not my work. It is this Bhanu's work". It is these endearing qualities that made RD a great music composer, a humble person, a great human being.

Gulzar the lyricist and RD were good friends, it was during the recording of Gulzar's first song "*Mera gora rang lai le*" from *Bandini* they met and friends they remained. Together they created magical music, if one can say so. Sometimes Gulzar would pull RD's leg regarding his Hindi. Gulzar very fondly remembers, "Pancham was an excellent singer. He knew the nuances of classical singing. For my films, he sang only a couple of songs. But he has lent his voice ever so often to other songs. For instance, in Jabbar Patel's *Musafir,* the boat man's voice over, is Pancham! As a singer he would perfect a tune by singing it repeatedly. "

Together they made spellbinding music. Even today we find the same effect continues. RD's music is special as it had all the flavors or essence from around the globe, from Indian classical to rock, jazz, Mexican mariachi, Brazilian boss nova and many more.

After many years of highs there came a period where there was a slide in RD's music composer career. Upset over all the things happening he had a heart attack in 1988 and had to undergo bypass surgery. While in hospital he had composed many tunes but these unfortunately did not see the light of day. RD in his last few years died a very sad man as the music compositions in Bollywood were changing. This was according to Asha Bhosle.

Vidhu Vinod Chopra had in 1993 signed RD for his film *1942 – A love Story* as music director and when to sell the music composition of his film one music company refused as they wanted a new generation music composer. But Vidhu Vinod Chopra stuck to his guns and we all know the results. He won the third Filmfare Award posthumously as the movie was released after his death. The other Filmfare Awards were for *Sanam Teri Kasam* 1982 and *Masoom* in 1983.

RD, Rahul Dev or Pancham as he was lovingly called died on the 4th of January 1994. The percussion guru was comfortable with playing any instrument; he has used a spoon against a glass, desks and bottles filled with water at different levels. He has used folk music both from India and Europe in his compositions. He is the one who ushered in modern trends in our Hindi music. Brahamanand Singh a film maker has made a fim on Rahul Dev called *Pancham Unmixed- Mujhe Chalte Jaana Hai*. Pancham's music carries on and it never become old or stale as they say, whether the original or remixed ones. The magic continues as the music remains alive in the hearts of his fans from all over the world.

Folk Tales

38

Folk Tales

Apfuho

(Nagaland)

'Apfuho' is a mythical mischievous character of the Lhota Nagas. He seems to be always naughty and trying to fool others. Though naughty, Apfuho means little harm to his people. In the tribal stories he is called Mache by the Angami Nagas, the Lohtas call him Apfuho, the Sema Nagas call him Iki, the Western Rengma Nagas call him Che and the Eastern Rengma Nagas call him Ichu. The character is similar to the rascal we have in Mizoram - Churra. No one knows where these rascals came from but there is similarity between all the rascals and they definitely make interesting reading

Here is a tale about Apfuho.

How the Villagers tried to kill Apfuho

The village people were fed up of Apfuho's tricks and decided they would do away with him. They took him to the biggest pond in the village saying they would have fun there. When they reached the pond some of them began swinging from the creepers near the fishpond. Most of them took turns to swing and asked Apfuho to do the same. The villagers made sure Apfuho was the last to swing.

Apfuho was enjoying the cool breeze while swinging and initially did not realise he was alone. Apfuho after some time realised; everyone had left and gone back to the village. Apfuho continued to swing enjoying the cool breeze but later got tired and was looking around for someone to stop him.

At a distance he saw a young couple; the woman was wearing a lot of ornaments and the man had a mithun (domestic bison) tied to a rope with him. Apfuho called out to the couple, "Hello, there is a beautiful breeze up here which makes swinging very pleasant. Take your ornaments off and put them on the water side, also remember to tie up your mithun to a tree. After that come and pull me in and then get a good swing". The couple did as Apfuho asked and were enjoying themselves. Later the couple asked Apfuho to pull them to the land, but Apfuho did not do this, he allowed them to fall into the water and both drowned.

In a while Apfuho put on the ornaments and took the mithun with him to the village. The village people were shocked to see him and asked Apfuho where he had got the ornaments and the mithun. Apfuho replied he had got it from the middle of the pond. He said if they wanted he could take them there to show them the exact location. The villagers eagerly said, "Take us there, Apfuho". A few days later Apfuho took all the villagers to the pond and said, "The ornaments are in the middle of the pond, you all will have to go very carefully" saying this Apfuho threw them one by one into the pond. Apfuho kept telling them the one who goes down quietly will get less ornaments and a weak mithun, the one who goes down struggling in the water will get good ornaments and a strong mithun. Saying this he allowed the villagers to drown. Apfuho went back a satisfied man as he had his revenge.

Churra
(Mizoram)

Tribal stories very often have rascal characters that are no different from the modern day rascals or villains. The same applies to the North Eastern region. The characters are known for their playing pranks on others and getting out of tricky situations. They of course cannot be compared with today's tricksters, who are mean, dishonest and at times evil. The tribal tales are full of stories that bring a smile to most of our faces, we rarely hate these characters nor does it leave distaste in the mouth.

Chhoora or Chura of the Mizo Hills seems to be slightly different from the other 'Seven Sister' state's rascals. (Chhoora reminds one of the North India 'chora'- the rustic village lad who is up to all sorts of mischief but means no harm). The Mizo Chhoora is also quite childlike in his behaviour. His pranks don't hurt anyone. Chhurbura or Chura, the most popular of Mizo folk heroes was very often troubled by his brother Nahaia, this quixotic character goes through the most mind-boggling adventures we have ever read.

Here are a few escapades of Chhoora/Chura:

Chhoora and the Chins

Chhoora was one day chased by the Chins but he managed to escape unhurt. The Chins were smarter and decided to catch him in his 'jhum' hut. ('Jhum' is shifting cultivation; most people of the North East practice this type of agriculture). The Chins thought they would hide in Chhoora's hut and wait for him to come back. Chhoora one day was returning to his 'jhum' hut from the cultivation area. However, he slowed his speed as his sixth sense told him there was danger, and his enemies might be close by. So Chhoora decided to call out 'Oh! House'. There was no response, he again called out loudly, 'My house always responds to my call. I don't know why it is not responding now; there must be someone inside that is why my house is not replying'. The Chins decided to answer back so that Chhoora would come in. As Chhoora called again the Chins responded and this only confirmed Chhoora's fear. Chhoora made fun of the Chins and called out 'You fools, do you think I would come in after this to be captured', yelling this he ran into the thick forests. This is how Chhoora escaped.

Chhoora and Whistling

One day Chhoora thought he would visit a relative who lived in a far away village. Since this was his first visit, Chhoora decided he would leave home early in the morning. Very early in the morning he set out and reached his destination by the afternoon.

While he was going through the forest he heard a whistle and liked the tune as it appealed to him a lot. Chhoora looked around to see who was whistling, it was the work of a young man walking a short distance ahead of him. Chhoora went up to him and said, "Sir, I like this tune, can you teach it to me"? The man said yes but with a condition that Chhoora would have to give him three 'mithuns' for teaching him the tune, and Chhoora agreed to the condition. Chhoora picked up the tune and was very satisfied with himself as he could whistle the tune as and when he wanted. Chhoora spent the whole day and night practising the tune in the village he had gone to visit. Next morning he decided to go home and on the journey back he kept whistling the recently learnt tune, little else mattered to him.

Chhoora did not look where he was going and slipped and fell down. He got up and tried to whistle, to his horror he found he could not. Chhoora tried very hard to remember but the tune did not come back. He sat on a rock and tried to see if he could get the tune back but to no avail. He looked around to see if he could find it lying in the grass. A stranger saw him crouching on the ground and asked Chhoora, "What have you lost, Sir"? Chhoora got angry and answered, "You fool if I knew what I had lost I would not look for it". The stranger got very irritated and tired of all this sat down on a rock and started whistling. Chhoora came running back to say, "This is what I had lost". And thanked the man profusely for helping him to remember the tune. Chhoora went back whistling home, a very happy man.

Chhoora and Household Chores

One morning Chhoora's wife had to go to the jhum to tend to the crops, after finishing her chores in the hut she asked Chhoora to look after the hut, the baby and the evening cooking. She instructed him to start when the setting sun rays fell on the leaves of the banyan tree. Chhoora in the evening climbed up the tree and tried to cook on the branch where the sun rays fell. As he climbed on to the branch he crashed down and badly injured himself and that was the end of the evening meal!

As he crashed down he could hear the baby wailing and hurried to see why it was wailing, Chhoora located the head and pressed it down too hard and the baby in shock died. In the evening when Chhoora's wife came back she found the baby cold and not breathing. She touched the face it was cold so she told Chhoora to wrap the baby in a mat and bury it in the nearby cave. Chhoora did as his wife asked; he rolled the baby in the mat and went to the cave, while walking the dead baby slipped and fell and lay on the path, Chhoora did not realise this. While returning home he saw the baby and did not recognise it, he only asked himself "Whose baby is this? Can't be mine as I have just left mine in the cave".

While walking back to the village he touched his ears and found them to be rather cold, Chhoora thought he was a dead man. So he walked back to the cave and lay down next to the mat in which he thought his dead baby was. At that time an old lady came in to the cave and saw a man lying still. She asked:

O, you of the dead

I wonder what you are doing.

Chhoora thought he had to reply back and said "What do you think I am doing? I am supposed to be dead". The old lady was horror struck as she did not expect the dead to reply. She ran out as fast as her legs could take her screaming at the top of her voice.

After a few days Chhoora's grandfather died and once again Chhoora decided to bring the corpse to the same cave. On the way as he was weary so he put down the corpse against a tree in a sitting position. A cowherd was passing by with his mithuns (a mix of a cow and buffalo) and Chhoora thought he would play a prank. He yelled out to the cowherd "If your mithuns knock down my grandfather who is not well, you will have to give me one mithun". The cowherd was not quick enough to control his mithuns and one of them knocked down the old man. The cowherd had to pay the penalty, which was one male mithun. Chhoora was very happy and after burying his grandfather he went back home. On the way the mithun passed water and Chhoora thought the mithun was leaking so he left it behind and went home. His wife when she heard this was very angry and sent Chhoora back to get the mithun. When Chhoora went back to the forest he found the mithun had been eaten by a tiger. Chhoora mistook the tiger for a brown dog and trashed the tiger with a stick and the tiger ran away. Chhoora went home a very sad man as he could not get the mithun back. His wife when she heard the tale asked him to stay clear of all brown things. After a few days Chhoora found something brown in his hut and without looking carefully he attacked the brown object till it was in shreds. His wife came home from the jhum area to find her brown 'puan' (skirt) cut into pieces.

Sharing the Mithun

Chhoora and his younger brother Nahaia jointly owned a mithun and both decided they would look after it jointly. They mutually consented to divide the work of looking after the mithun, that is the front and the back part and each would look after their own portion. The younger brother thought he was a smart fellow and so decided to give Chhoora the tail portion while he took the front part.

Every morning Nahaia would remind Chhoora that he had to clear the dung as the back part belonged to him. After sometime Chhoora got fed up and asked for a change, a reversal of roles. This carried on for sometime and Chhoora was happy.

In a few months time a calf was born and Nahaia claimed the calf was his as the back part belonged to him. Chhoora argued but all the arguments fell on deaf ears.

One fine morning Chhoora thought out a plan, he told his younger brother Nahaia that he wanted to take his share, the head away. Nahaia was stunned and realised that if the head was taken away he would lose everything. So Nahaia apologised for being stubborn and agreed to jointly own the calf.

These are some of the stories about Chhoora and one wonders if he was actually an idiot or an intelligent person.

Duhmanga and Dardini
(Mizoram)

Duhmanga and Dardini are the Romeo Juliet of the Lushai Hills. Like Romeo and Juliet they both loved each other but could not live together because of their families. Two young lives were lost because of family feuds.

A long time ago there lived Duhmanga and Dardini who were young and very much loved each other. Duhmanga was the chief's son and Dardini was the daughter of an ordinary widow, with very little money. Duhmanga's parents were against the relationship as they felt he was marrying a person below their status. However Duhmanga refused to listen to his parent's wishes and married Dardini and brought her home.

Duhmanga was a great hunter and sportsperson and quite often would be out of the house for a fair length of time, hunting in the forest. On one such trip when Duhmanga was out for a long time his parents got Dardini divorced from Duhmanga and sent her back to her mother. Dardini was very lonely and often would sit outside her hut and sing.

"How brave is my Duhmanga out there in the wilderness,
Does he feel hungry under the scorching sun, I wonder,

if only I could send him some sugarcane and
tender yam to lighten his weariness".

When Duhmanga returned he found his love missing from home, so he asked his mother where she was. The mother replied she had gone to her mother's place. It was only after a few days Duhmanga realised Dardini was forcibly divorced during his absence when he was out hunting in the forest. Duhmanga was very sad and distressed by all these happenings. As he could not live without Dardini he went back to her hut and brought Dardini back to his hut and married her again. This was much against his parent's wishes.

After a few days Duhmanga had to go out hunting again and left home with a sad heart as he had to leave Dardini behind. The parents-in-law of Dardini as soon as they got a chance chased her out. Dardini was again divorced and sent back home to her mother. Duhmanga's parents this time quickly got Duhmanga married to the neighbouring chieftain's daughter as they felt she was from the status. When Dardini saw her ex-husband she wept and said "Your parents have finally married you to a girl from your rank and must be very happy. All that I have is sorrow and tears". Hearing of this Duhmanga felt sad and unhappy and decided he would divorce the chieftain's daughter within three days of the wedding and marry Dardini again. Both lived happily for some time but this happiness was not meant to last as Duhmanga's parents were waiting for an opportunity to throw out Dardini. Once a rogue elephant was troubling the villagers, the elephant destroyed crops and broke anything that came in its way. Duhmanga, the hunter was requested by the village people to kill the rogue elephant. He had to go to the forest to kill it. His parents who were waiting for such an opportunity immediately reacted and again got Dardini divorced from Duhmanga and sent her home.

Dardini's mother who was now fed up with the number of times Dardini was divorced from Duhmanga now decided to get her married to someone else to get rid of the shame that poverty was bringing them. A man from a distant village had come visiting Dardini's mother and this seemed a good opportunity for the mother to marry Dardini to him. So Dardini went away to her new home with a heavy heart as she still could not forget Duhmanga.

When Duhmanga came home from the forest after disposing off the rogue elephant found to his horror that Dardini had again been divorced and sent back to her mother. When he went looking for her in her mother's hut he was told Dardini had been married off to another man. Duhmanga wanted to know where she was and the mother replied "Your parents have been very harsh to Dardini and have divorced her from you so many times; she was in great pain as she felt very humiliated and sad. So I decided to marry her off very far away from this village".

Hearing this Duhmanga went away a very sad man, for three long years he kept pining for her and hoped Dardini would come back one day to the village, but this did not happen.

One day when he could not bear the pain any more, Duhmanga decided he would visit Dardini in her village. So he set off for her village, on reaching Duhmanga found quietness near her house which unnerved him. He asked a few people what was the reason for the gloom. He was told that Dardini had died in childbirth, which was the reason for the unnatural calmness in the village. Duhmanga wept his heart out at the thought that Dardini was no more in this world.

Dardini had been lying in her coffin for three days as was the custom in those days. Duhmanga requested the people around to allow him to see her once and stay with her for the night. So the tomb was opened for him and the villagers allowed him to spend the night with her. The grief stricken man kept muttering to himself saying "Life has no meaning without you". Muttering these words he stabbed himself in the heart a number of times and died. The two were buried in the same grave. Thus, ended the love story of two unlucky lovers. Duhmanga and Dardini could not live together in this world but were united in death.

Lichao's Daughter
(Nagaland)

The Nagas in the olden days believed in Lycanthropy. Lycanthropy is a psychiatric state of mind in a person where he identifies himself with an animal. The animal could be a tiger, wolf or leopard or any other beast which is dangerous in that region. We find this belief in lycanthropy; it goes back to ancient times. The Greeks and the Romans believed in this superstition, even in Europe we find stories about the 'werewolf' quite popular.

Here is a tale related to lycanthropy.

Once upon a time a farmer found his fields damaged by wild pigs, so he went to hunt them down. He could wound one with his spear and started tracking them down. In the jungle while tracking the pig he came across the house of Lichao, the guardian of wild pigs. In the house he found two beautiful maidens feeding the pig he had wounded. The young man hesitated to tell the old man Lichao the truth, so instead he said he wanted one of the girls as his bride. The old man thought for a while and asked the young man to come back the next day.

Lichao next day made his slave girl dress up in his daughter's clothes and his own daughter in rags. But the young man was not to be deceived. He loved only Lichao's daughter and would not take any other girl as his bride. Little did the young man know that Lichao turned into a tiger at night and devoured human flesh? Lichao set difficult tasks for the young man so that he could consume him. The daughter realised this and told the young man to do whatever the father asked him. One day Lichao set a very difficult task for him, it was to pick up the leaves of 'kotyoh' and 'koremyoi' bushes (both are very thorny) without a scratch on his body. The young bride finally told her would-be husband her father was a tiger and at the slightest pretext would eat him up. So the young man picked the leaves of the tree without a single one being torn, he also came back without a scratch. After a lot of difficulties Lichao finally allowed his daughter to go with her new husband.

The young wife in her husband's house became very weak as she had no human flesh to eat. The worried young husband asked his wife, "Why do you look so weak, everyday you seem to become weaker"? The girl replied, "I don't get the food here as I was used to in my father's house". So the young bride sent her groom to her father's house to fetch a parcel of meat wrapped up in leaves, also warning him not to look inside. After eating the meat the wife became healthy and plump. But without human flesh for a few days she again lost her health. Finally, out of sheer curiosity he waited for the day he could open the parcel. Lichao understood the son-in-law's curiosity and so sent a bird with the package. The little bird told the son-in-law, "If you open the packet I will tell grandfather". The wife when she got the packet eagerly went into the hut and opened the packet to eat. The husband hid to see what it was and to his horror found she was roasting human fingers to eat. The man was very upset and so asked his wife what meat it was. Finally, the girl had to say that it was human flesh, and that she was a tigress. She said, "When I turn into a tigress with claws and fangs, slip a basket over me quickly. If you do not I shall devour you". The husband tried his best to slip the basket on the tigress's head but failed. So he was caught and eaten by the tigress. Alas! Thus ended the life of a brave husband.

Love and Lightnings
(Tripura)

Long time ago in a village by a rushing brook there lived a man called Champarai Sardar, his wife Khulumati and their son Nagurai. One day Khulumati while bathing in the river found the body of a young girl floating in the water. Immediately, she called out to her son Nagurai to come and save the girl. The son dived into the water and saved the girl. The life of the girl was saved and Khulumati brought up the girl as her own. Champarai and Khulumati named the girl Nakapili.

Nakapili blossomed into a beautiful girl and Nagurai fell in love with her. The two when they went to their 'jhum' fields would sit together, totally engrossed in each other. So both Champarai and Khulumati decided they would get married as the two young lovers. A doubt remained in the minds of the seniors as the parentage of the girl was not known. But since Nagurai was adamant the wedding was fixed.

At the wedding people from near and far were invited and soon there was a big gathering. One of Champarai's relatives had come with his wife and daughter and soon the daughter recognised the bride as her half sister. The relative had married the second time as his first wife had died due to some illness. The step-mother like in all tales use to ill treat the girl and very often humiliated Nakapili in front of visitors and would make her work the whole day. Fed up with such a life Nakapili decided she would commit suicide and so jumped into the river. Later Khulumati found her floating in the water. The daughter of the relative went and told her parents about this and soon there was an uproar amongst the guests as marriage with relatives is taboo.

The bride and bridegroom were devastated at the situation and both Nagurai and Nakapili took off their wedding dresses and the sandalwood paste on their foreheads. Nakapili could not stop her tears and kept weeping the whole night. The guests to drown their sorrow kept drinking the whole night. The young lovers decided they would elope and when all were drunk and fast asleep they vanished into the dark night. Both decided to settle in a far off place where they would live as a married couple. But fate had other things in store. Champarai the father of Nagurai had been looking for his son and one day the people of the village gave him the good news that his son had been seen in some far off village. Champarai and Khulumati went to bring back their son and when they saw him they pleaded with him to come back as social customs forbade such marriages, they promised to get him married to a beautiful girl from their village. Nagurai refused to go back with his parents. When all pleading failed Khulumati started abusing Nakapili, Khulumati screamed that it was all the fault of Nakapili and that she should die. Hearing this Nakapili sobbed and touched the feet of Khulumati and said, "I shall die now but I pray in my next life I have Nagurai as my husband". After this Nakapili jumped down the mountain side, Nagurai when he saw this also ran after Nakapili.

The villagers and the parents saw a very peculiar sight, the two lovers instead of going down rose up in the air and soon dark clouds had covered the sky and there was thunder and lightning all around. Even today when there is thunder and lightning the Tripuri people talk about their Nagurai and Nakapili.

The Fate Line
(Tripura)

People of Tripura believe that the fate of an infant is written by Bharya Purush or the 'Lord for writing the fate of the new born on the forehead', it is on the sixth night that this takes place.

Long long time back there lived a king who was blessed with a daughter and was very happy. The king was waiting for the sixth day or 'Shasti' as they say; he was keen to know the baby's future. The king had put guards near the door where the baby was sleeping and was eagerly waiting for the Bharya Purush. On the sixth day a man came and asked the king to remove all the guards. The king asked the man who he was and the man in reply said, "I am the scribe who writes on the forehead of new born babies their fate. I have come here to write this child's fate". On hearing this the king allowed the man to enter the room. The man after writing was about to come out when the king asked him to reveal what he had written. The man hesitated and said he could not disclose the details. The king kept insisting and after some time the man said the baby will have a very sad life and that was the reason he did not want to reveal the secret. The king got very sad and in anger asked, "How can you write such sorrowful things on the forehead of an infant"? The scribe said, "I am only a messenger, I only hold the pen, God dictates and the pen moves". Curious father that he was the king insisted on knowing the fate of his daughter. Finally, the scribe had to reveal the truth and say that the new born princess would be a lonely bride as she would marry a dead body. The princess would live in a solitary palace. The stunned king could only keep the secret to himself.

The baby grew up to be a beautiful princess and soon she was ready for marriage. Many offers did come from royal houses for her hand but nothing materialised. The worried father now realised that possibly her future was bleak. The king set out on a long journey with the princess and travelled far and wide, crossing rivers, mountains and unknown cities. One day they found themselves in a dense forest and after exploring the area found a broken down palace. The ramshackle palace had a beautiful pond with lotus in it. The princess sat at the side of the pond and drank its cool water. The princess wanted to rest for some time and asked her father to gather some fruits and berries for them to eat. The king went but told his daughter not to move around.

Very soon the princess out of curiosity went looking around and peeped into the old palace windows, initially she could not find anything interesting. Next she tried opening the doors but they wouldn't. Finally, she came across one door which at the slightest touch flew open and the princess could walk in. The princess in one of the rooms found a cot with a young handsome man lying down; it almost seemed he was sleeping. Looking carefully she saw he was dead. The room had all kinds of fruits and sweets; it seemed they were meant for the dead. The scared princess started crying and hoping her father would come back soon.

The king came back with fruits and berries for his daughter and called out for the princess but got no reply at first, then he heard a faint sound and realised it was his daughter replying. The king followed the sound and it led him to the old palace, looking he found his daughter all alone with a lot of fruits and sweets around her. The king now realised that fate had overtaken her. He told the princess that this was her fate and she would have to stay here. The king went back sobbing to his kingdom leaving his young daughter to her fate.

The princess tried to overcome her problems and looked around to see what was around the room; she found the body had not decomposed as under normal circumstances it should have. So she decided she would take care of the body and everyday bathe the body and looked after it. Days and months passed and the body remained in the same condition. Actually it was a prince who had been cursed by God; he would remain in that condition for a certain period and only the care and love of a princess could bring him back from the other world. This was the fate of the prince.

One fine morning the prince opened his eyes when the time bar was over, he found a beautiful girl in front of him. The prince fell in love with her at first sight and stretched out his arm to her and the princess reciprocated by giving her hand. Suddenly everything came to life, the trees had flowers, the birds were chirping, the servants were working happily; their prince had come back to life and there was happiness all around. The prince and princess returned to the princess's kingdom and the prince asked the king for the hand of the princess. Finally, a grand marriage took place and the prince and princess lived happily ever after. This was their fate, as they say 'whatever will be, will be. ' Or '*Que sera, sera*'.

The Sweetest Singer and the Best Dish
(Arunachal Pradesh)

Long, long time ago the Sun held a festival called Thung and invited one and all, both people and animals to the party or festival. Everyone was happy to attend the party and prayed to the Sun to shine brightly so that men, animals and plants would be happy to live; the Mishmis take the Sun as a female figure as it gives warmth through sunshine. Since the festival had a happy note the Sun asked all her people, 'Who can sing the best?'

Hearing this Makao bird quickly said, "I can sing the best". The Sun asked her to sing and the Makao sang out loud and clear in her hoarse voice which irritated the goddess. The goddess picked up the bird and threw it into a bush of wild flowers and the birds head and neck got smeared with the white flowers. Till date the Makao has a spotted body.

Next the Sun asked others if there was anyone who could sing well and finally after a lot of hesitation a Jerai, a cheerful little bird dared to answer, "I sing the most melodious song from my group". The Sun asked her to sing and out came a croaky voice, the Jerai in all earnestness sang a lively song but the Sun was not pleased and in anger put some black juice from the Shiram tree on the Jerai's body. The Jerai has remained as black as ever since then.

After this no one had the courage to sing in front of the Sun, finally Kuwei, the cuckoo bird came forward bravely and declared, "I can sing the best in the woods". So the Sun agreed to hear the cuckoo bird and the cuckoo sang sweetly in happiness. The Sun was very happy to hear a voice so sweet that it touched your heart, everyone around stopped to hear her sing. The Sun in happiness stroked the head and body of the cuckoo and from that day the Mishmis believe the cuckoo started having a firm body.

The Sun was glad that she had found the best singer for mankind and now was looking for the best dish or food for human beings. So, the first one to be questioned was the rat. The Sun asked the rat, "How many offspring can you breed at one time"? The rat proudly said she could breed four to five at one time. The Sun was not happy as this was too little for so many people. So again the Sun went looking for specie that would be adequate for all. After a lot of deliberation the Sun called the fish and asked, "How many offspring can you breed at one time"? The fish in reply said, "I am not sure as I have lost count, my children coming out from my left side fill up the left bank of the River Tulu and from the right side the right bank". The Sun was very happy as now all could get adequate food. She proudly declared, "From this day fish shall be the best food for mankind". After this people eat fish on every occasion. People do not hesitate to eat fish as the Sun has given us permission and today even the priestly class in the East eat fish.

U Shulong
(Meghalaya)

Shillong, the capital city of Meghalaya gets its name from a mountain peak which lies near to the city. There are many legends as to how the city got its name. The most loved one is it got the name from a handsome man who was called U Shillong.

The first story: U Shillong they say was born to a virgin mother Lir by name. The mother Lir was slightly strange and lived alone in a small village called Bisi. Bisi lay close to Myllieum which is close to Shillong. One day Lir found she had become pregnant and no one knew who the father of her child was. Lir had no answer to the questions asked as she did not know the answer herself and this was the reason why people said she was virgin. Lir finally gave birth to a still born child. Later Lir buried the child in her garden. Many years had gone by when one night Lir was woken up from her sleep by noise created by many people talking outside her house. So Lir went out to see what the noise was about and found a crowd, from the group a tall handsome youth came forward and said, " Mother, don't you recognise me? I am the same infant whom you buried in your garden. I have come to help the people of the area and whenever my services are required I will be here. Do not be afraid of me as I will not let any harm come to you since you are my earthly mother". The name of the young man was Shulong ('the one who grows naturally'). It is believed the young man was the Shillong deity. The words 'Khot Shillong'/ 'Call Shillong' can still be heard when people are in trouble. It is like calling out to God when one is in trouble.

The second story: There was a cave not far from Shillong Peak called 'Krem Marai' and was supposed to be the home of the Shillong deity, a God like creature. The Shillong deity ruled over a large territory and mere mortals were scared of him. To appease the deity people would make offerings and perform religious rituals. The deity blessed those whom he favoured. Many years later they say people had seen a beautiful girl in and around the cave. Some say that they had seen a young maiden sitting on a rock sunning herself. Some shepherds said they had seen a beautiful girl when they were grazing their cattle; she was so beautiful that some thought she was more a figment of the imagination, almost dreamlike but no one dared to go close to her or near the cave.

A lot of people had heard about her name and beauty and a young man though very practical seemed to be very curious about this tale of a beautiful girl. One of the young man's friend had seen her and said her beauty was unparallel, you all felt she could only be imaginative. The man belonged to a group called Mylliemngap and was also called Mylliemngap, decided he would find out for himself and went close to the cave the girl was supposed to come out from. He hid himself behind bushes and waited. With the early sun coming out, the forest area seemed to have come to life. Birds were chirping and gentle breeze made the flowers sway, it almost as if they were dancing. From out of the cave the girl had also come out to appreciate nature. Mylliemngap could not believe his eyes, she was so close to him. He could not take his eyes off her, so beautiful she was, fair skin, black hair flowing down to her waist, her body in perfect form, she was truly God's daughter. The girl went from flower to flower flitting around taking in the sweet smell, almost like a bee trying to suck the nectar from flowers. To Mylliemngap it seemed she was the daughter of the God in fact the Shillong deity. Immersed in her beauty he suddenly realised the girl was no longer there.

Mylliemngap wanted to see her again and so he got a bunch of flowers the girl admired and tied it to a pole and put it near the cave entrance, he waited for her at a distance, hoping against hope she would come back. Suddenly he saw movement and found the girl was trying to reach out to smell the flowers. He very gently kept pulling out the pole and gradually he could bring her out of the cave, next Mylliemngap jumped and caught hold of the girl's hand and would not let her go. He took her home and brought her up as his own daughter.

People believe that the girl called Pasyntiew or in the local language 'Lured by Flower' was the ancestral Queen mother of the Shillong kingdom. They say Pasyntiew was married to a man called Kongor Nongiri and had three children. It is believed the royal family of the Shillong kingdom started with her. Hers was a period of the 'Golden Age' where there was all round development from agriculture to etiquette. Pasyntiew also taught the people how to dance, sing and the very art of eating 'betel nut' or 'tambul and pan'. The kingdom flourished under her care and one day when her children were grown up and ready to take on their own responsibilities she told them her secret that she was the daughter of the mountain god 'U Lei Shyllong' and had her father's permission to come down to earth and be with the human race, now time had come for her to go back to her old place or realm. When she felt her human responsibilities had been achieved Pasyntiew went back to her cave. 'Krem Marai', she was indeed the daughter of the Shillong deity. Her descendents are the two known chiefs of the Khasi families -Khyrim and Mylliem and are still called the 'Syiem, Chief of Shillong. '

Both the stories are interesting and Shillong peak and city are there for us to see.

Select Readings

1. *Abhiyatri* by Nirupama Borgohain
2. *Adi Bari: A Performing Art* by Talom Rubko
3. *Ahom Buranji- From the Earliest Time to the End of Ahom Rule* Translated and edited by Rai Sahib Golap Chandra Barua
4. *The Ahom Rulers and the Neighbouring Tribes* by Dr Arun Barua. (NE Book supplement)
5. *Ahom Tribal Relations* by Laksmi Devi
6. *Among the Luminaries of Assamese Biography* by Anjali Sarma
7. *An Assamese Film on the Life of Azan Fakir* by Dr Syed Ahmed
8. *Assamese Women in Indian Independence with a Special Emphasis* by Guptajit Pathak
9. *Assam – Political Cohesion* by Bimal J Dev and Dilip K Lahiri
10. *Atan Burgohain and his Times* by Dr SK Bhuyan
11. *Babruvahana* from Wikipedia
12. *Battle of Saraighat from Wikipedia.* Barman, Sivanath (1999)
13. *Bhupen Hazarika – The Roving Minstrel* by Arup Kumar Dutta
14. *The Brahamaputra* by AK Dutt
15. *Buddhism Reincarnation and Dalai Lama of Tibet* by MG Chittoor
16. *Communal Riots in Post-Independence India* by Ashgarali Engineer
17. *The Court Chronicle* by Saroj Nalini Paratt
18. *The Court Chronicle of the Kings of Manipur* by Saroj Nalini Parratt
19. *Dalai Lamas of Tibet: Succession of Births* by Inder L Malik
20. *Early History of the Vaishnava Faith and Movement in Assam-Sankardeva and His Times* by Maheswar Neog
21. *Encyclopedia of North East India* by Col Ved Prakash
22. *Essays on the History of the Mizos* by Sangkima
23. *Folklore of Assam* by Jogesh Das
24. *Haipou Jadonang : A Freedom Fighter* by Thunbui Zeliang and Romeo Palmei

25. *A History of Assam* by Edward Gait
26. *History of the Church in Mizoram* by J Meirion Lloyd
27. *A History of the Mizos* by CG Verghese
28. *History of Zomi* by T Gougin
29. *History, Religion and Culture of the North East India* by S Gajrani
30. *India's North East Frontier in the 19th Century* by Verrier Elwin
31. *Indigenous Writers of India- Introduction and Contribution* by Ramnika Gupta
32. *Industrial landscape of NE India* by Basanta Kumar Sarma
33. *Jadonang – A Mystic Rebel* by Gangmumei Kamei
34. *Jyoti Prasad Agarwala's Dramatic Works* by Dr Kutubuddin Ahmed
35. *'Kabui Messiah': The Jadonang Movement in Manipur* by John Parratt and Saroj N Arambam Parratt
36. *The Khasis* by PRT Gurdon
37. *Lachit Barphukan and his Times* by SK Bhuyan
38. *Lamas of Tibet* by Inder L Malik
39. *Lokopriya Gopinath Bordoloi, An Architect of Modern India* by LM Baruah
40. *The Land Where the Bamboo Flowers* by JD Baveja
41. *The Language and Literature of Meghalaya* (edited compilation)
42. *The Lasting Values of Sankaradeva's Teachings* by HV Sreenivasa Murthy
43. *Legends of Culture from India's North East* by Jyotiprasad Aggarwala by Dipankar Banerjee.
44. *Literary Vision* by Basavraj Naikar
45. *Lushai Chrysalis* by Major Anthony Gilchrist McCall
46. *Manipur and the Naga Hills* by Sir James Johnstone
47. *Manipur, Past and Present* by Naorem Sanajaoba
48. *Maniram Dewan* by Benudhar Sharma
49. *Meghalaya by Hargovind* Joshi
50. *Michael Aris' Work on the Sixth Dalai Lama*

51. *Mishmi Folk Tales of Lohit Valley* by Obang Tayeng
52. *Mizo Chiefs and the Chiefdom* by Suhas Chatterjee
53. *Mizo Drama* by L Khiangte
54. *Mizo Freedom Fighters* by PR Kyndiah
55. *Mizoram* by Animesh Ray
56. *Mizoram Dimensions and Perspectives* by Jagdish Kumar Patnaik
57. *The Monpas of Tawang-Arunachal Pradesh* by Tsewang Norbu
58. *The Nagas in the 19th Centuary* by Verrier Elwin
59. *Origin and Growth of Christianity in Tripura: with Social Reference to the New Zealand Baptist Missionary Society* by Sukhendu Debbarma
60. *The People of Meghalaya* by BS Rana
61. *Political Life in Assam During the 19th Century* by BB Hazarika
62. *Primitive Faith Tries to Fight Back in Arunachal Pradesh* (edited compilation)
63. *Queen Empress Vs Tikendrajit, Prince of Manipur* by John Parratt and Saroj Parratt
64. *Raven Crown* – the Origins of Buddhist Monarchy in Bhutan
65. *The Relevance of Rani Gaidinliu in Current Context of Naga Society* by Jagdamba Mall
66. *Sachin Kartar Ganer Bhuban* by Khagesh Dev Burman
67. *Sankaradeva* by Vasudev Sharan Agrawal
68. *Saraighatar Subachani* by Dr SK Bhuyan
69. *Sattriya Dance* by Mrs Devika P Borthakur and Mr Pulak J Sethi
70. *The Sixth Dalai Lama* by Tsyang Gyatso and Paul Williams
71. *Songs of Love, Poems of Sadness: the Erotic Verse of the Sixth Dalai Lama*
72. *Srimanta Sankaradeva Sangha* Home Page
73. Srimanta Sankardeva from Wikipedia
74. *Status of Social Sciences in the Vernacular Languages in NE India* by Jaiprakash Singh
75. *Status of Women* by Lal Dena

76. *The Story of Tibet* by Thomas Laird
77. *The Story of Tibet* by Thomas Laird
78. *Strangers of the Mist* by Sanjoy Hazarika
79. *Sufism and Azan Fakir of Assam* by Rahena Saikia
80. *Tales of a Dalai Lama* by Pierre Delattre
81. *Tantric Buddhism and Altered States of Consciousness* by Louise Child
82. *The Mizos* by Lal Biak Thanga
83. *Traditional Institutions of Mehgalaya: A Case Study of Doloi and his Works* by LS Gassah
84. *Tripura* by Omesh Saigal
85. *Tungbhungia Buranji*- Compiled by Dr SK Bhuyan (History of Assam: 1681-1826)
86. The *Turquoise Bee* by Rick Fields, Brian Cutillo and Mayami Oda
87. *An Unsung Colossus: An Introduction to the Life and Works of Sankaradeva*, Forum for Sankaradeva Studies, Gauhati 1999
88. *U Tirot Singh – A Khasi Drama in English* by Victor G Bareh
89. *U Tirot Singh* by Hipshon Roy
90. *Where the Sun rises When Shadows Fall* by Geeti Sen
91. *Wings of the White Crane: Poems of Tsangs Dbyangs Rgyo Mtsho-Tshans-Dbyans Rgya-Mtsho* by Gary Wayne Houston
92. *Women in Naga Society* by Lucy Zehol
93. *Zikirs of Azan Faquir: Assamese Devotional Songs and Inter-community Relationship* by Abu Nasar Saied Ahmed

Index

25. **Manas Defence Year Book 2010-2011** *(Fully Coloured Illustrated)*	General Padmanabhan, General VK Singh, Lt Gen S Pattabhiraman, General Deepak Kapoor, Air Chief Marshal PV Naik, Air Chief Marshal Fali Homi Major, Admiral Nirmal Verma and other Top Officers
26. **Do You Know Administration?**	Dr Chandrika Singh, Dr Suraj Singh Sisodiya
27. **The Folds of Insurgency**	AP Maheshwari, IPS *(Foreword by: Prakash Singh, IPS)*
28. **CBI Top-Cop Recalls**	SK Dutta, IPS *(Former Director – CBI)*
29. **India at 60:** A Rediscovery	Ambassador PK Budhwar
30. **The 1857 Jihad**	Shesrao B More
31. **The ISI Game Plan**	A Novel by Brig Yash Mohan, VSM
32. **5 Years Guarantee:** How to make India Richer	Shrawan K Vikram
33. **Effective Interrogation:** Naxalism, Police, Intelligence	G Chatterjee *(Former Intelligence Officer)*
34. **Intelligence, Security & Asymmetric Warfare**	Dhirendra Singh, IAS & Lt Gen DB Shekatkar
35. **Reforming Bureaucracy**	Dr Chandrika Singh
36. **White Collar Crimes X-Posed**	Thakur Shailendra Nath
37. **Travels in Assam**	John Butler
38. **India and China:** Strategic Energy Management and Security	BK Sikdar
39. **India's External Intelligence:** Secrets of Research and Analysis Wing (RAW)	Major General VK Singh *(Ex-Jt Sec - RAW)*
40. **India's Quest:** Leadership of a Powerful Nation	Lt Col (Retd) Jaswant Singh Marwah *(Father of General JJ Singh)*
41. **Changing India:** Straight from the Heart	Lt Gen SK Sinha, PVSM *(Former Governor - J&K, Assam)*
42. **Threat to Security:** How Secured is India from within	PC Dogra, IPS *(Former DGP, Punjab)*
43. **Who Owns CBI:** The Naked Truth	BR Lall, IPS (Retd) *(Former DGP-Haryana & Jt Dir-CBI*
44. **Tribes of Arunachal Pradesh (2 vol set)**	Col DS Grewal (Retd)
45. **Folk Culture of Manipur**	Padma Shri Dr M Kirti Singh